SOLOS

SOLOS

photographs by Linda Connor

Apeiron Workshops, Inc. · Millerton, New York · 1979

Published by Apeiron Workshops, Inc.

Copyright © 1979 by Linda Connor

Library of Congress Catalog Number: 78-70695
ISBN 0-934354-04-9

First Edition

to my family

FOREWORD

I can clearly recall watching the clouds moving past my window and perceiving, for the first time, their passage around the earth; my breathless investigations of snowflakes on my sleeve before they would melt; the intricate patterns of an Oriental rug which, decades later, I would recognize again instantly.

As a child I was alone amidst the substance and power of the world, an awed and fascinated witness. Photography reestablishes that state of absorption and wonderment, of unfiltered experience. It both grounds and nurtures my imagination.

Discipline and an attitude of openness provide the proper medium for the flow of creative energy. It is a privilege to serve and transform this elusive force; it enriches my life, surpasses my knowledge, and remains far more profound than I.

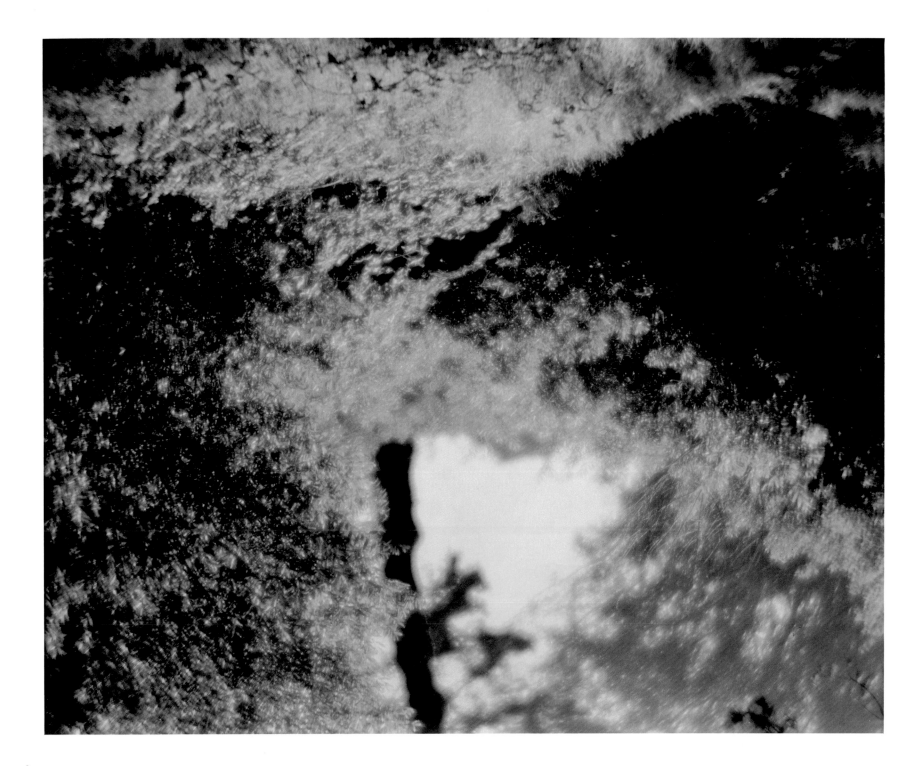

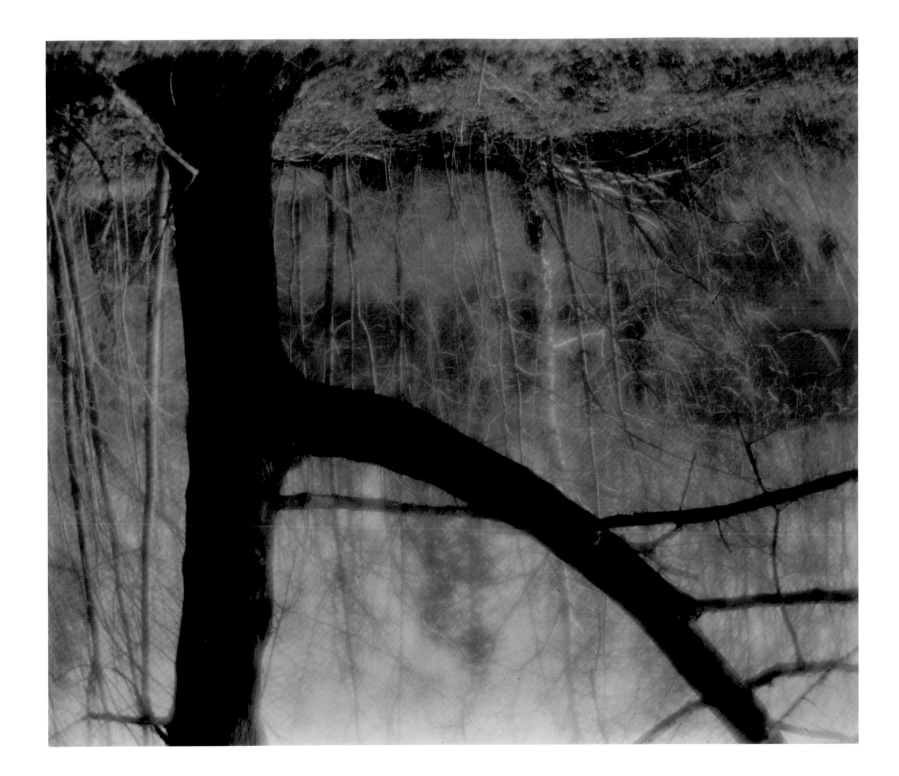

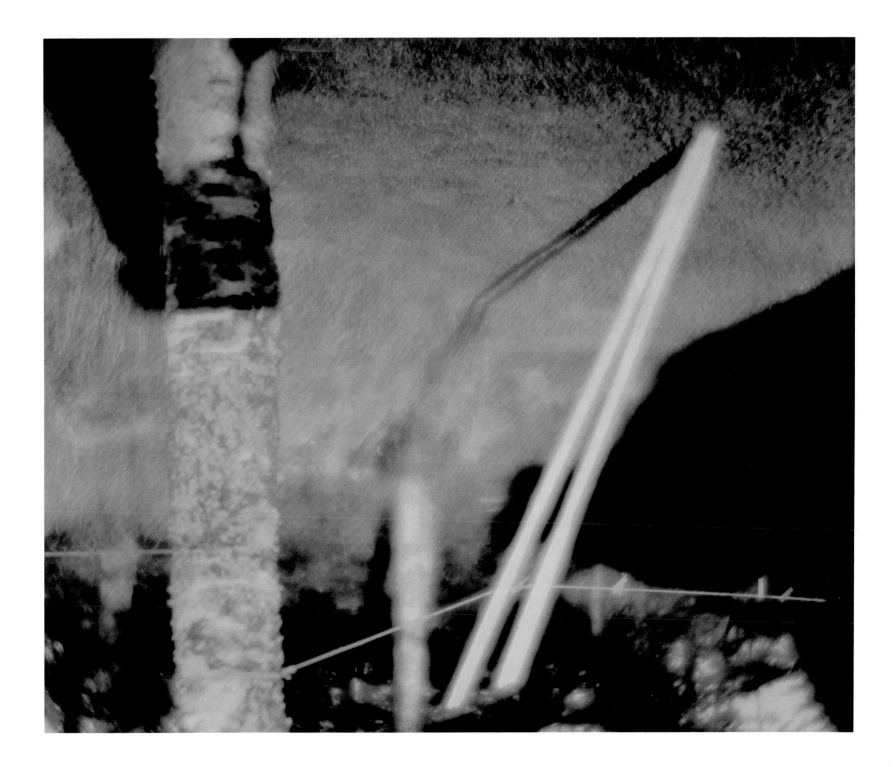

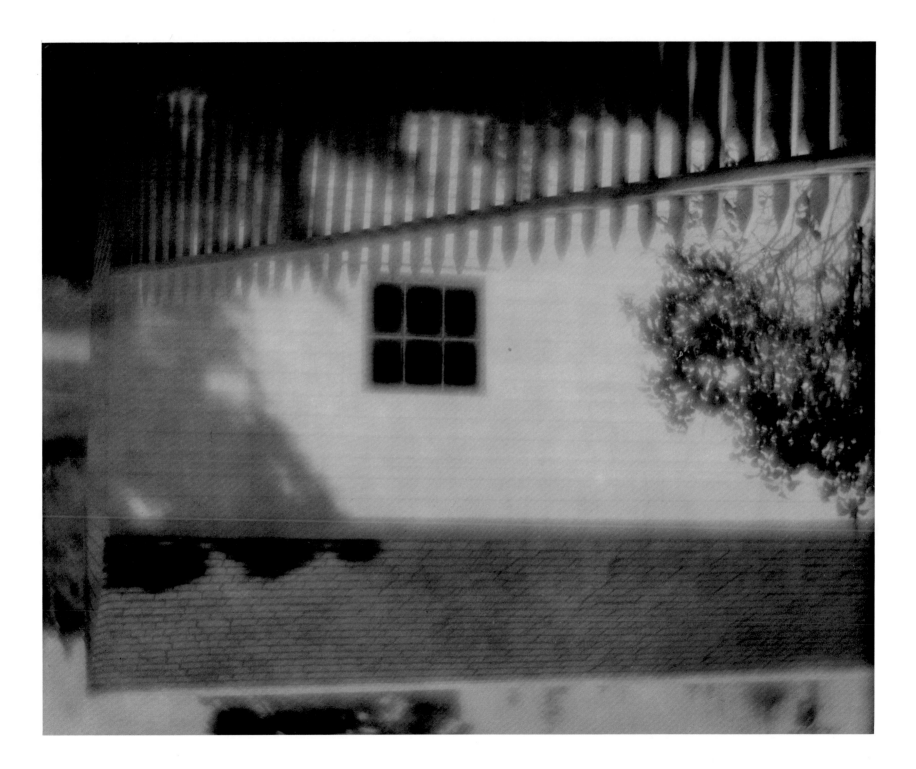

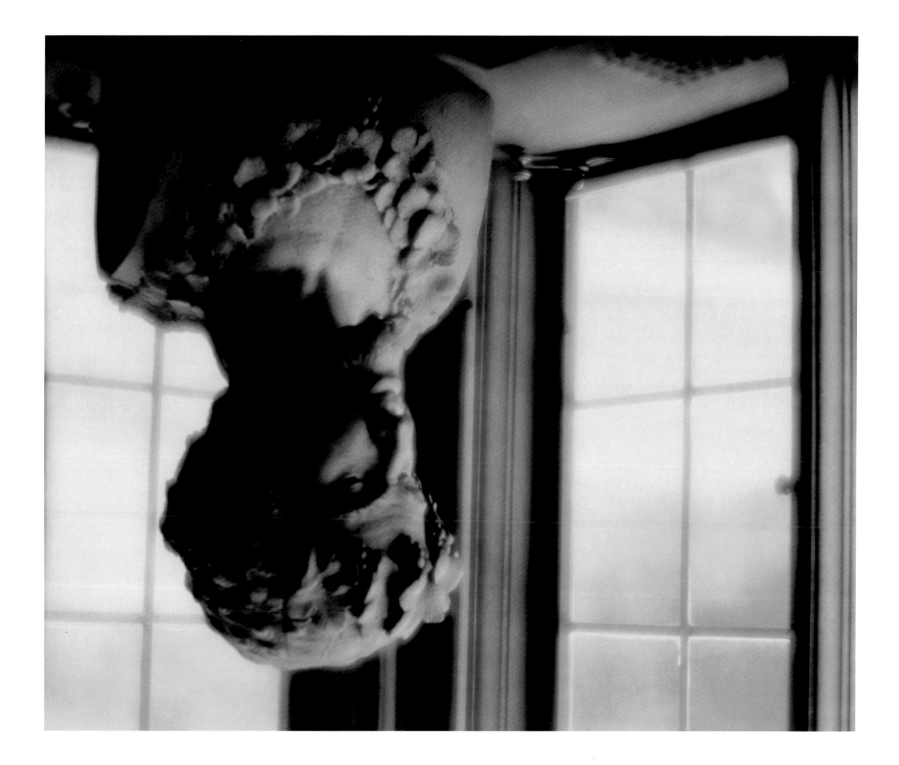

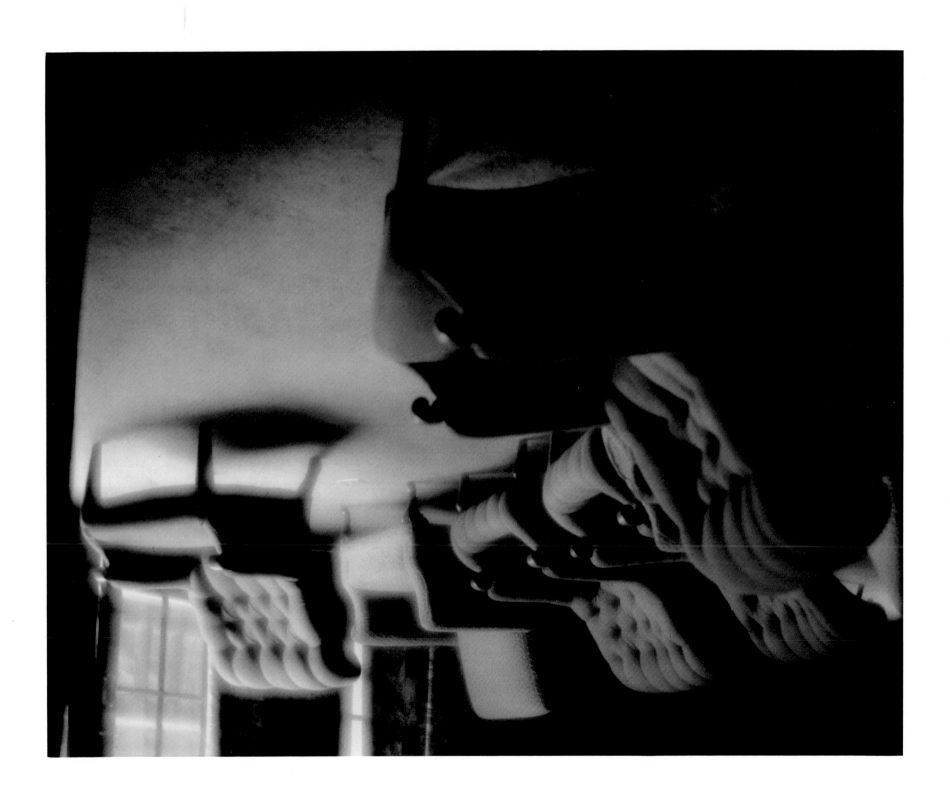

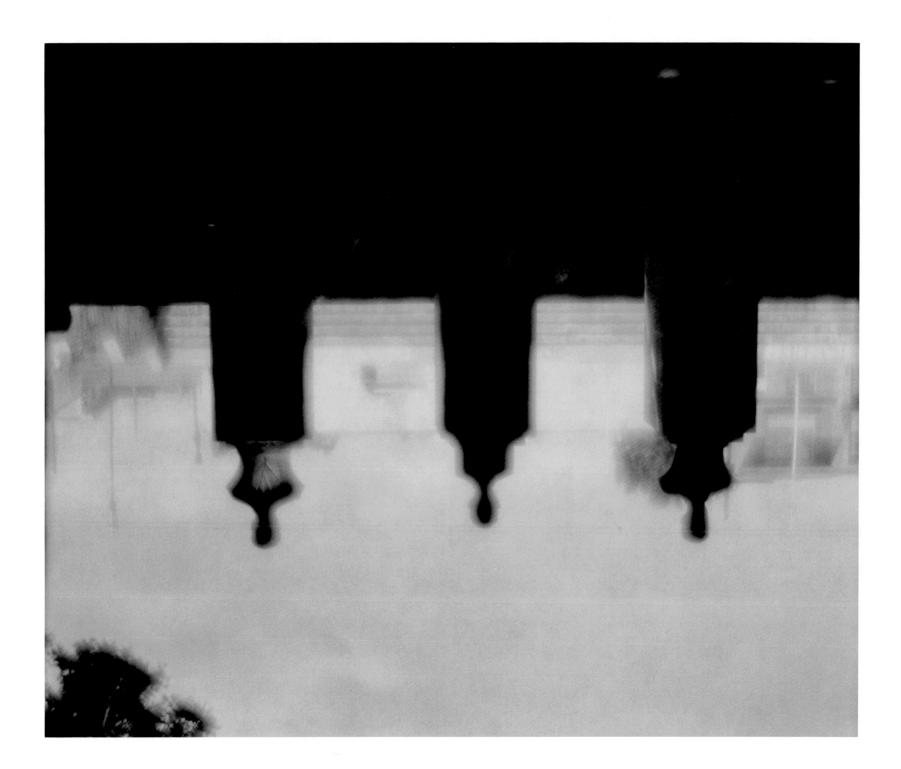

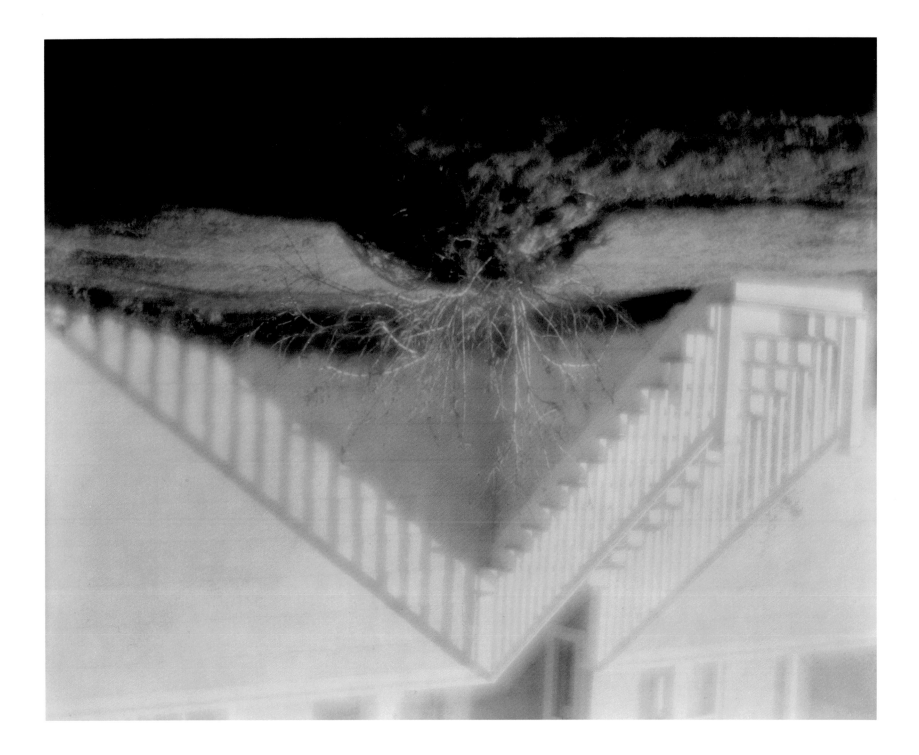

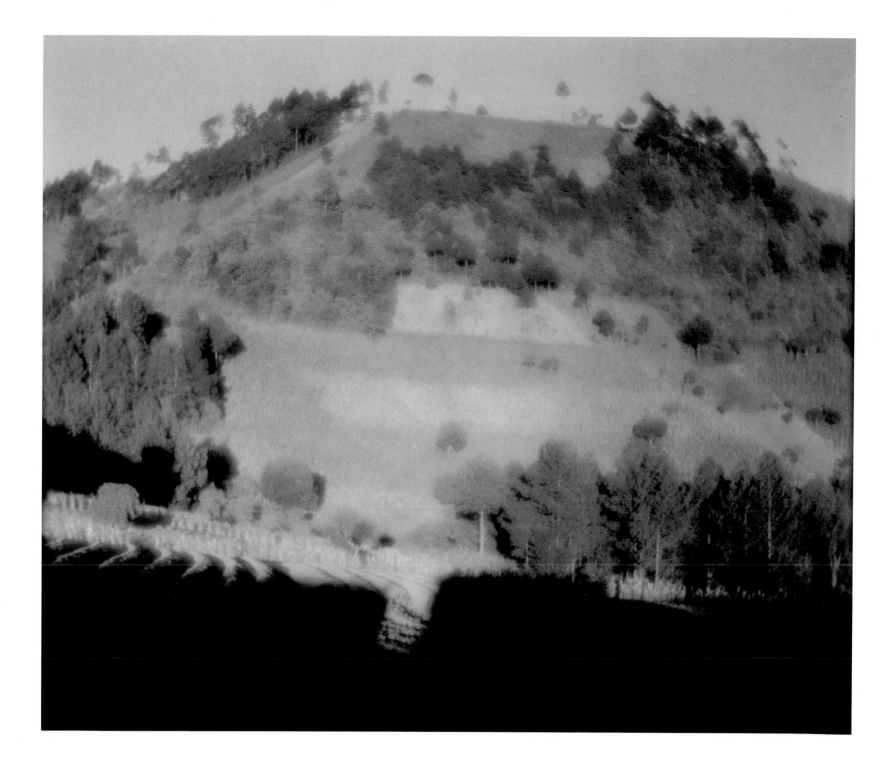

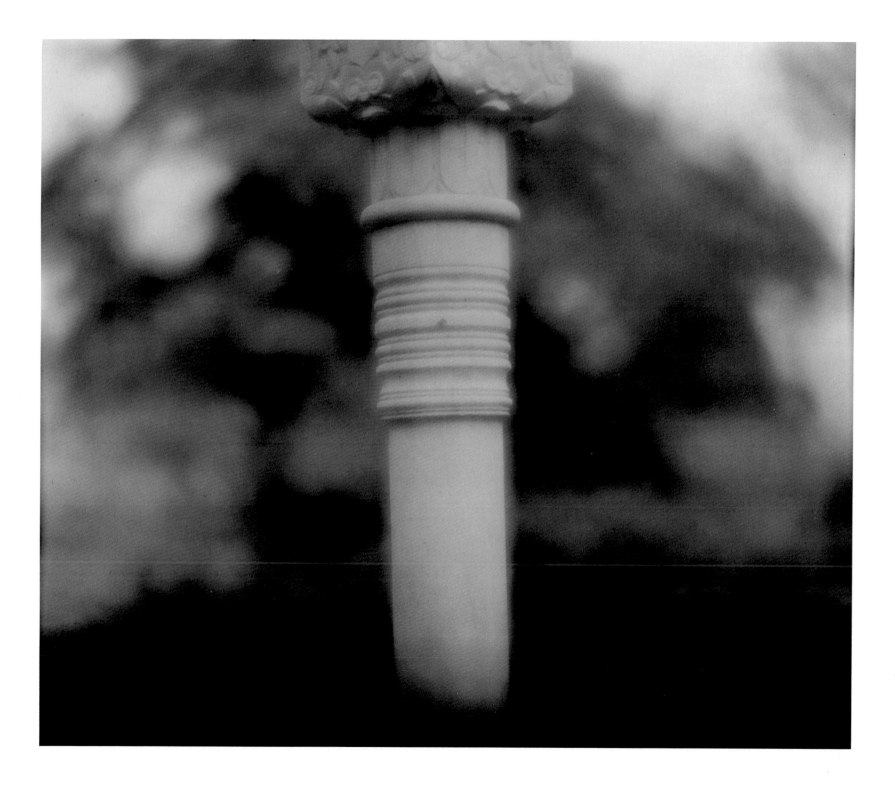

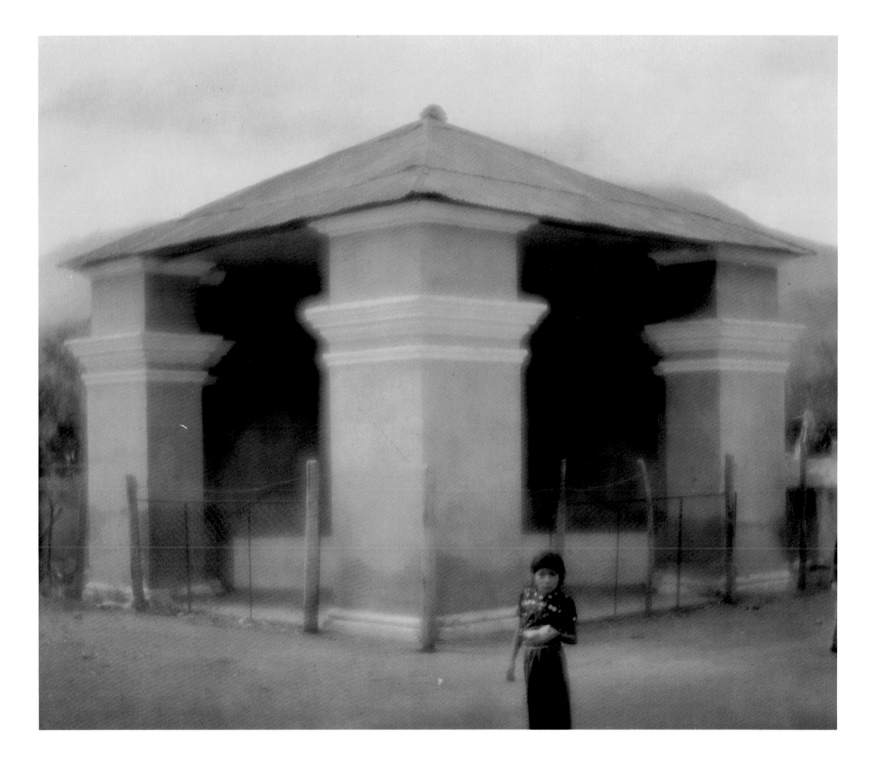

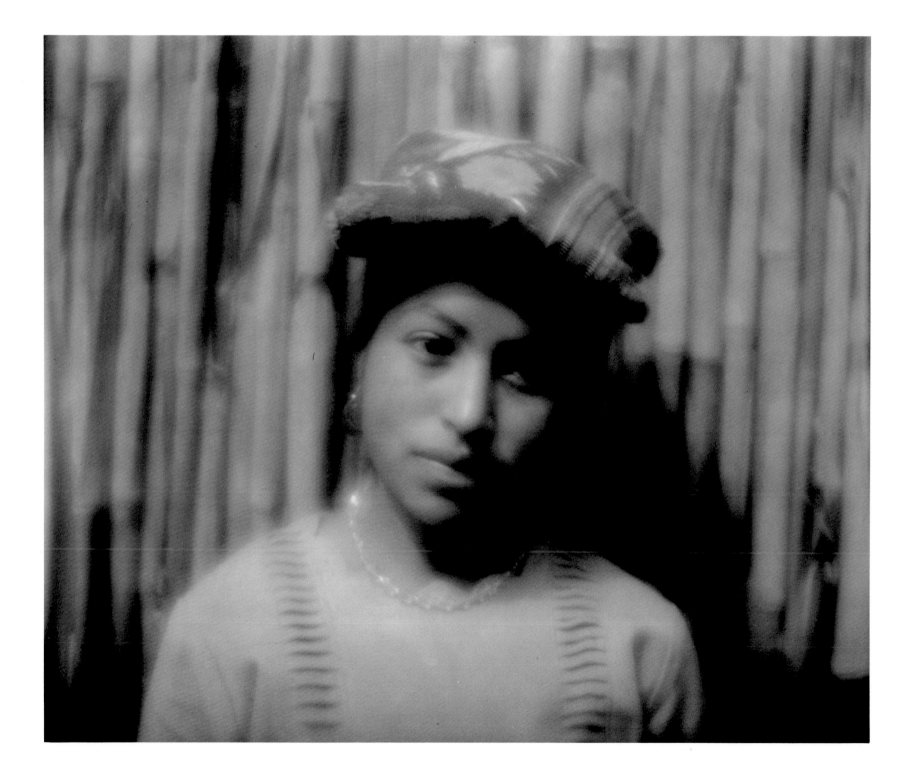

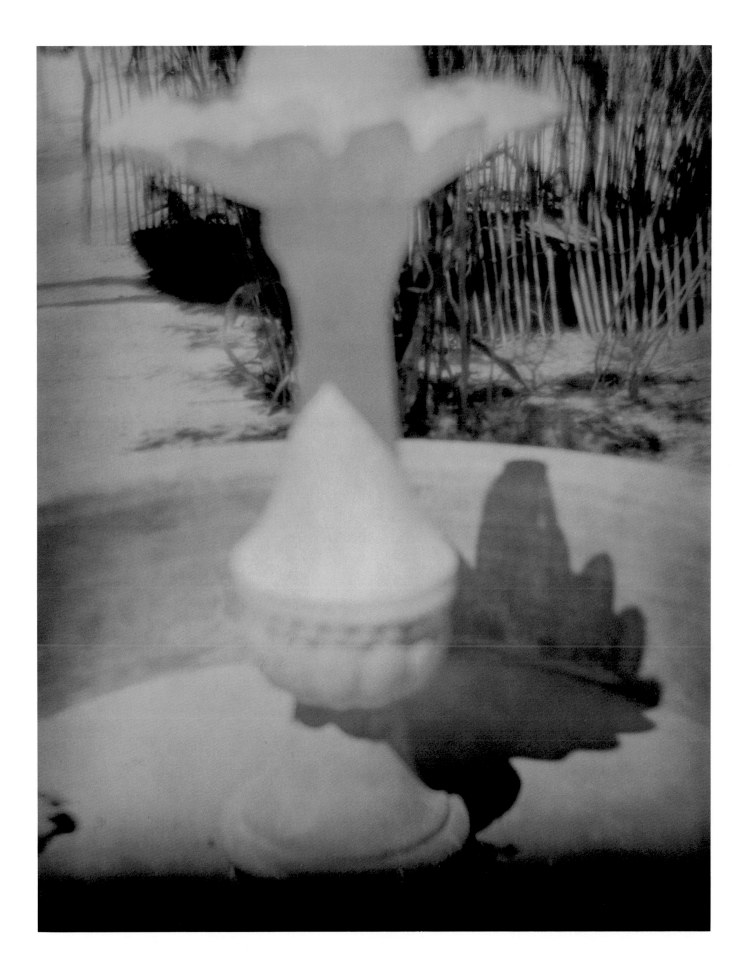

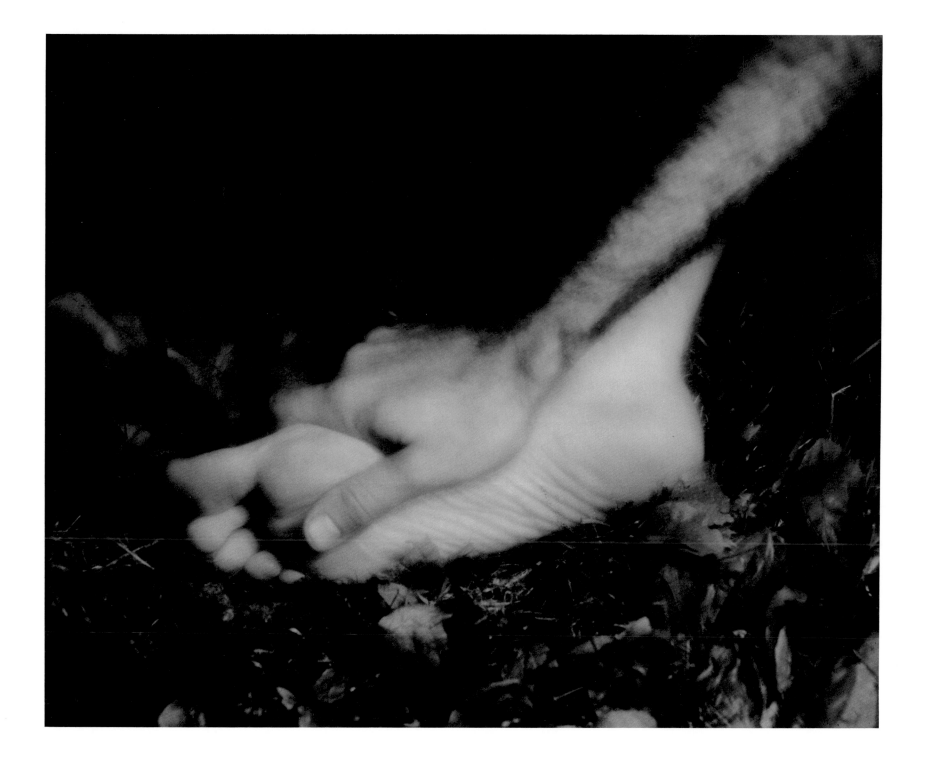

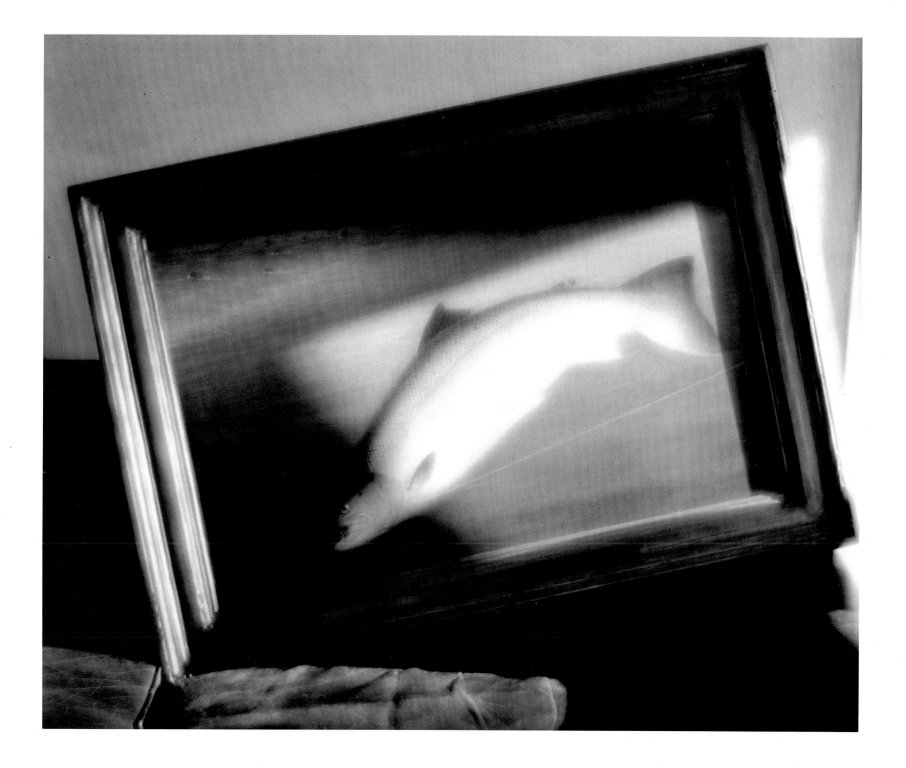

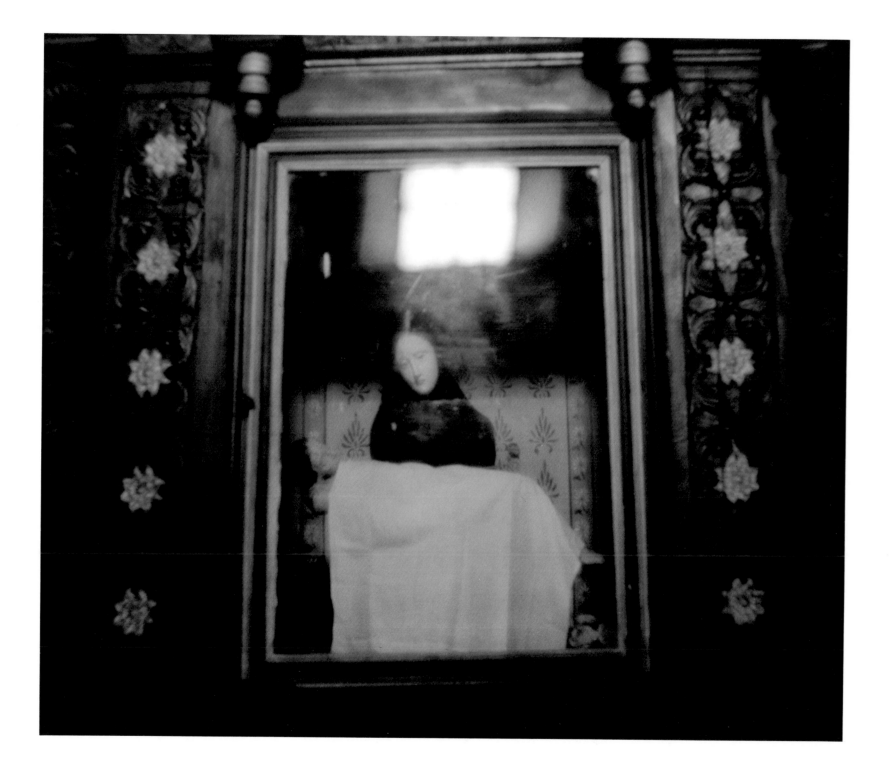

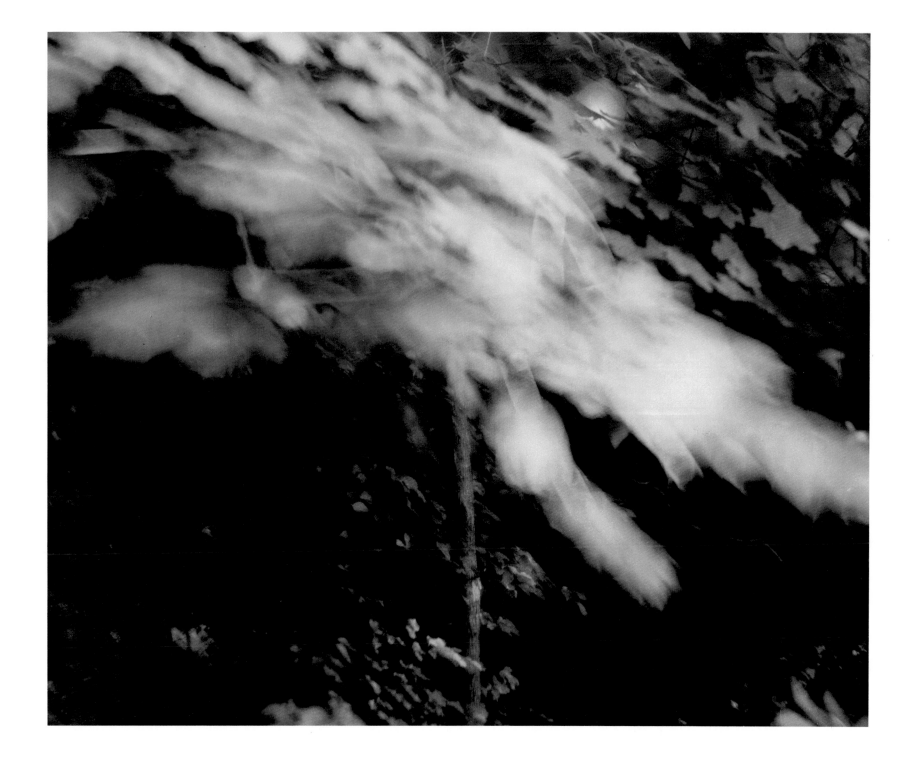

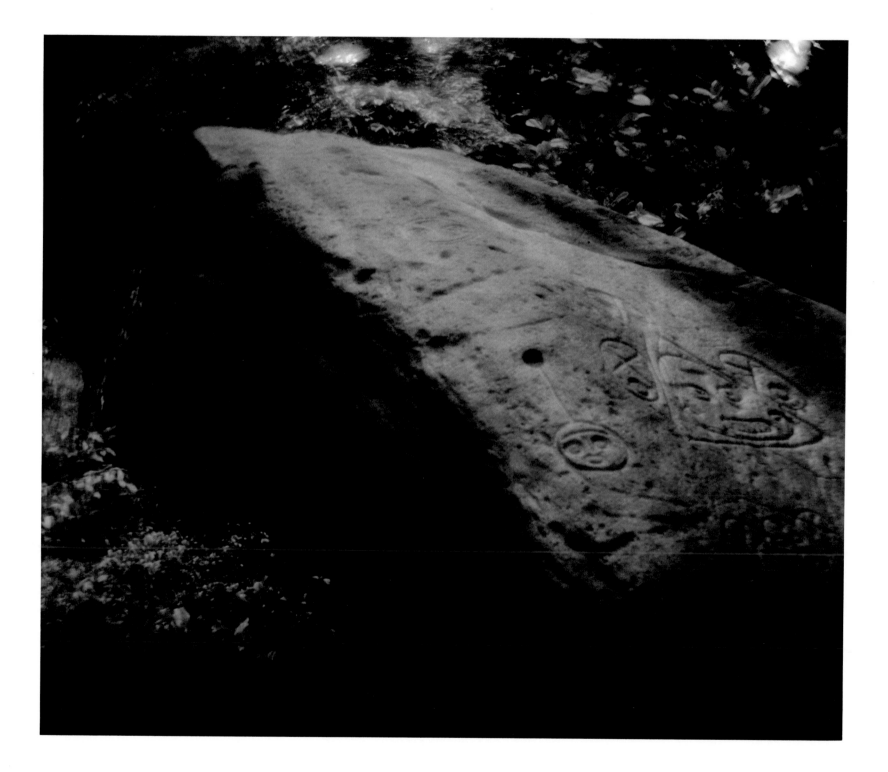

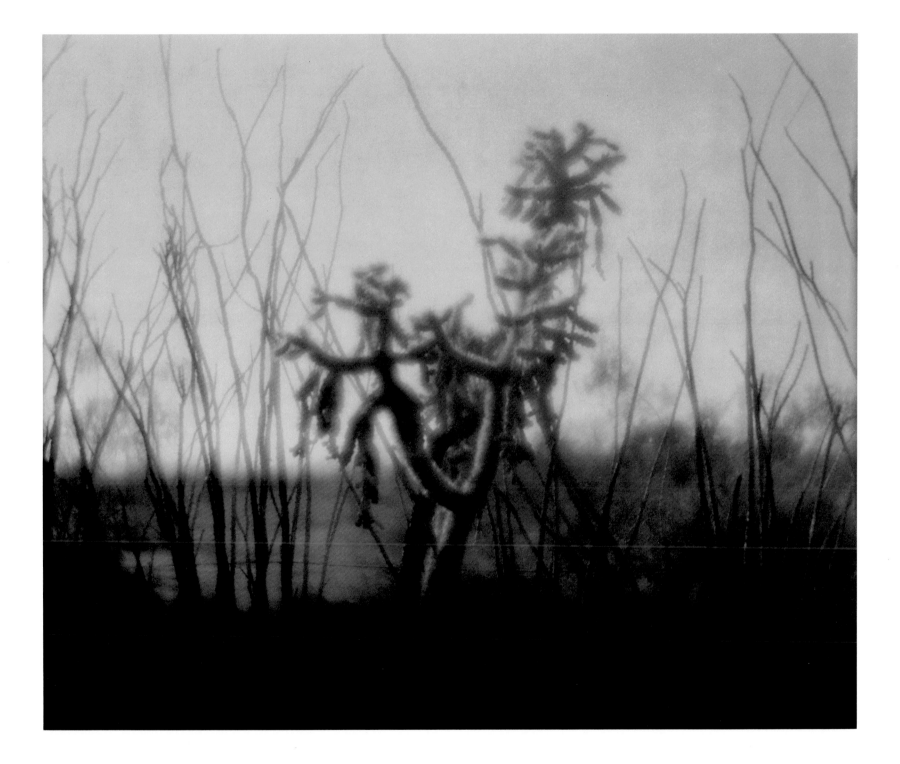

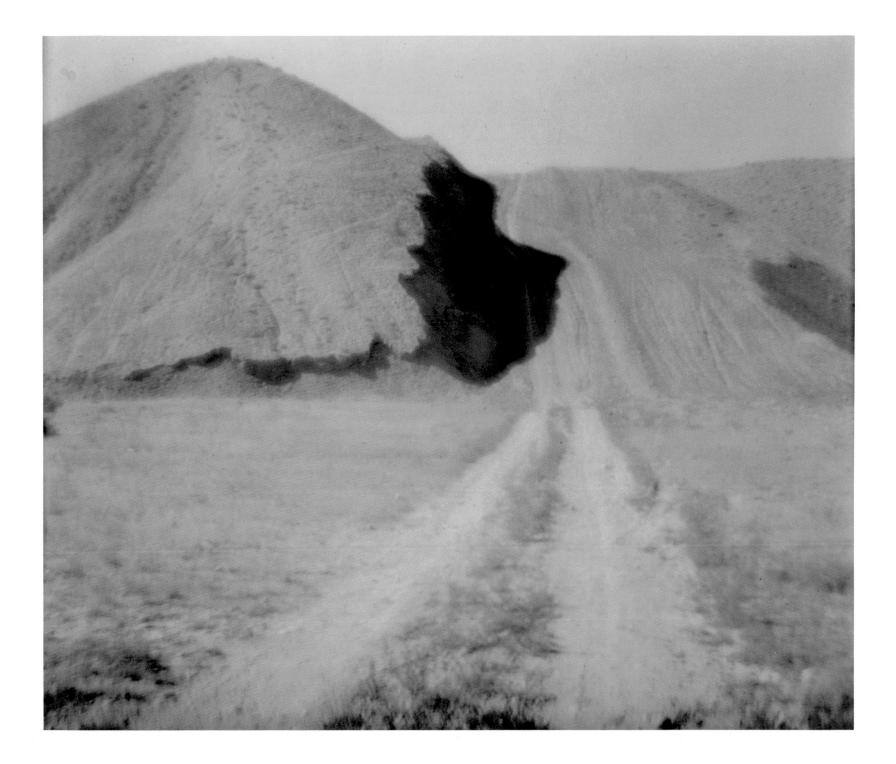

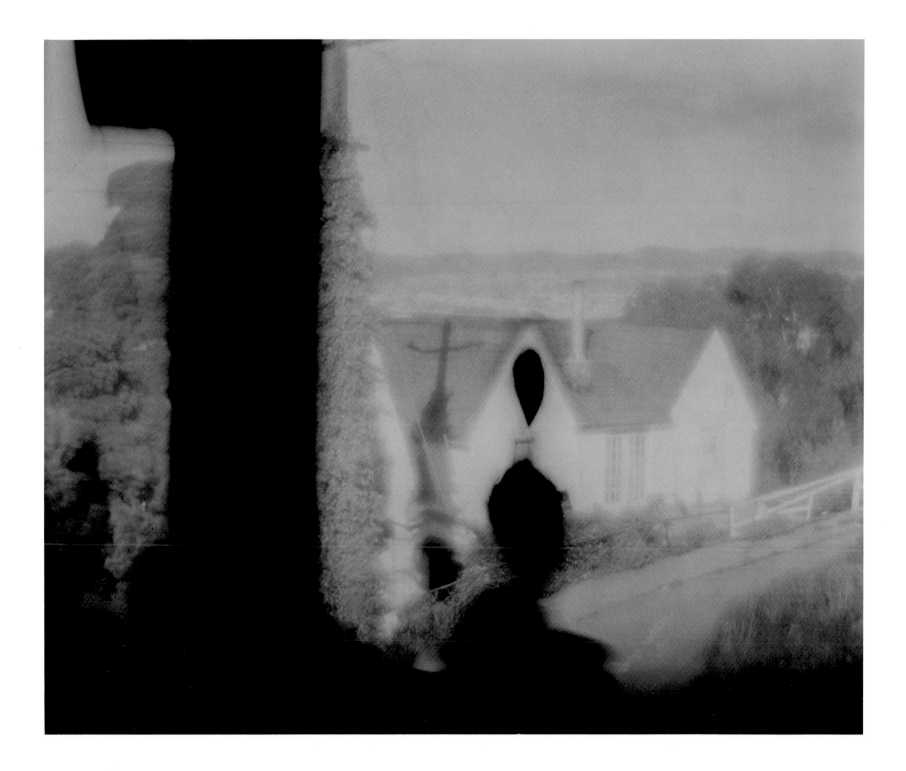

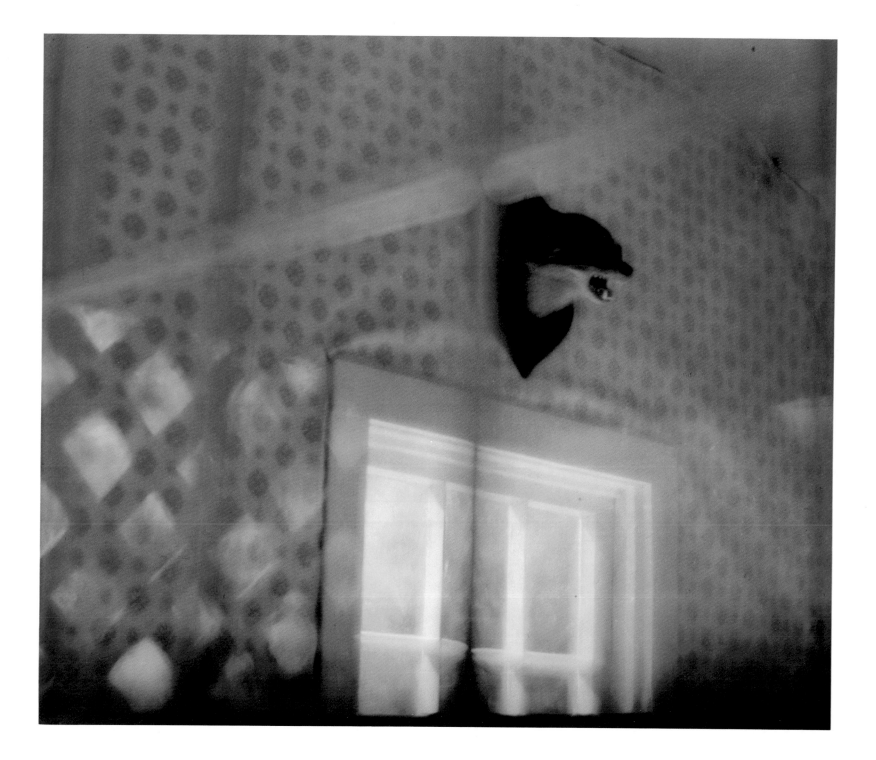

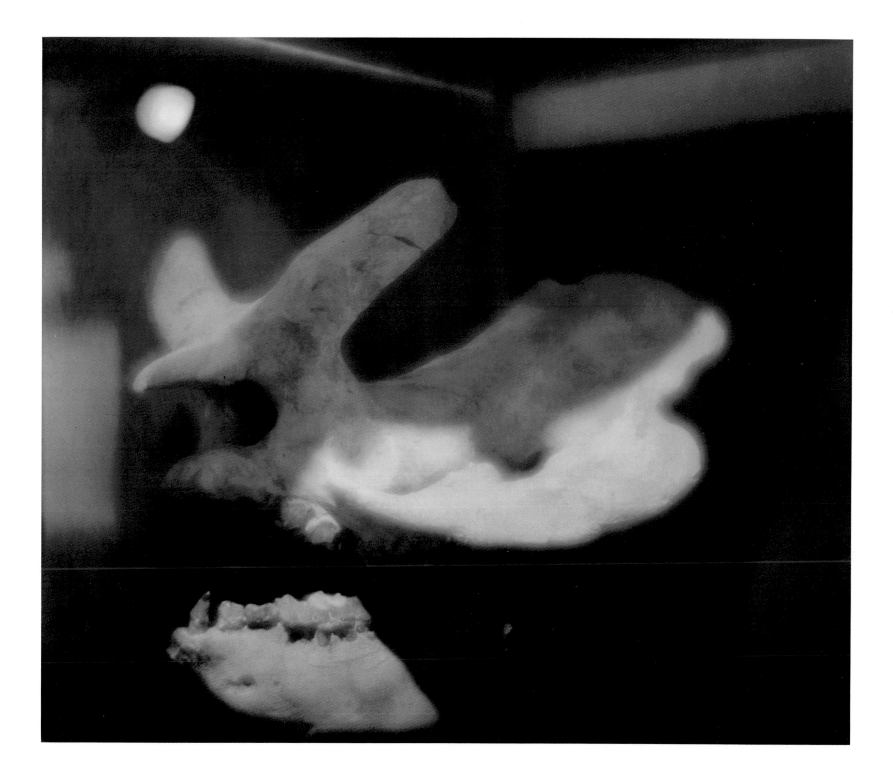

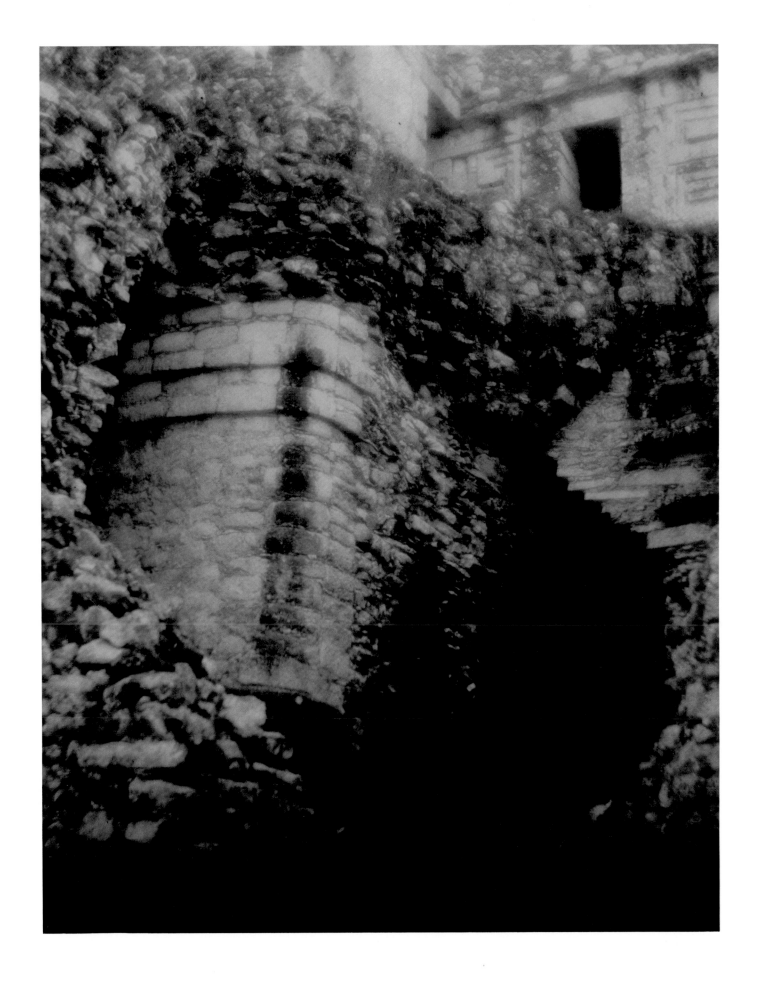

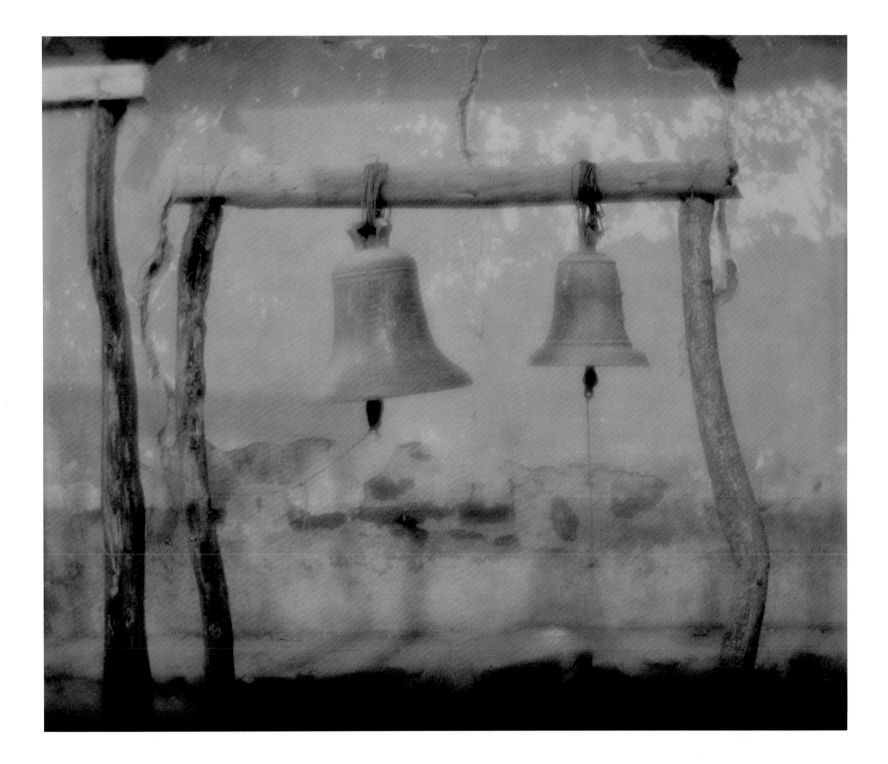

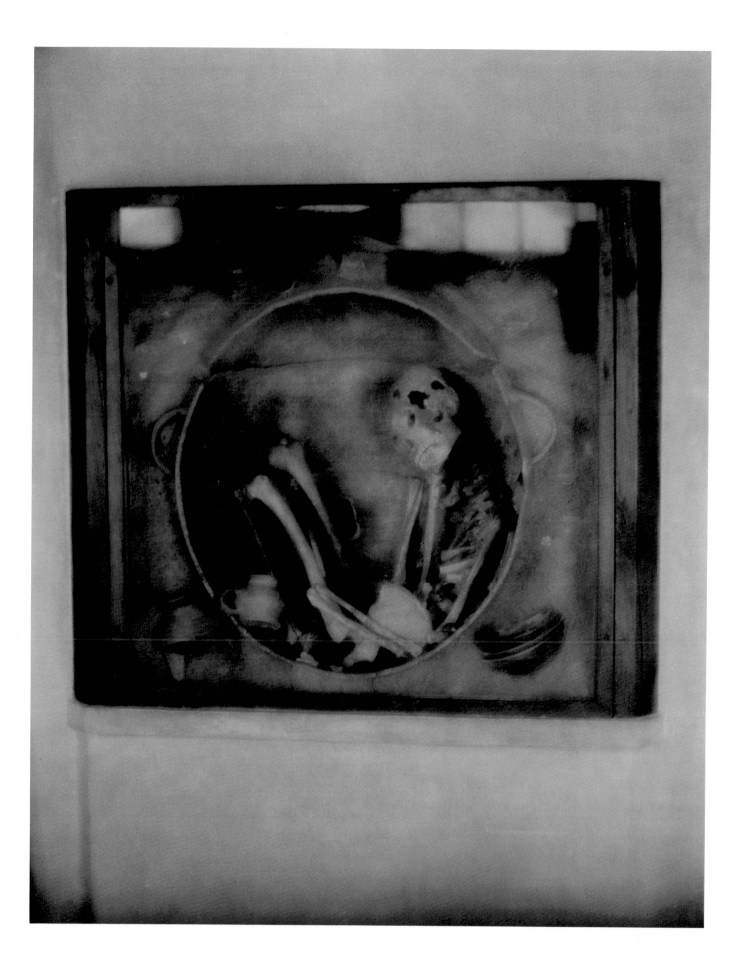

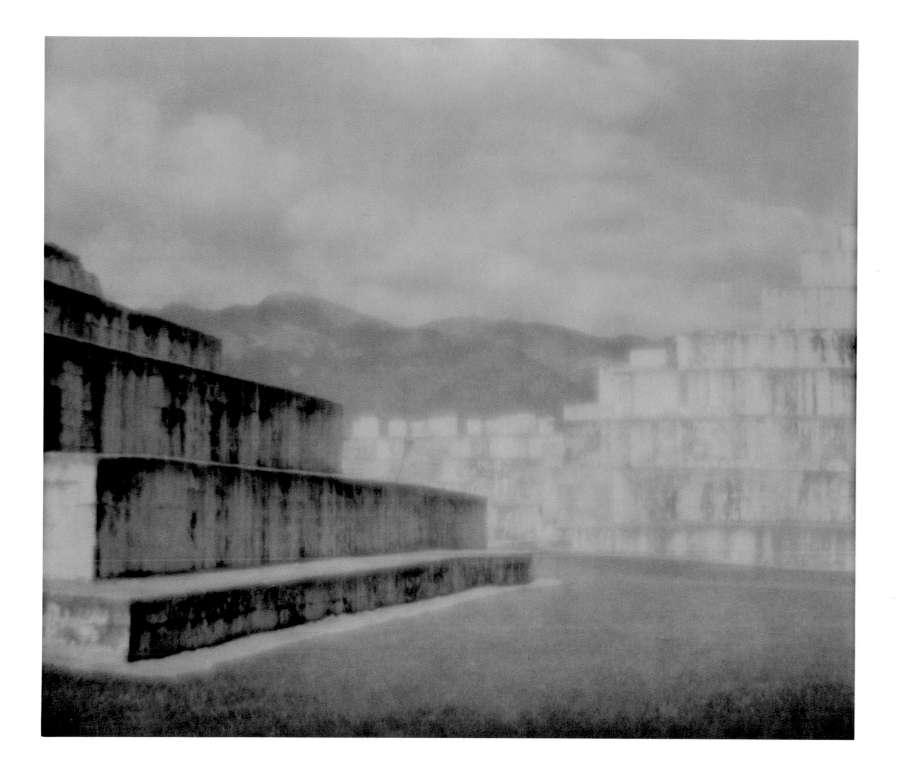

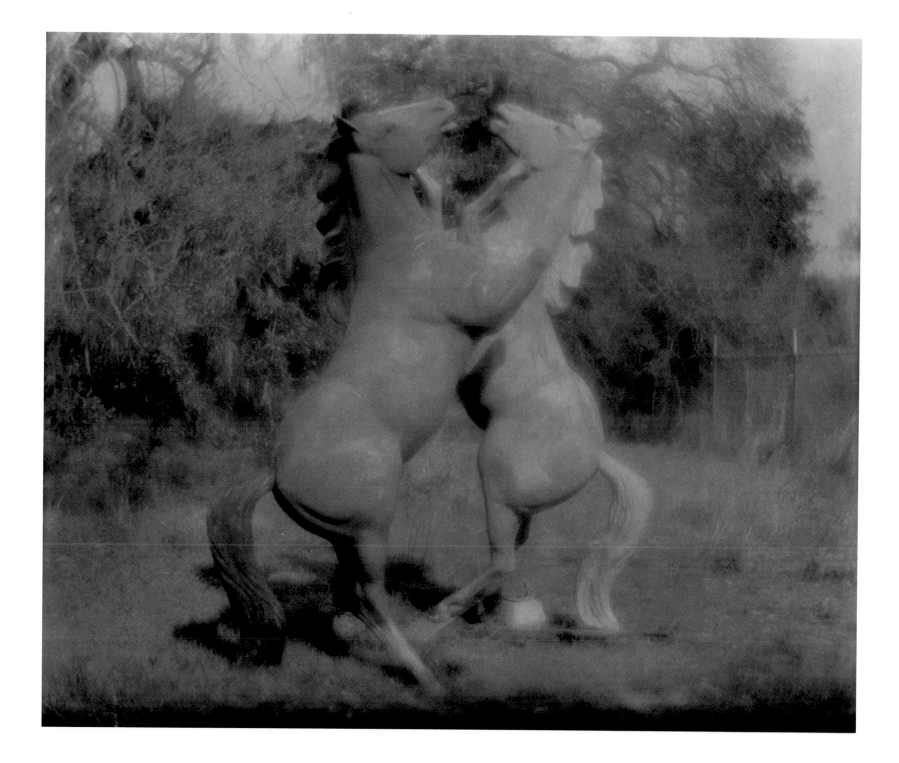

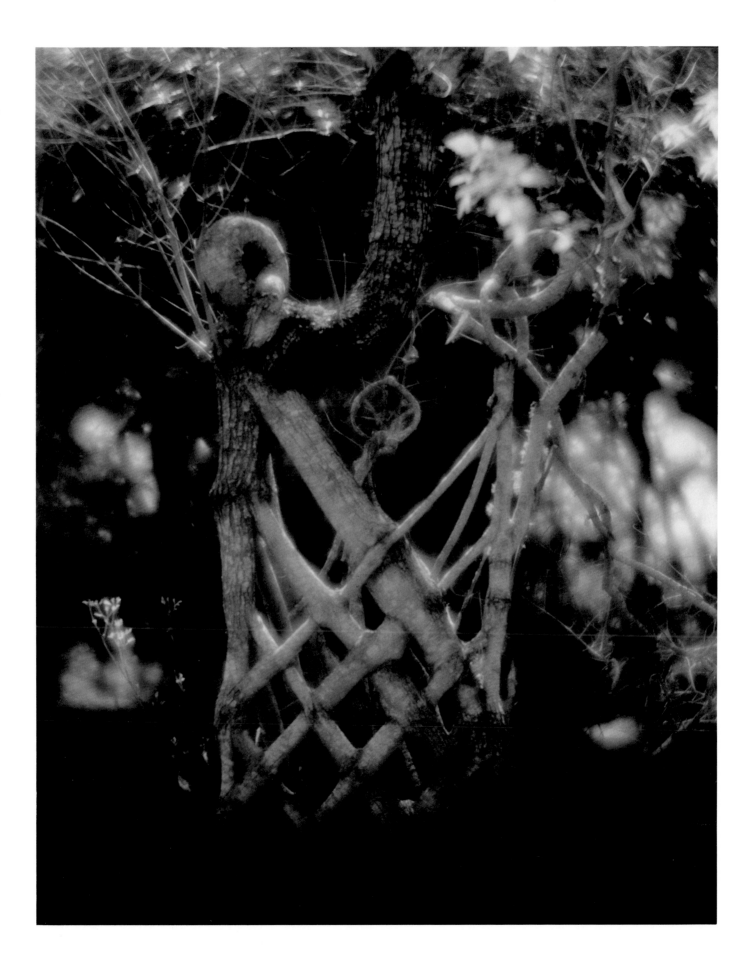

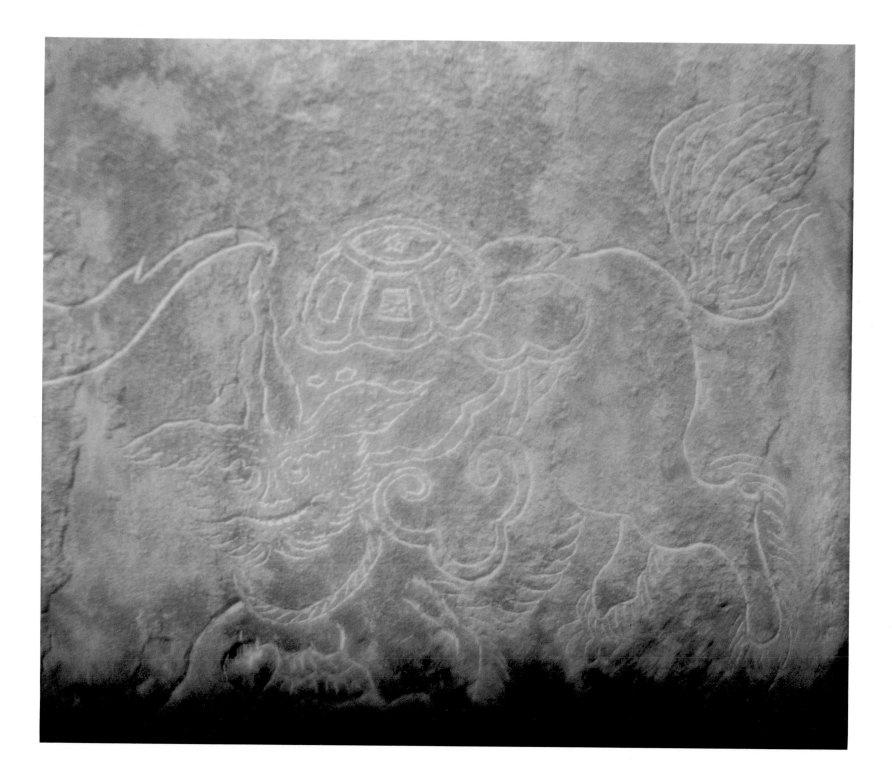

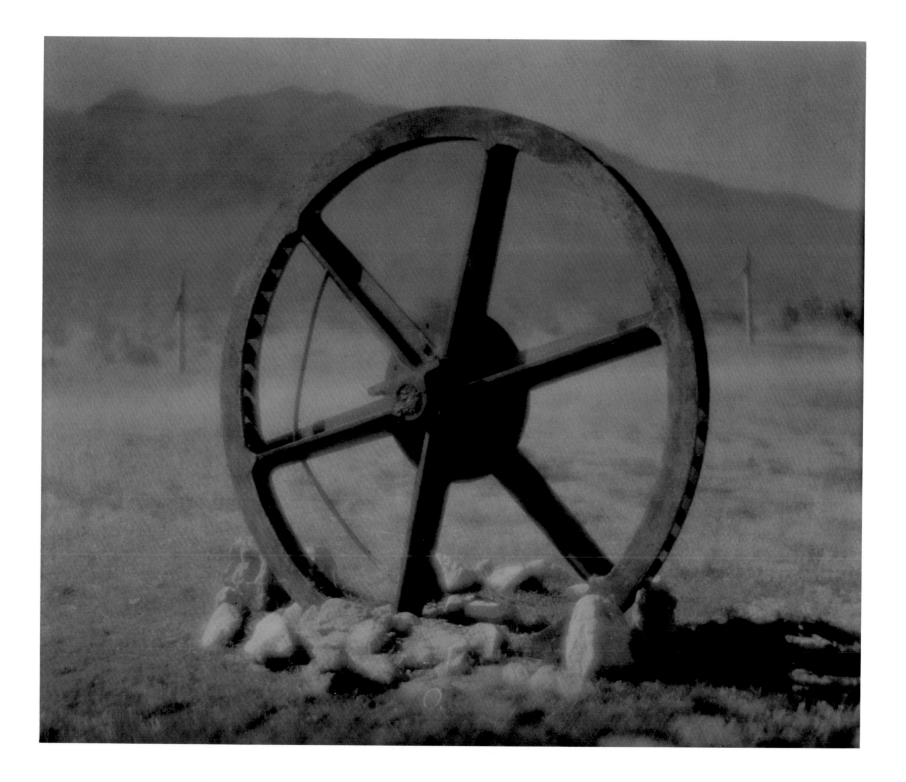

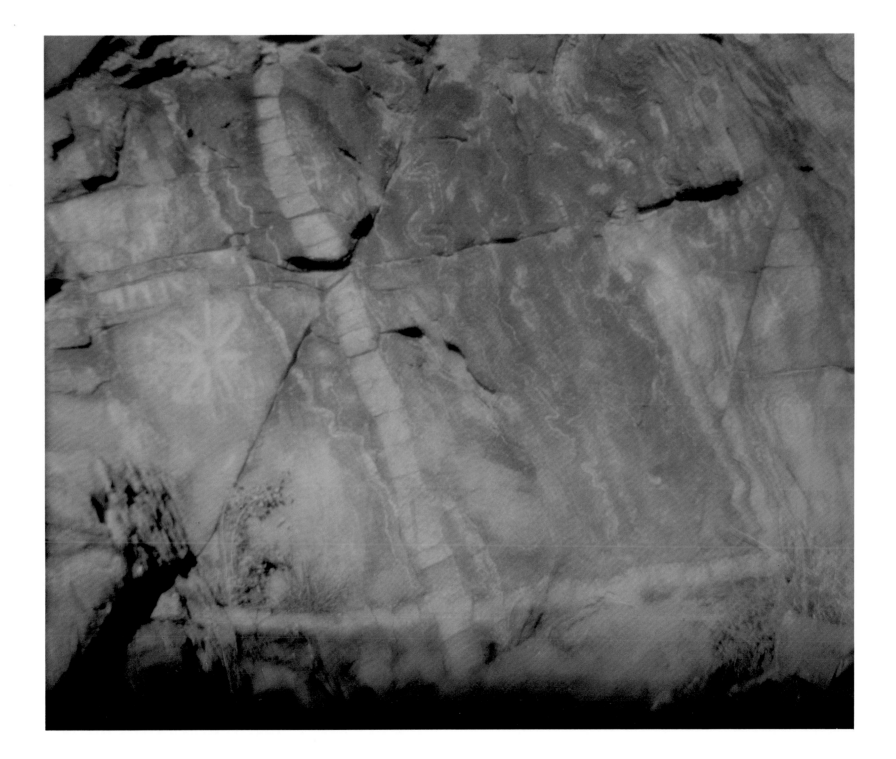

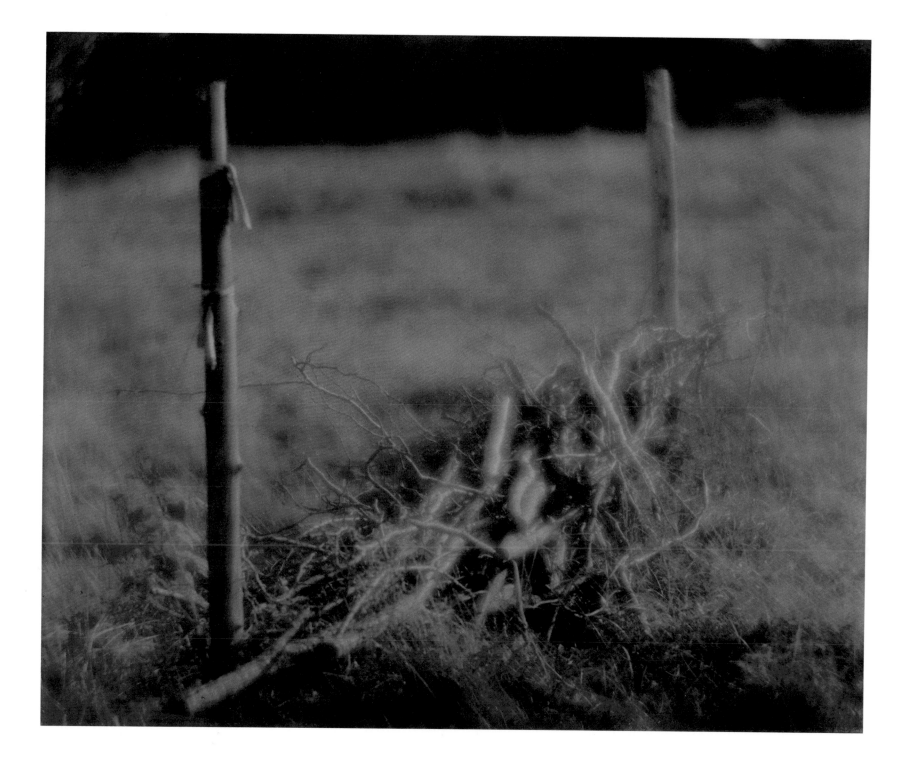

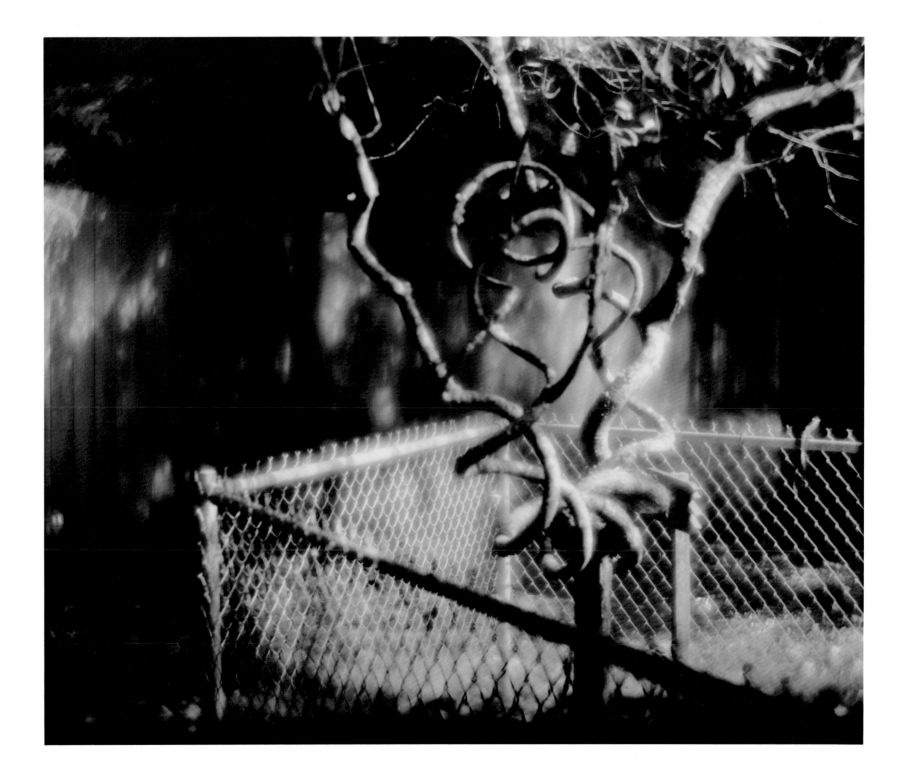

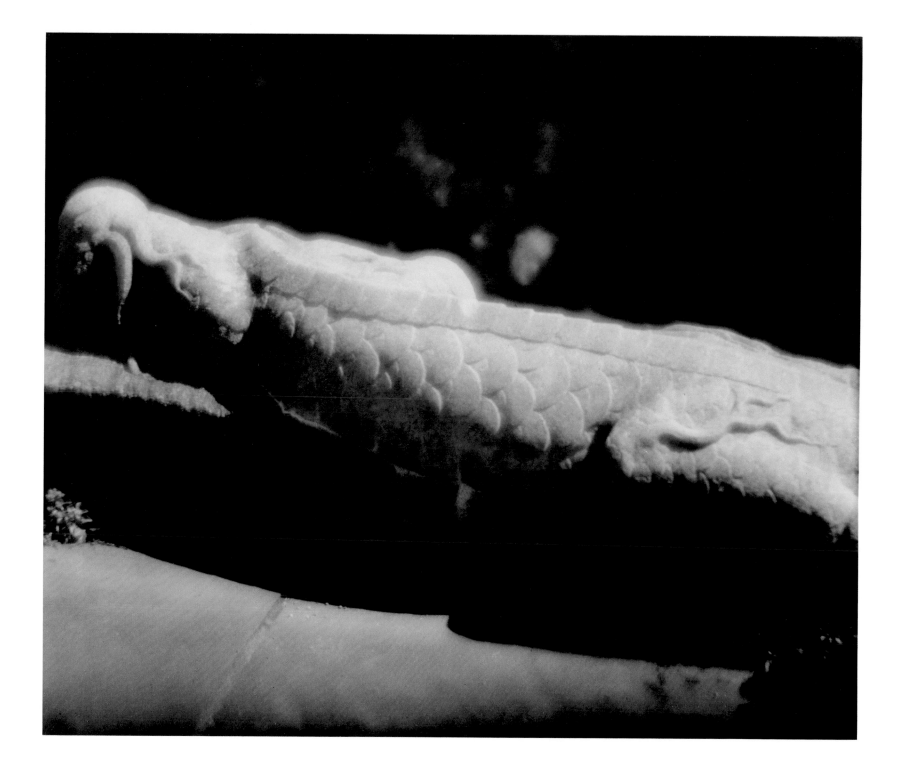

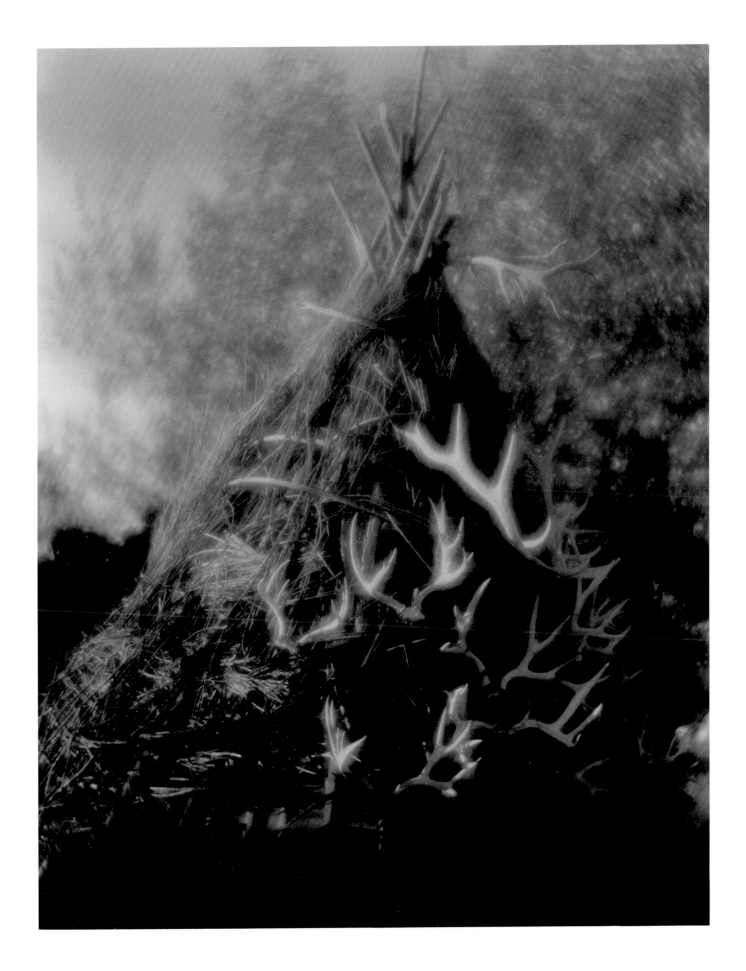

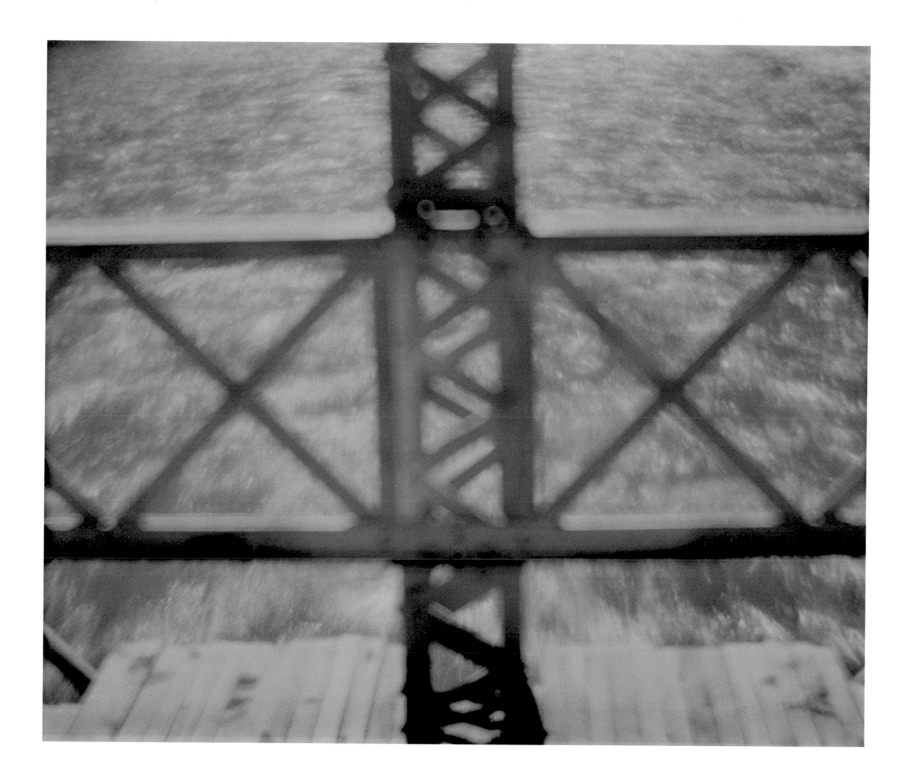

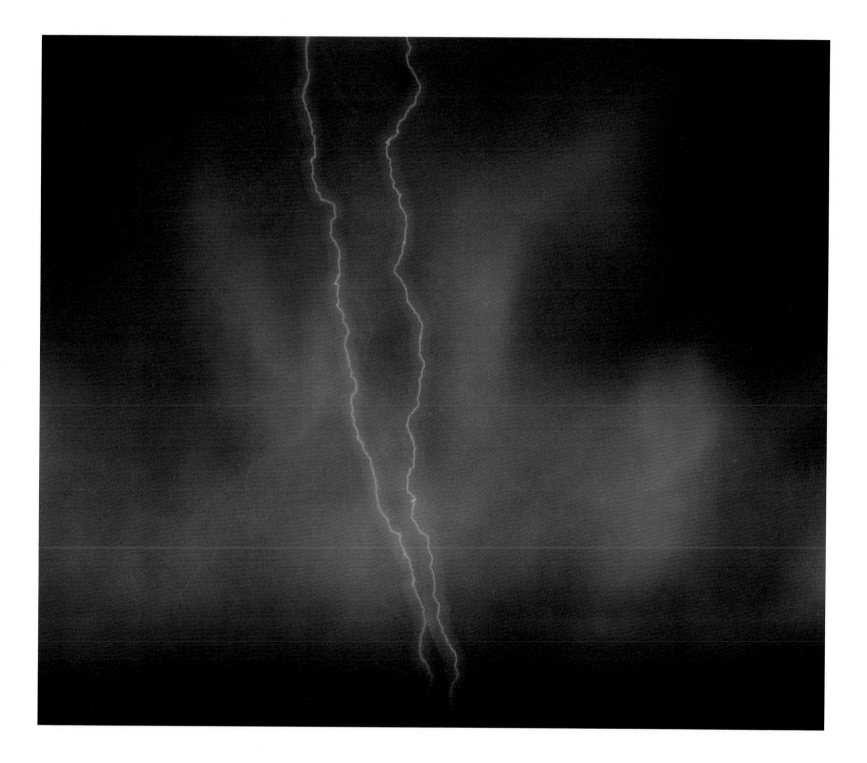

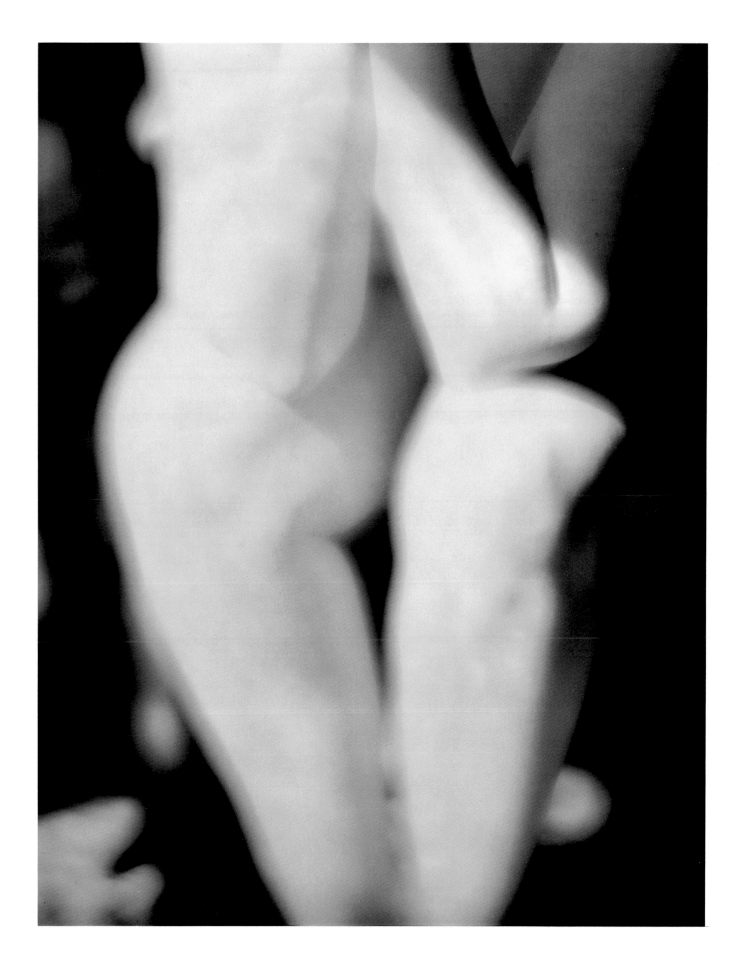

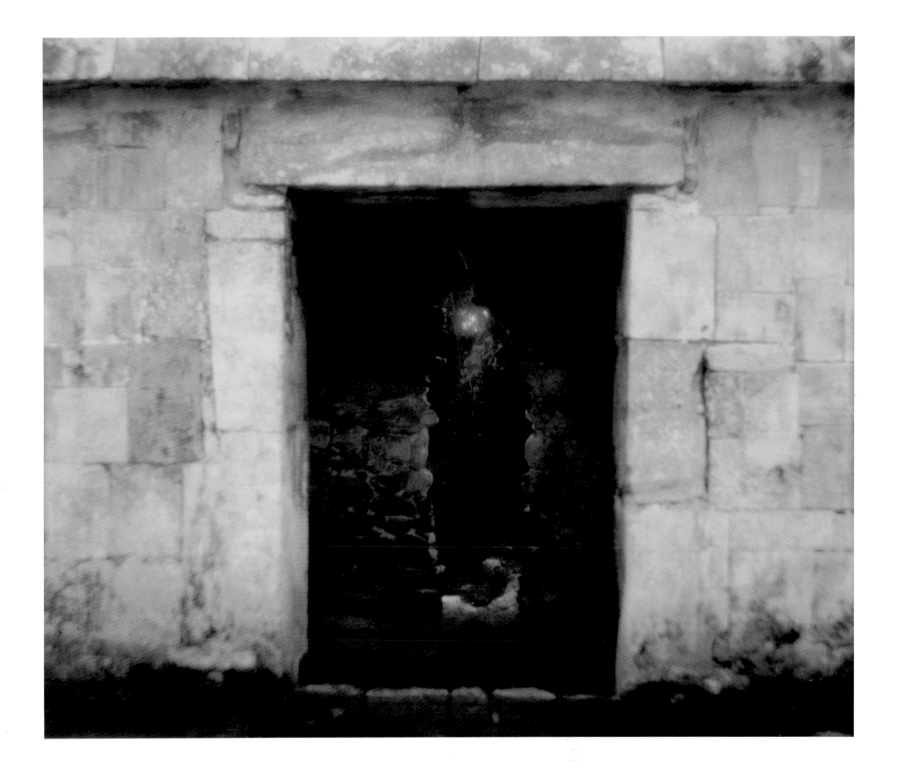

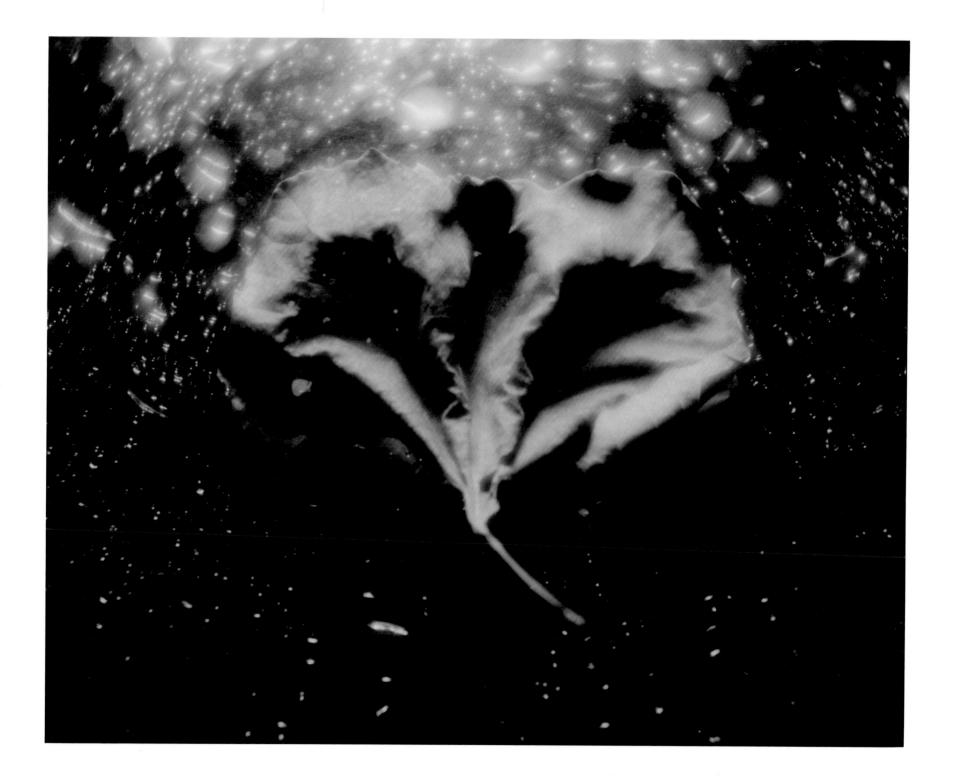

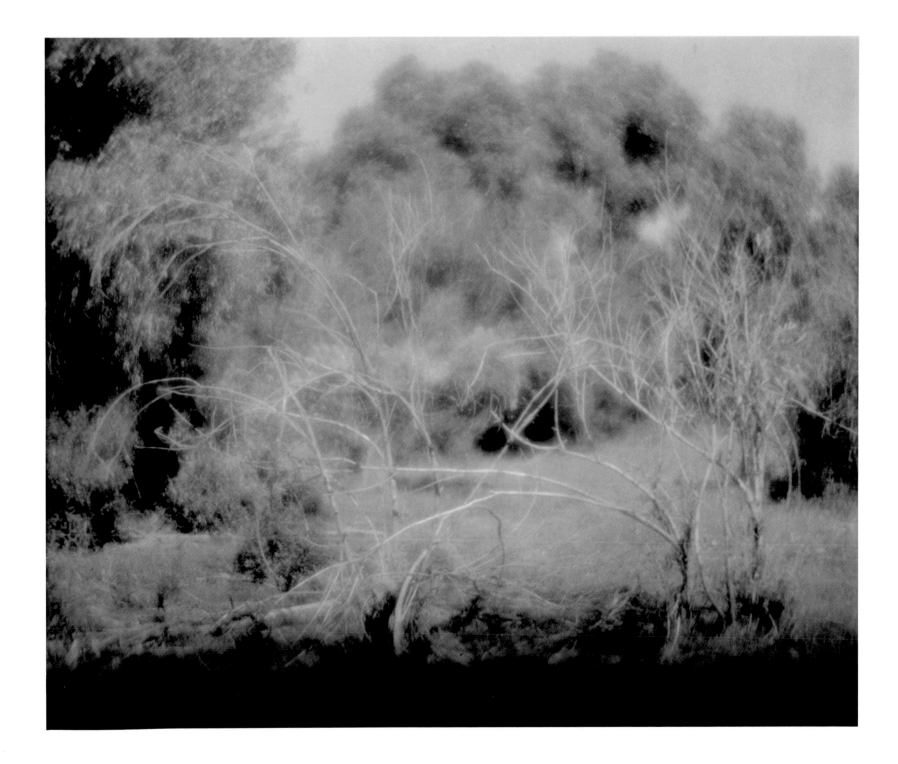

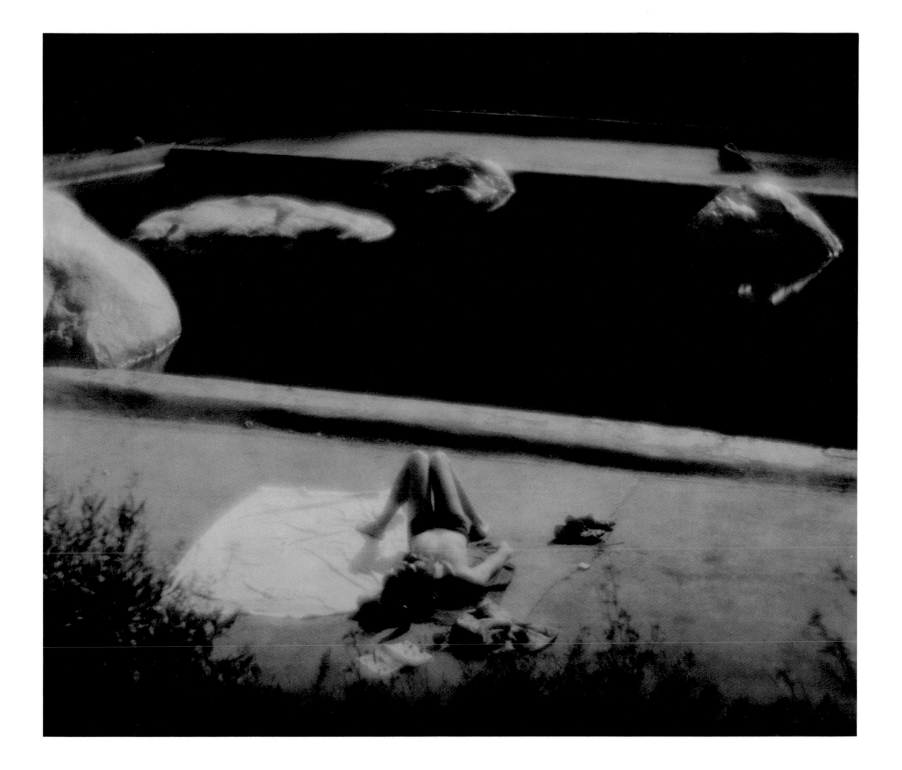

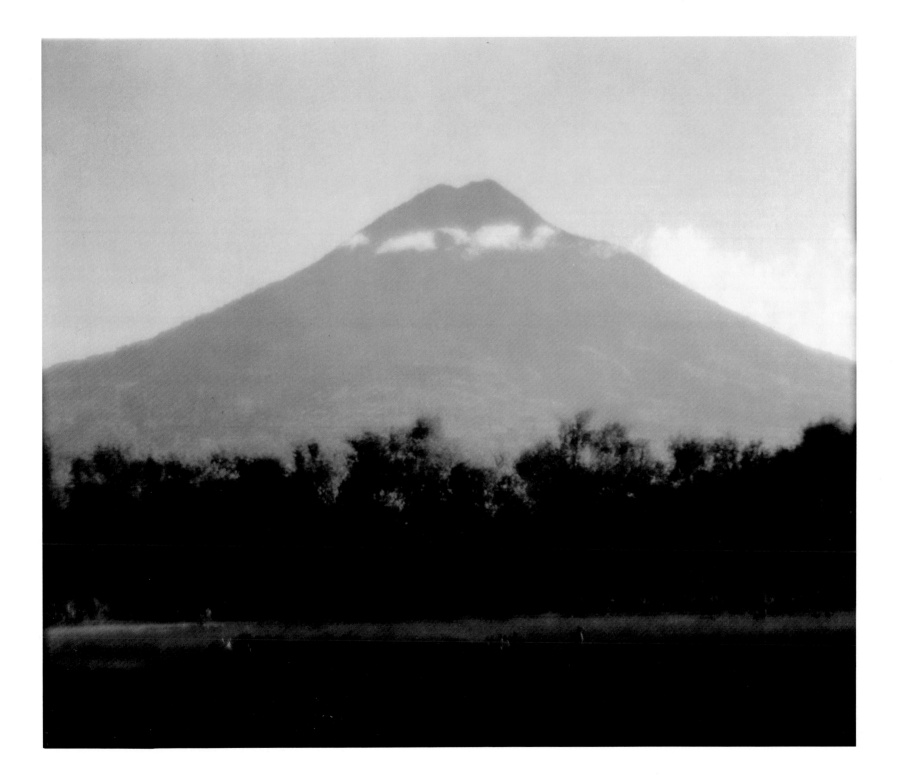

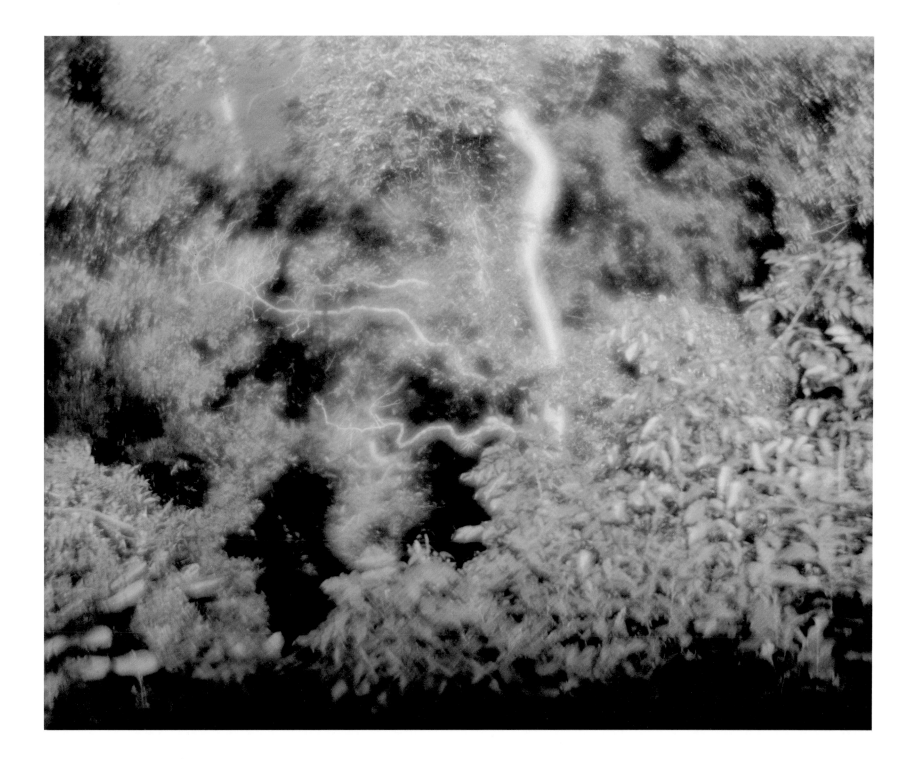

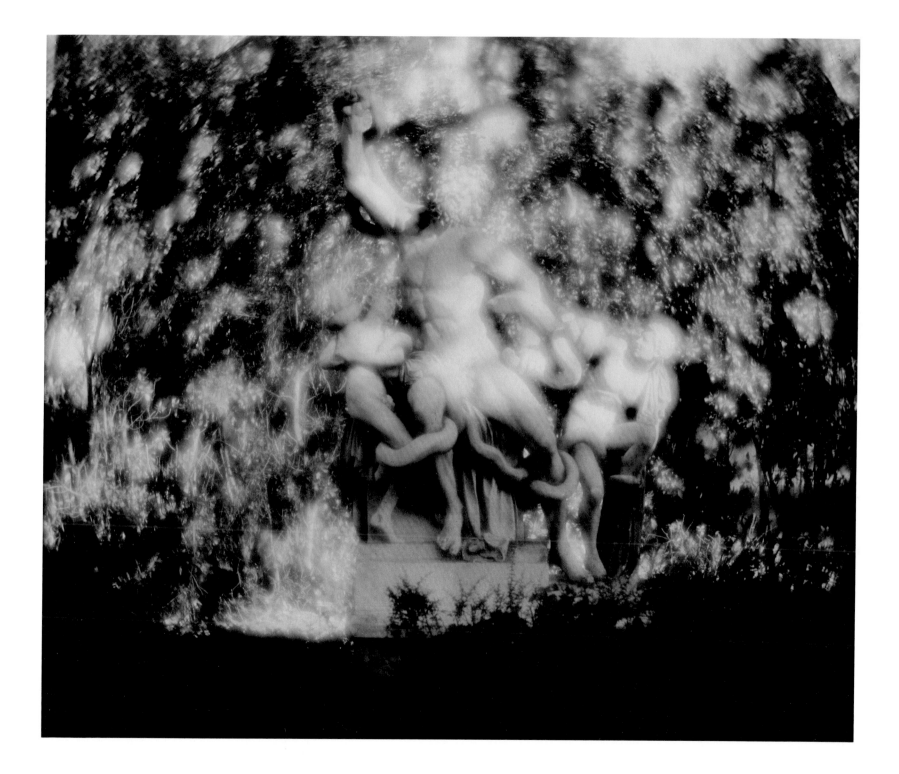

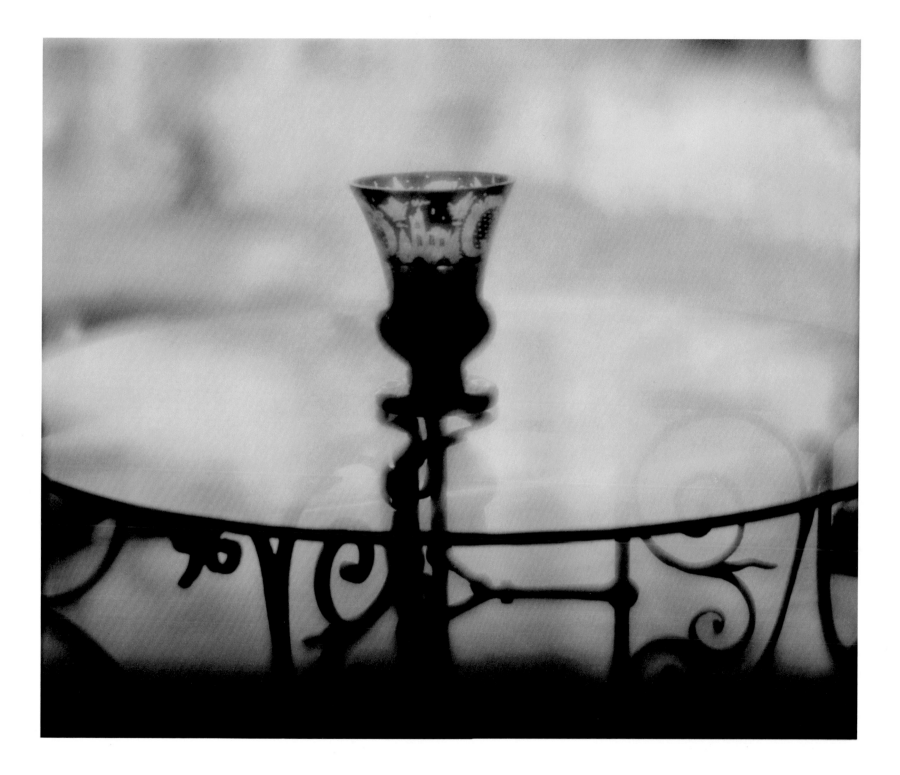

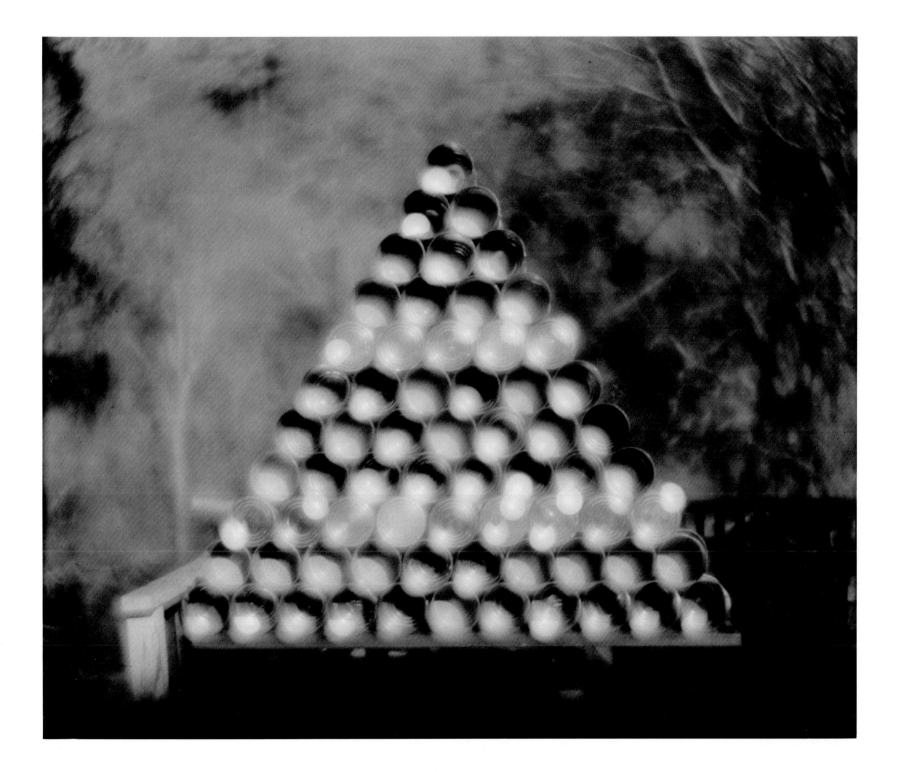

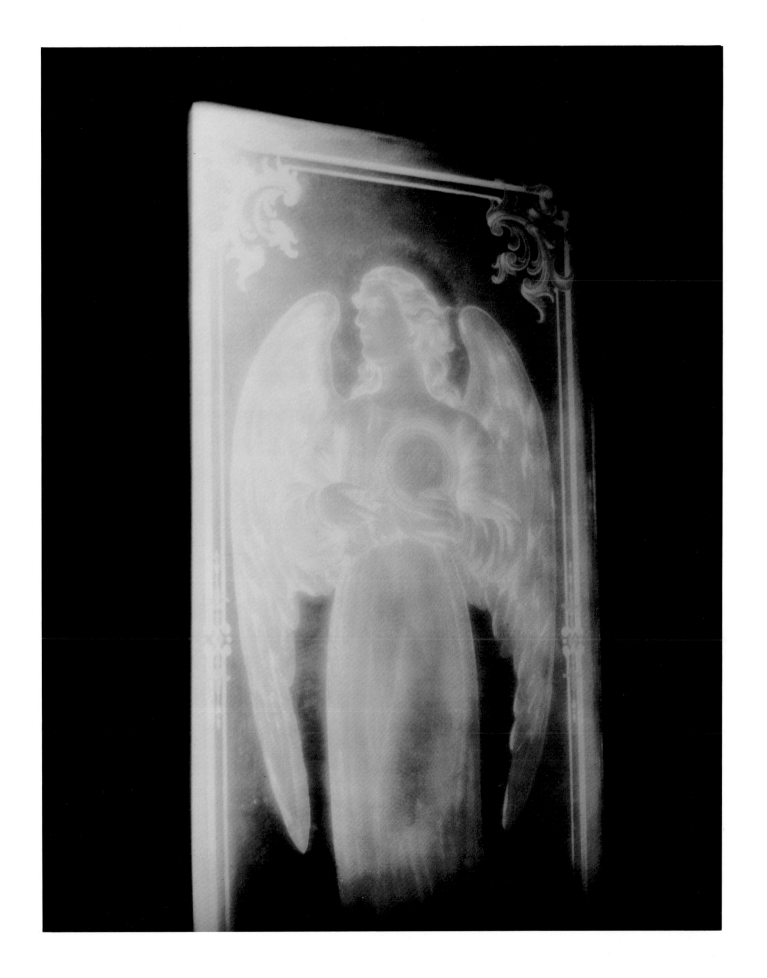

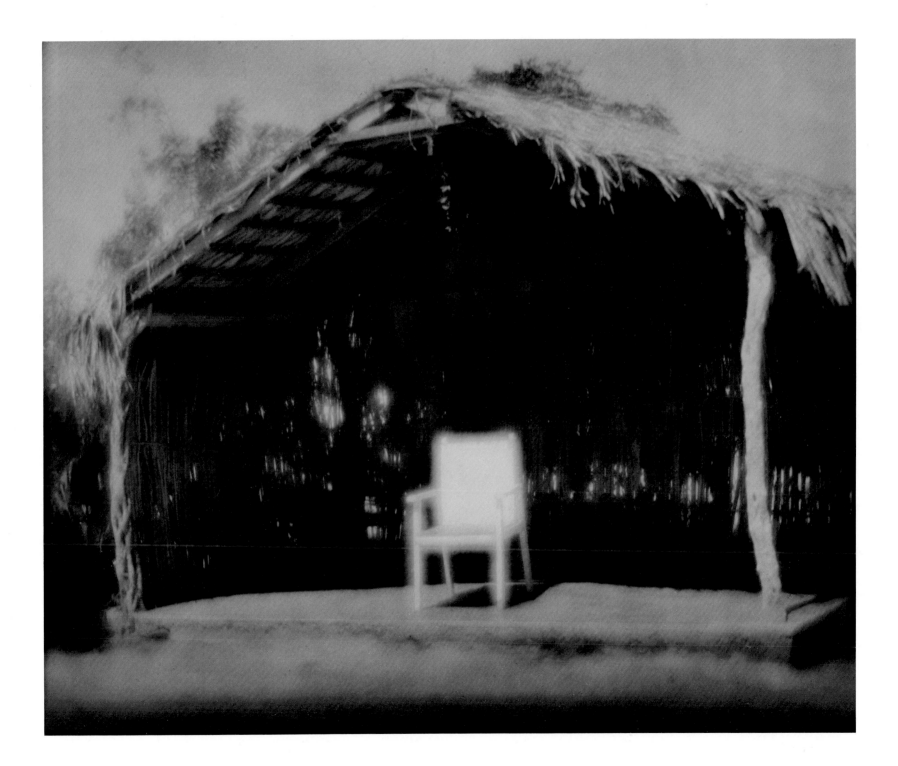

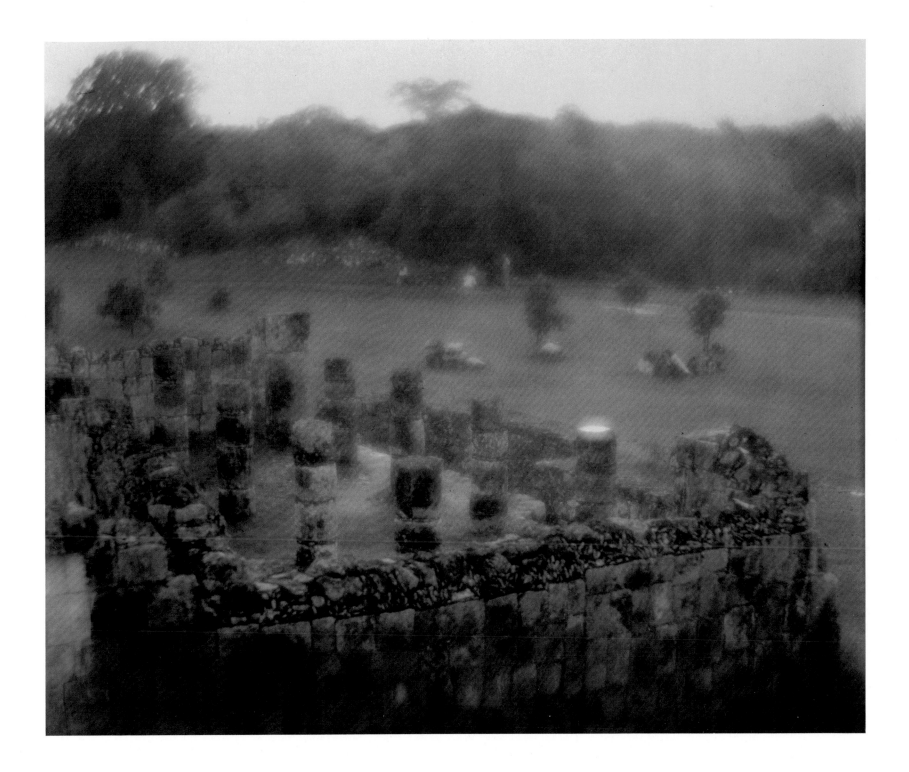

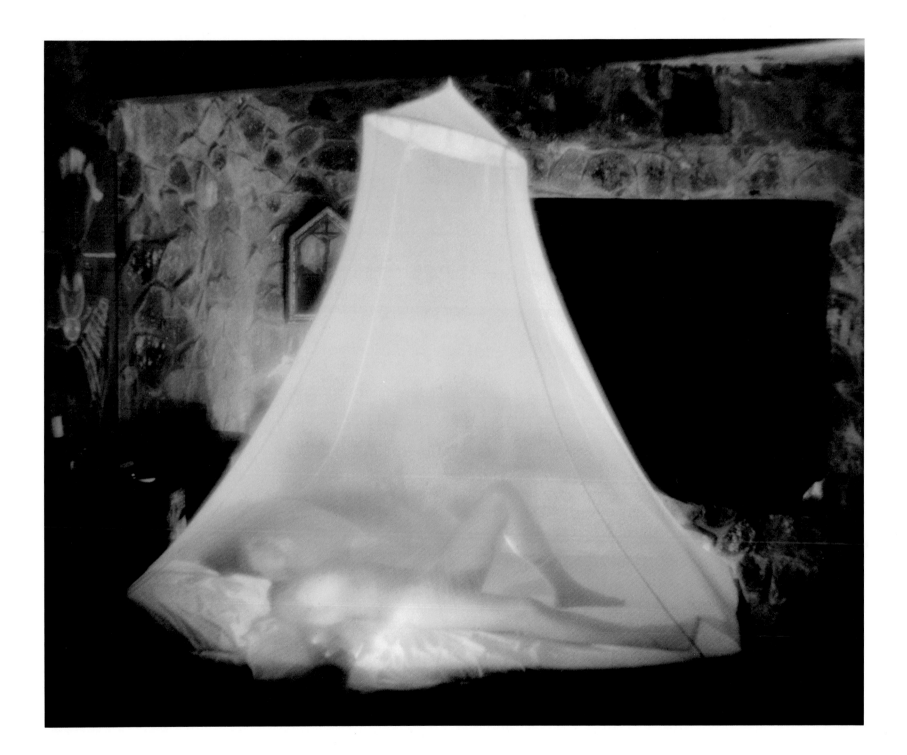

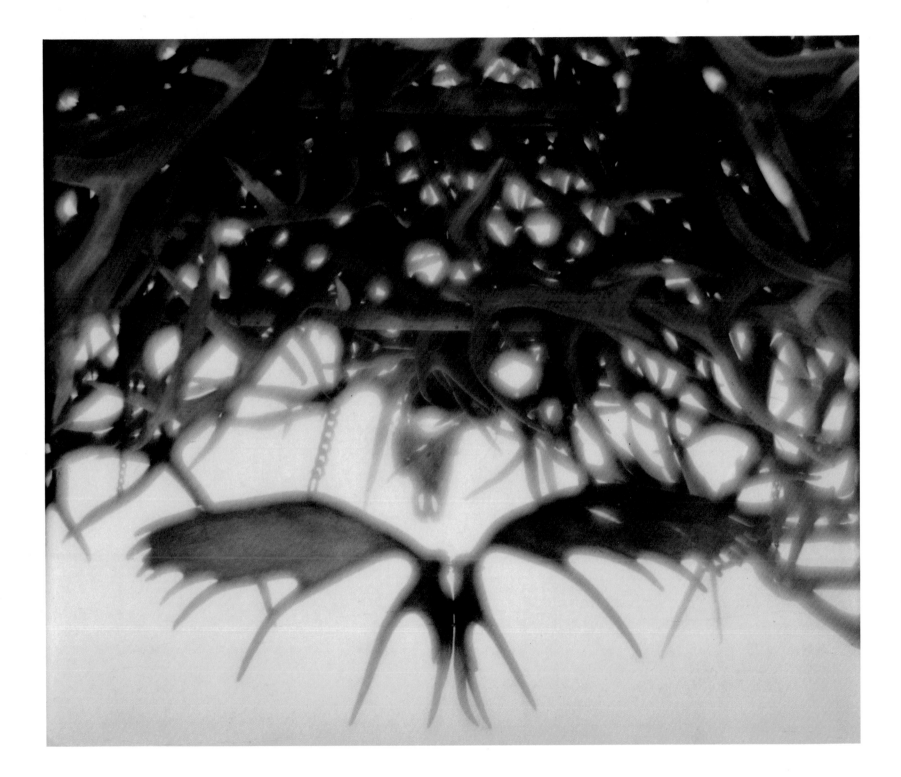

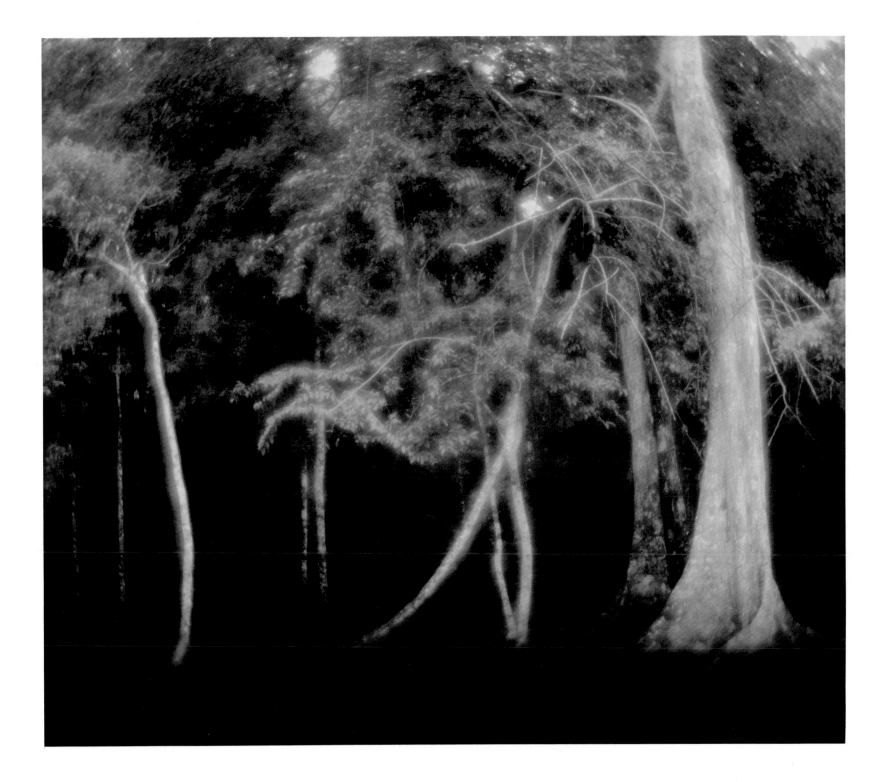

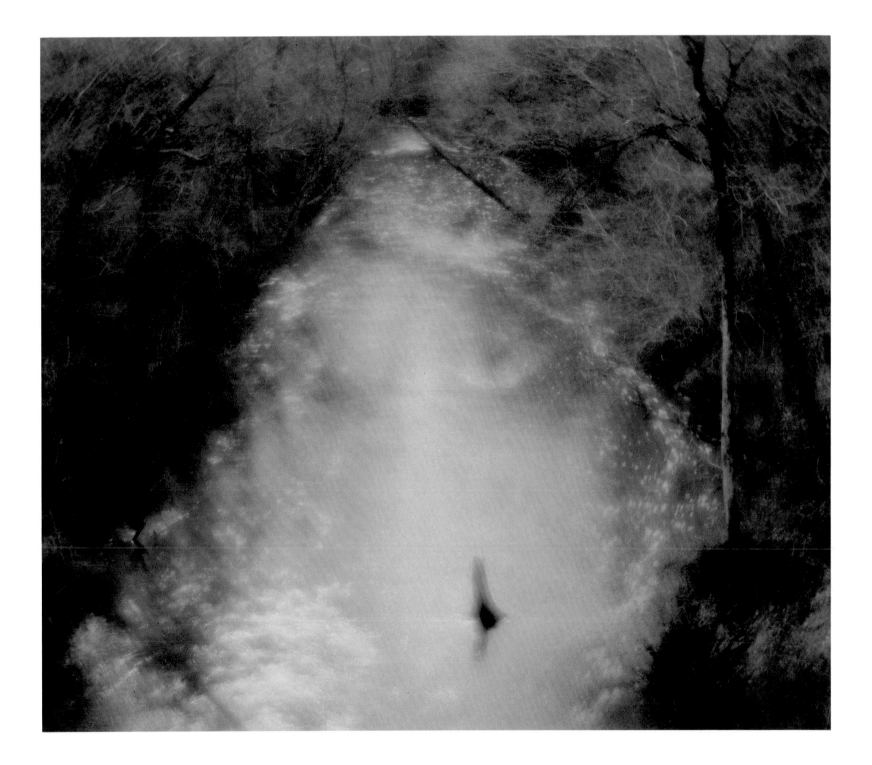

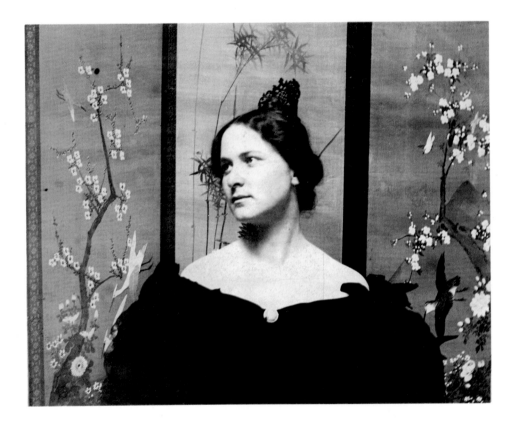

In 1905, Ethelyn McKinney became interested in the art of photography, and enrolled in a class with Clarence White. Along with her Century 8 x 10 view camera, she ordered a custom-made portrait lens from England, a soft-focus "semi-achromatic."

My aunt and uncle gave me their Aunt Ethelyn's camera in 1972. From my first look through it in their garden, I was enchanted. All of the images in this book were made with that camera and lens.

Thank you, Ethelyn.

This book would not have been possible without:

A grant from the National Endowment for the Arts, Washington, D.C.

The generous support of Ralph and Jean Connor, and Celeste Barnes

The editorial and production assistance of Peter Schlessinger and the staff at Apeiron Workshops

SOLOS

was designed by Katy Homans

typeset by Thomas Todd Company

printed by the Meriden Gravure Company

bound by Robert Burlen & Sons

WORKING DOGS

WORKING DOGS

Carrie Owens

Prima Publishing

PRIMA PUBLISHING and colophon are registered trademarks of Prima Communications, Inc.

Cover photo courtesy of Carrie Owens.
Back cover photos courtesy of: Carrie Owens (top left),
Big Feat Entertainment (top right), and Michael Haumesser (bottom photos).
Author photo courtesy of Carrie Owens.

Library of Congress Cataloging-in-Publication Data

Owens, Carrie.
Working dogs / Carrie Owens.
p. cm.
ISBN 0-7615-1978-5
1. Working dogs Anecdotes. I. Title.
SF428.2.095   1999
1636.73—dc21   99-40940
CIP

99 00 01 02 03 04 GG 10 9 8 7 6 5 4 3 2 1
Printed in the United States of America

How to Order
Single copies may be ordered from Prima Publishing, P.O. Box 1260BK, Rocklin, CA 95677;
telephone (916) 632-4400. Quantity discounts are also available.
On your letterhead, include information concerning the intended use of the books
and the number of copies you wish to purchase.

Visit us online at www.primalifestyles.com

Contents

Acknowledgments

The author would like to thank Vickie Andreassi, Pamela Berger, William Berloni, Peter Bloeme, Constance Bracewell, Cassandra Case, William Russell Case II, Heather Cameron, Mike Cash, Bernice Collins, Kevin Dailey, Ben Dominitz, Lisa and Jerome Dupree, David Ferland, Steve Fischer, Rochelle Fabb, Terry Glover, Melvin Graves, Steve Gregson, Molly Hayden, Dan Hayter, Cheree and Tiara Heppe, Dorne Huebler, Jackie Kaptan, Tara Kennedy, Roy Key, James Krusoe, Barry and Jean Larkin, Ella Levitskoya, Glenda Manucy, Don McGee, Michelle Melville, Bill Mott, Roy Neely, David Nilsen, Ted and Jana Ondrak, Daniela Ortner, John Oulton, Boone Owens, Sonya Owens, Deborah Palman, Jim Parks, Brent Phelps, Candace Pirnak, Gregory Popovich, Thomas Prendergast, Dana Provost and the Flying Colors Flyball Team, Debbie Seymour, Carolyn Scott, Caren Schwenkmeyer, Michael Snell, Andrew and Marilyn Solarz, Jeffrey Tennyson, Rick Spring, Art Resnick, Mary Rice, Rachel Rosenthal, Sara Sockitt, Mark Taverniti, Andrew Vallas, Barbara Van Deusen, Antonio Velatti, Liz Ward, Christina Wessell, Charlie West, William Wegman, Gregory Wood, and, especially, Michael Haumesser.

Preface
Labor of Love

WORKING DOGS COME FROM ALL WALKS OF LIFE. Some are purchased for thousands of dollars, others found abandoned with no price tag but the one that says "love me." Some working dogs sleep on the pillows of their owners' beds, others sleep alone in kennels on the other side of the world. Some of them perform back flips for millions of fans, others quietly save the lives of children they'll never meet.

Traditionally, working dogs were hunting dogs, herding dogs, and guard dogs. In our modern times, the jobs of dogs are much more diverse: cancer detection, professional sports, land mine detection, therapy, even performance art. Although many jobs call for the use of dogs' incredible noses—they are 1,000 times more sensitive than man's—the skill sets of working dogs are expanding every year. Some dogs have inexplicable talents. Just how does a dog detect an impending epileptic seizure? No one knows.

While the work may be as varied as the careers you'd find in any small town in America, working dogs have more in common than you may think. What they share is the reason for doing the work. Dogs work for their supper. They work to earn play time. But mostly, dogs work to keep the people they love happy.

There's a mysterious connection between people and their working dogs—amplified perhaps because they spend so much time together. It's a connection that defies explanation. By relying on dogs for their livelihood or well-being, people's lives are enriched in ways they had never dreamed possible. And the dogs seem to truly appreciate having something to do—they are creatures who shoulder responsibilities well. When I was a child someone told me dogs were put on this earth to teach humans how to love—not the way humans typically love each other, with strings attached, but the way love was meant to be—unconditional and steadfast. As I wrote this book that childlike idea kept coming back to me because if dogs are teachers, working dogs are professors.

It doesn't matter if someone calls his dog an asset and a portable machine, or if he is someone who relies on his dog so much that the loss of the dog stops the man's life cold. Through their working dogs, people learn a little bit more about love. And maybe even a little bit more about the nature of God. Whether his reward for a hard day's work is a tennis ball or a hot dog, if you really look, you'll see that what a working dog most wants is his human's praise, affection, and kindness—and he'll work his tail off to get it.

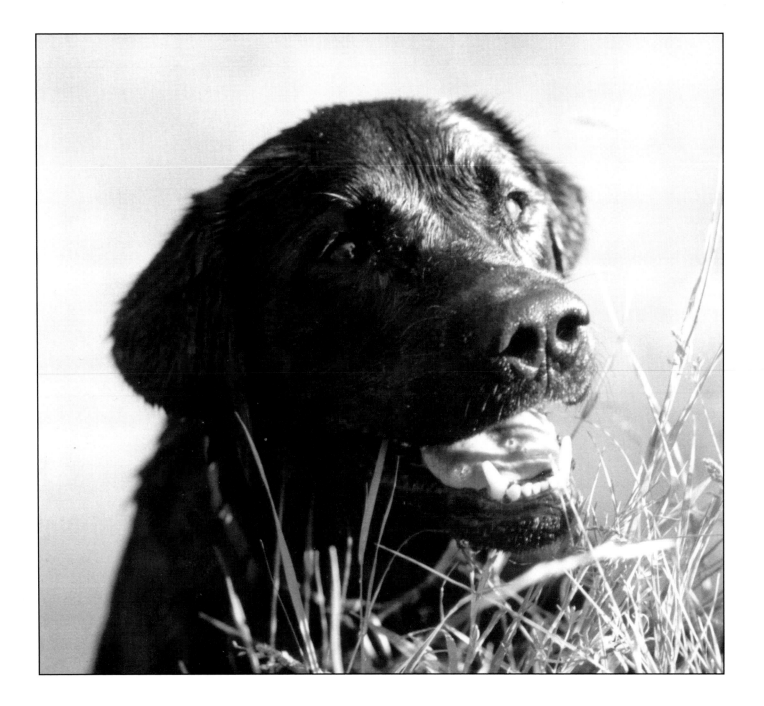

TESSA

Hunting Retriever

HUNTERS KNOW THAT DUCKS JUST FALL OUT OF the sky if you shoot them; retrievers know to go into the water, find the ducks, and gently carry them to the hunters. For this classic team—hunter and dog—there are few activities filled with greater pleasure than a day spent shooting and retrieving ducks.

When Barry Larkin's wife, Jean, brought Tessa home, they agreed to give her a good life. They looked at the little Labrador puppy and decided that there would be no strenuous training. She could sleep on their bed. Any hunting work she performed would be a bonus. But, as often happens, Tessa has shown Larkin that she loves to work, and that their hunting together is as much for her enjoyment as it is for his.

Larkin spent a lot of time with Tessa their first winter together, tossing a stick for her and taking her on walks and rides in the car. When the ice went out, he started throwing a stick into the river, but it took her a month to get over her fear and swim out to get the stick. Larkin never

> TESSA IS A WATER DOG.

3

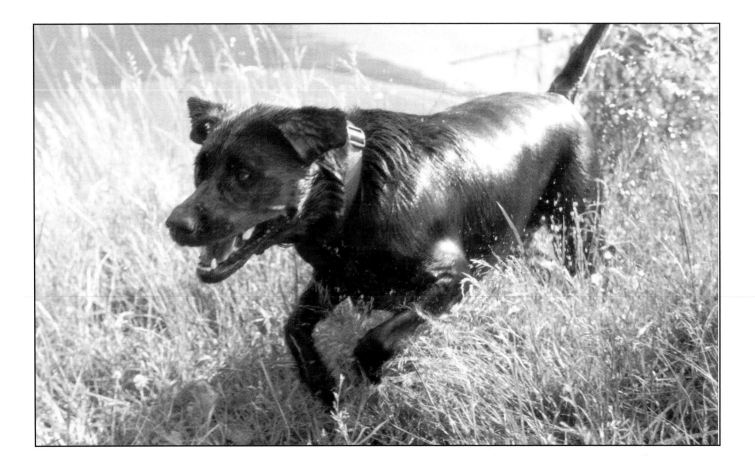

pushed her, he just kept throwing the stick until she decided to get it herself. By summertime, she loved swimming and fetching sticks, and the two went walking together nearly every day.

When hunting season arrived, Larkin took Tessa duck hunting. He had never fired a gun around her and was concerned it might frighten her. Nonetheless, while sneaking into a swampy area, he shot a duck. Tessa immediately went into the water and grabbed the bird. She brought it back to Larkin and that was that: Tessa was a water dog.

Later Larkin tried her at pheasant hunting, and she was just as excellent at flushing and kicking out birds for Larkin to shoot. When he takes the dog ice fishing, she grabs the fish after he throws them onto the ice and helps him put them into a bucket. She even chases and hunts rabbits. These are activities Tessa does on her own—without being taught. All Larkin has to do is put her in a hunting situation, and she takes it from there.

LABRADOR RETRIEVERS ARE THE MOST popular dogs in America. They were developed in nineteenth-century England as hunting dogs, and are known for being outgoing and loyal. Because they are still bred to encourage their ability to retrieve, many people consider them to be the last great working breed in America.

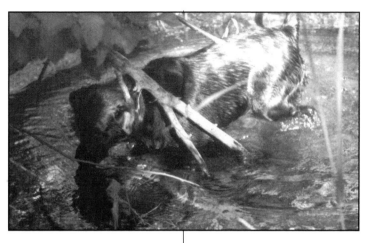

ALL LARKIN HAS TO DO IS PUT HER IN A HUNTING SITUATION, AND SHE TAKES IT FROM THERE.

Tessa is as affectionate as most Labradors. She approaches life with caution, always watching to see what is expected prior to bounding into a situation. Perhaps that is a lesson she learned as a puppy, when she jumped out of a moving car and broke her leg. She and Larkin are so close that she tells him with her eyes when she needs to go outside. Larkin lets Tessa sleep on his bed, and if she migrates at night and ends up on his pillow, he just gets another one for himself.

Last summer, Larkin planted six tomato plants in his yard and was surprised to see Tessa spend time sniffing them each day. When the fruit was just beginning to turn red, Tessa ate it. Throughout the summer, she ate every single tomato just as it ripened. For the remainder of the season, the Larkins enjoyed watching her do it. This year, they're planting even more tomatoes for Tessa. After all, they did promise her the good life.

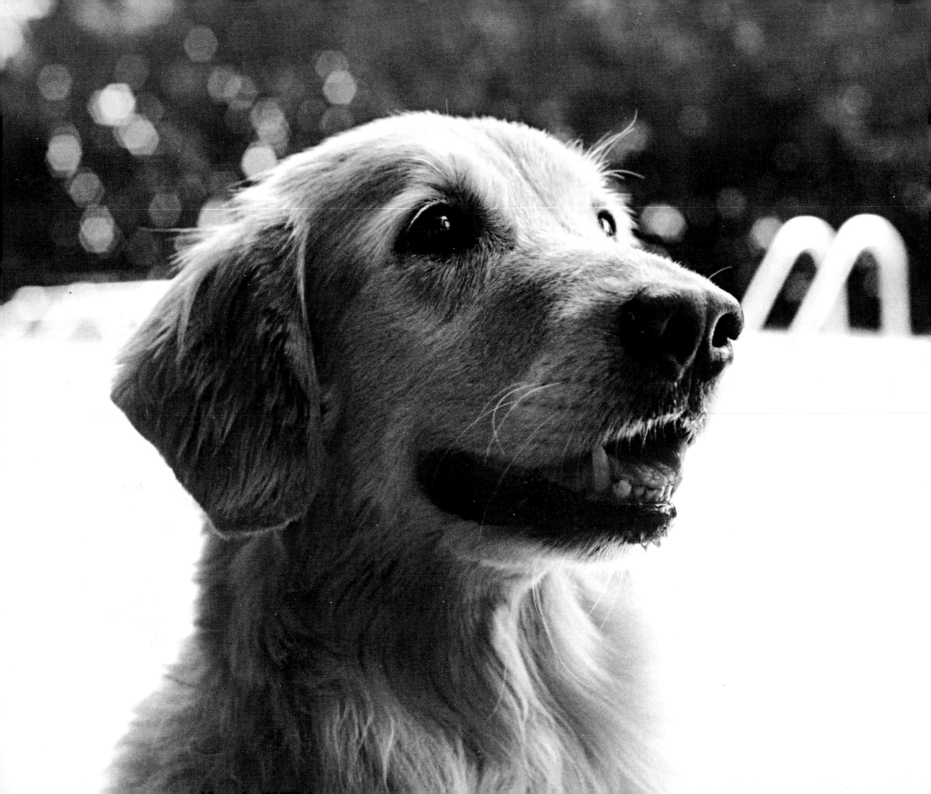

BREEZE

Cancer Detector

BREEZE IS THE ONLY FEMALE GOLDEN RETRIEVER who has earned all three important AKC titles: Utility Dog Excellent, Obedience Trial Champion, and Master Hunting Dog. But when her owner Glenda Munacy asks Breeze, "Ready to find cells?" she's doing another kind of work entirely. Breeze is searching for cancer. There's no title for finding cancer, but if there were, Breeze would have it. She works with 100 percent accuracy.

It all started in 1994 when a Florida dermatologist teamed up with a local police K9 trainer to see if dogs could be trained to detect cancer. Breeze was pulled into the testing because she was such a well-trained dog and was excellent at scent work. Breeze knew how to communicate, or alert, by sitting down when she found what she was searching for. All she needed to learn was the scent of cancerous cells; her training and her nose would do the rest.

Munacy taught Breeze the scent of cancer cells by putting a fresh biopsy sample into a piece of plastic pipe with holes drilled into it. Munacy hid the pipe and told Breeze to find the cells. It was a game, and Breeze was good at it. Munacy hid the pipe under the couch, in

7

a cabinet, all over the house. Breeze proved to be as adept at finding the cancer samples as she was at tracking game or lost people.

Once Breeze knew the smell, and could find the hidden pipe, Munacy transferred the melanoma sample to a test tube, which she put into a stand with nine other test tubes. By putting items such as tape and plastic gloves into the other tubes, Breeze learned to ignore related smells and focus on the scent of cancer. By alerting only to the biopsy test tube, Breeze was able to differentiate between cancer cells and other common hospital aromas.

To teach Breeze to search on a person, Munacy placed the biopsy between two Band-Aids and attached it to people. Breeze learned to touch a person's skin with her nose to show Munacy the exact location of the cancer. Eventually, Breeze was allowed to search a real patient, still alerting to the scent of melanoma. Being a soft and gentle dog, people loved being examined by her. She searched seven patients and was accurate in every case, touching her nose to the exact spot where melanoma was found.

One of the patients Breeze searched already had a negative biopsy test result so the doctor expected no alert. In fact, he thought Breeze was wrong when she

> THERE'S NO TITLE FOR FINDING CANCER, BUT IF THERE WERE, BREEZE WOULD HAVE IT.

alerted to the spot. When Breeze alerted to the same spot again and again, the doctor went back and removed the entire lesion for further testing. Breeze was right—they found melanoma.

Breeze was also trained to alert to lung cancer. For these tests, they enlisted a local lung cancer doctor, who provided breath samples of patients both with cancer and without. The patients would breathe into a cloth that he then sealed in a test tube. After providing a few samples with cancer on them, the doctor sent blanks—breath samples from a person who did not have cancer. Breeze performed eighteen lung cancer searches and was accurate with every one, positive or negative.

In one unusual case, Breeze alerted to the sample of a person whose cancer had metastasized to the outside of his lung. Because the lung isn't considered to be porous, it was quite curious that Breeze could smell the cancer. No one was sure how she could do it.

AFTER THREE YEARS OF TESTING, THE DOCTORS WHO HAD been providing biopsies lost interest in continuing the research. Breeze had proven that dogs could detect cancer, but there seemed to be no interest from within the medical community to use that information.

Munacy felt people were concerned over liability issues. It's too bad, because one of the best ways to survive cancer is to find it early. A cancer-detecting session with Breeze is a much more relaxing experience than an x-ray or biopsy—and the chance for an accurate result seem a lot higher.

Now, Breeze only tests friends of Munacy's who wonder if they might have cancer. They'll call and ask, "Can she search me?" So far, Breeze has found only basal cells—cells in the deepest skin layer—that were turning cancerous and needed to be removed from one of Munacy's friends.

When working, Breeze wears special collars, and she knows by the collar Munacy puts on her what job she will be asked to perform. For hunting, it's a flat collar; for obedience work, it's a leather collar; and for cancer searches, it a chain collar. She is rewarded—with cheese and praise—every time she searches for cancer, not just when she finds it. Munacy is careful never to encourage false alerts.

Becoming a cancer detector didn't change Breeze. She's just as gentle and smart as ever. She's had so

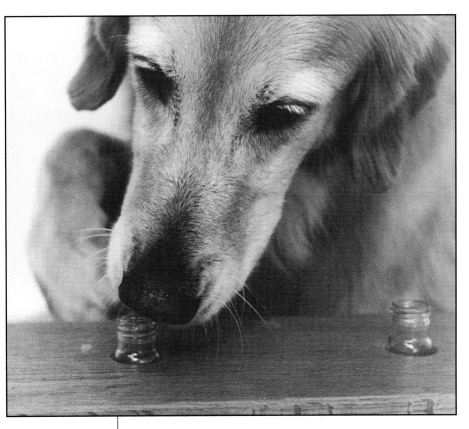

many excellent puppies that she has been awarded an Outstanding Dam certificate by the AKC. She loves to hunt at Munacy's farm; she swims in Munacy's pool. She may be a dog who knows how to pursue life-or-death matters, but for Breeze, this was all simply one more game to master.

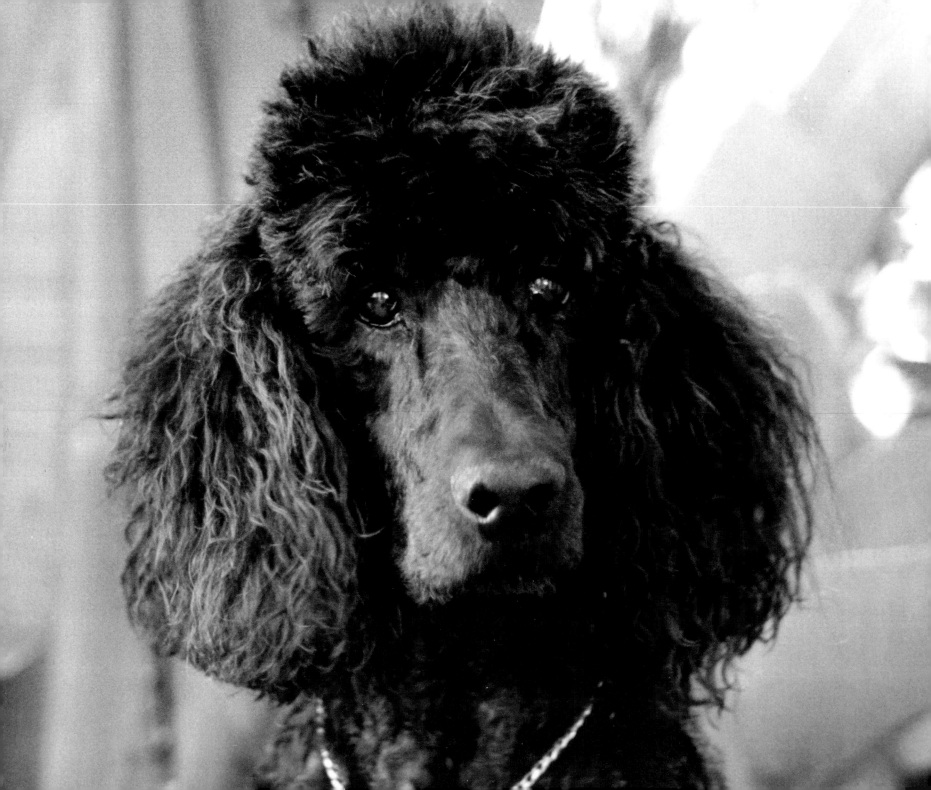

DUBONNET

Earthquake Predictor

LIKE MANY DOGS, DUBONNET LOVES TO EAT CAT FOOD. She is considered a great judge of character. She nibbles on shoes when unhappy and enjoys getting dressed in her red raincoat and rain boots—a fine contrast with her black poodle curls. She prefers sleeping on the velvet couch.

Unlike other dogs, however, Dubonnet warns her family of imminent earthquakes. This comes in handy, as the family lives in California, where, although they've been through a few bad ones, the Big One is yet to hit.

When you live in California—as in other places where natural disasters occur with frequency—you must keep a certain security blanket of ignorance around yourself as you go through your days. With Dubonnet in the house, however, that just isn't possible. Her family is always ready for the Big One, watching their poodle for signs. To warn of an earthquake, Dubonnet goes through five levels of unusual behavior, from losing her appetite to clawing at the front door. As she progresses from level one to level five, her family knows an earthquake is more and more likely. And they get ready.

11

Level One: When Dubonnet stops eating, they keep an eye on her.

Level Two: When she follows them everywhere and is constantly underfoot, they check the house to be sure everything weighty is on the floor or bolted down.

Level Three: When she starts whining, they check their supplies: water, canned food, and whistles. Certain valuables—crystal and china—are stowed in packing boxes.

Level Four: When she starts drooling, they think twice before traveling across town.

Level Five: When Dubonnet claws at the front door and is confused about whether she wants to be inside or out, they know an earthquake is about to strike, and they rely on their preparations and their faith in God.

ALTHOUGH SUCH BEHAVIOR AND ITS RELATIONSHIP TO earthquakes is considered a coincidence by most scientists, other cultures recognize the correlation and rely on animal behavior to predict earthquakes and evacuate cities. For instance, in 1975, upon noticing strange animal behavior, the Chinese evacuated the city of Haich'eng hours before a 7.3 earthquake struck—saving 90,000 lives. Of course, other earthquakes have occurred in China without warning, often with devastat-

ing effect. The U.S. Geological Survey claims there is no reliable method for predicting earthquakes with greater accuracy than chance.

ONE MAN WHO STUDIES ANIMAL BEHAVIOR AND CLAIMS 75 percent accuracy in predicting earthquakes is retired U.S. Geological Survey geologist Jim Berkland. He counts the number of lost pet ads in newspapers and correlates that information with lunar-tide cycles. If the number of lost pets rises during a seismic window caused by gravitational variations in the lunar cycle, he says earthquake, and, most likely, one will occur. The lost pet ads are key because they document animals who, like Dubonnet, are greatly agitated—and flee their homes in their confusion.

According to Berkland, Dubonnet is the most accurate earthquake-predicting dog alive. Other dogs he's known of with

> DUBONNET IS THE MOST ACCURATE EARTHQUAKE-PREDICTING DOG ALIVE.

this particular talent include Twiggy, a tea-cup poodle who hid under a fringed chair in the living room prior to an earthquake, and Cenji, a standard poodle who covered himself in mud and ate willow-bark before quakes. Originally bred to be hunting dogs in

Europe, poodles don't show any breed peculiarities that would explain this evidence of being earthquake sensitive, but they are considered to be among the smartest of dogs.

DUBONNET GAINED HER REPUTATION FROM HER REACTION to the 7.1 Loma Prieta quake, which shook Northern California in 1989. She was only one year old then, and this was her first earthquake. She began with her odd behavior: not eating, constantly underfoot, whining, drooling. On a Monday, she went to the office with her family, who owned an advertising agency, where her behavior intensified until the end of the day when she was frantically clawing at the door.

The earthquake struck.

As the building rocked and buckled, people dove for cover and objects jettisoned across the room. The twelve-foot-tall windows exploded, and the ceiling caved in. Fifteen seconds can last a long time, long enough to make everyone think that this was the Big One.

When the earthquake stopped, the electrical fires began. Dubonnet barked and jumped at the door. Everyone followed Dubonnet into the smoky hallway and the quiet chaos that is distinctive to disasters. As they made their way to the staircase, Dubonnet ran ahead, stopping every ten feet or so to bark and show

the way. She led them down four dark flights of a staircase that had ripped away from the wall. Once outside, and with everyone safe, she returned to normal.

Several days later, Dubonnet was in the car with her family when they drove over the San Andreas fault. Again she drooled and barked and clawed and whimpered. When the same behavior happened a third time, on their return trip, Dubonnet's family called Berkland. Now, when Dubonnet displays her earthquake warning behavior, her family calls Berkland straight away to assist in his research.

Those scientists who do believe animal behavior can warn of impending earthquakes have mixed opinions of how it happens. The animals could be reacting to changes in the electrical field, to a release of radon gas, or through plain old precognition. Because Dubonnet had a reaction in a moving automobile, Berkland believes that she reacts to electromagnetic signals caused by rocks fracturing deep within the earth.

Her family doesn't know how Dubonnet is able to predict earthquakes. She just does. When she is not busy with earthquake warnings, Dubonnet has a normal suburban life: She plays tag with the horse, Jet, and naps with the cat, Lulu, curled up on top of her. Dubonnet is a graceful dog, and she keeps her secrets to herself.

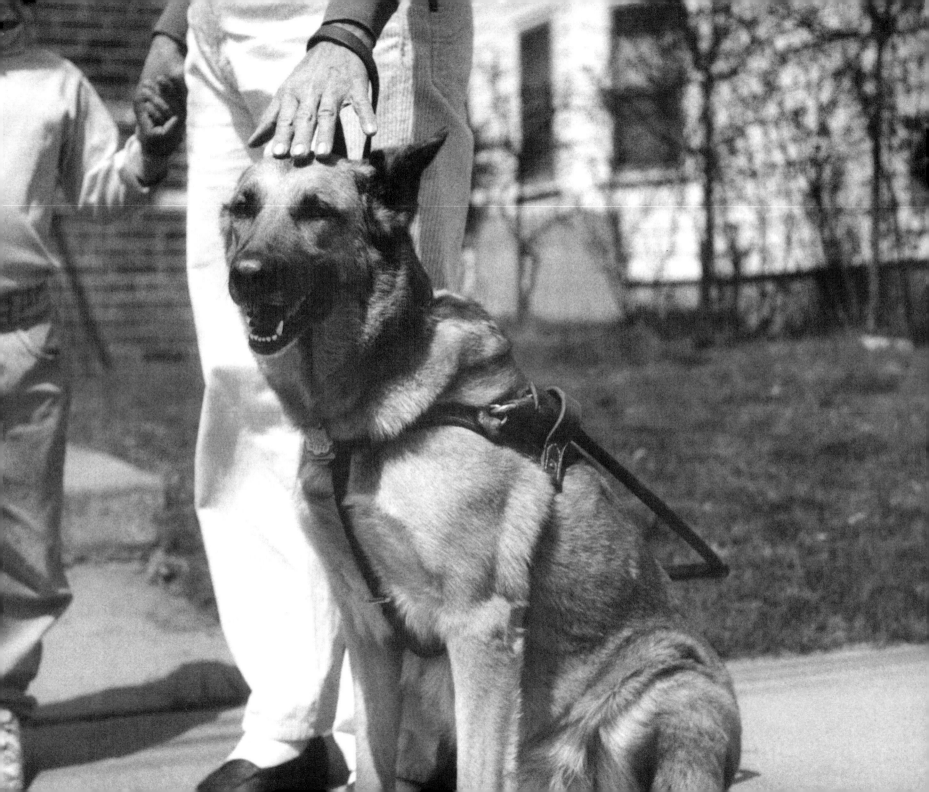

HAVEN

Guide Dog

WHEN CHEREE HEPPE ADOPTED HAVEN AT THE pound, the pound administrator told the dog, "See, little one, fairy tales do come true."

The administrator had shown Haven to Heppe only because the German shepherd was scheduled to be euthanized the very next day, and he was desperate to find her a home. Haven had been rescued from a burning building, where she was sheltering her litter of puppies instead of seeking her own safe exit. When their story was published in a local newspaper, all the puppies were adopted. Haven, however, was sent to the pound, where she contracted a respiratory infection. Despite that illness, Heppe admired the dog's strength and peaceful temperament. She took her home and named her Haven.

Some dogs have notable lives. Haven's life was about to get even more interesting, for Heppe trains guide dogs and is, herself, blind.

Heppe began by training Haven in basic obedience: sitting, staying, and fetching. Like many shelter dogs, she needed to learn everything. Through it all, Haven maintained her sweet calm. She wasn't bothered by the tapping of Heppe's white cane, and she was kind and patient with Heppe's small daughter, Tiara.

Over a period of six months, Haven learned to maneuver in traffic, retrieve objects, and use public transportation. She learned how to find empty tables in crowded restaurants and how to find the buffet table at a large gathering. She traveled on the train to New York City, Boston, and a petting zoo, where she touched noses with a giraffe. She was excellent at remembering places and knowing how to return to them.

When Haven began traffic work, though, Heppe was concerned. Haven lacked "intelligent disobedience," the highly valued ability in a guide dog to refuse to go where the handler directs when it is dangerous to do so. This ability can save someone's life if, for instance, she is directing her dog to walk across the street and a truck is headed straight for their intersection. Haven would sometimes walk directly into oncoming traffic, obeying Heppe's commands but not protecting her life.

BLIND PEOPLE HAVE BEEN RELYING ON DOGS TO GUIDE them for hundreds of years, and they've been training

> No ONE OTHER THAN THE PERSON RELYING ON A GUIDE DOG CAN KEEP THAT DOG WORKING SKILLFULLY, SO MANY PEOPLE TRAIN THEIR OWN GUIDE DOGS FROM THE VERY BEGINNING.

the dogs themselves, as well. One such owner was Abram V. Courtney, who acquired a dog named Caper in 1851 in Bangor, Maine. After training Caper to lead him through city streets and over country roads, Courtney was so fond of his dog that he wrote, "During the last five years he has proved so trusty a friend, that please God, he shall never be separated from me again while we both live."

After World War I, the Germans began an official program to train former war dogs to guide men blinded by war injuries. In 1927, an article about the German guide dogs appeared in the *Saturday Evening Post*. An American man wrote to the author, another American, named Dorothy Harrison Eustis, and she trained a dog named Buddy for him. This was the beginning of the Seeing Eye Foundation, a group that trains dogs to guide people who are blind.

HEPPE TRAINS HER OWN DOGS BECAUSE SHE CAN DO SO with great success. No one other than the person relying on a guide dog can keep that dog working skillfully, so Heppe, and many other people, train their own dogs from the beginning.

When Haven's training period was complete, she went through a one-month evaluation, during which time Heppe would decide upon Haven's future. Despite her training, Haven continued to walk into traffic occasionally. Heppe realized Haven would most likely need to be placed in someone's home as a pet, and she started making inquiries with friends.

BECAUSE OF THE STRESS AND INSTABILITY OF THEIR FORMER lives, dogs from shelters often have difficulty learning to be reliable guide dogs. It is quite amazing, given this, that Haven is as peaceful as she is, maintaining her composure even in stressful situations. It is also quite clear that Haven loves Heppe with the incredible loyalty of a dog who, after many travels, has found her place in the world. But still, Haven needed to learn better traffic skills in order to be Heppe's guide dog.

To give Haven a full chance, Heppe enlisted the help of some friends in further correcting Haven's traffic work. Heppe tried to walk Haven directly into traffic and then praised her for her resistance. Also, as her friends walked behind and reported on Haven's conduct, Heppe was able to strongly correct the dog's behavior. With continued work, Haven's traffic skills finally improved. The question was: had they improved enough?

As Heppe was trying to decide on Haven's future, and working in her office, Haven suddenly came to her and, with great urgency, pushed her hands off the keyboard. Heppe kept working; the dog did it again, with even greater insistence. Thinking Haven needed to go outside, Heppe got up and walked to the front door. On the way there, Heppe realized she didn't hear Tiara. She called her daughter and the toddler answered from outside the formerly locked storm door, where she wasn't allowed to be by herself. Heppe heard the swish of a tail as Haven returned to her resting place on the rug, and she realized Haven had warned her that Tiara was in danger. She gathered her daughter back into the house.

Heppe made her decision. She took Haven to the vet to get an implanted microchip—a seed-sized identifying chip that most service dogs wear these days. The chip ensures that a dog can be identified and returned if she were ever lost. Now Haven was officially an important animal. She had become a guide dog, one half of a loving and successful team.

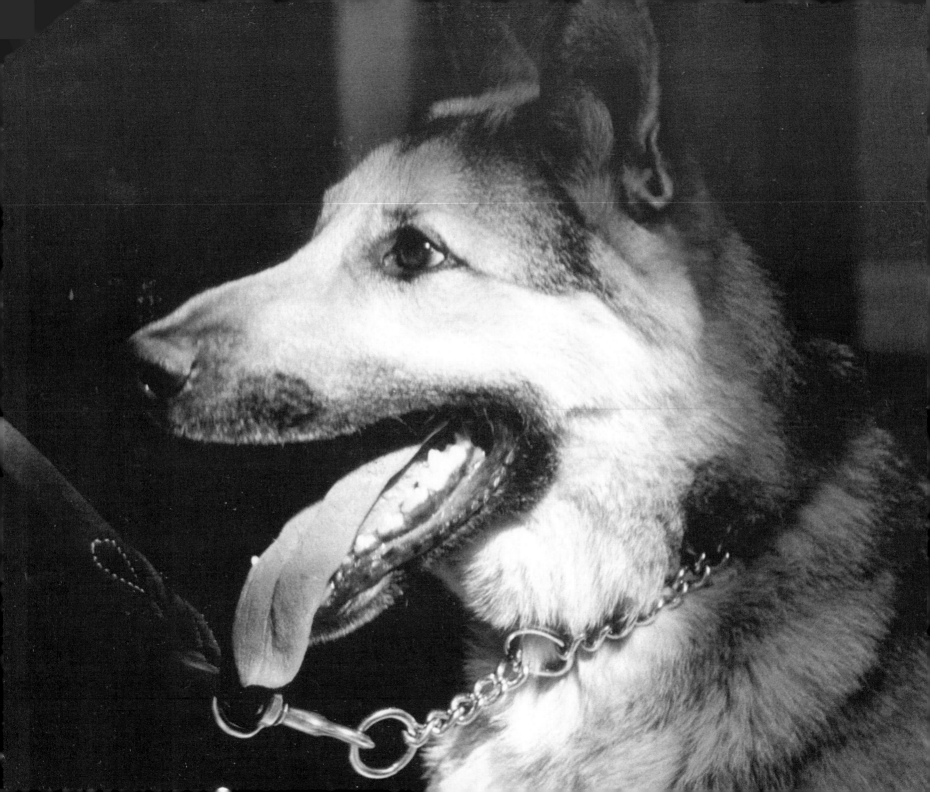

KOJAK

Drug Detector

WHEN KOJAK ATTACKED A PACKAGE DURING A routine sweep of the international mail center, his partner, Canine Enforcement Officer Steve Fischer, threw the dog a towel and got to work. Fischer sliced open the punctured box and found four sealed tin cans labeled "Pumpkin Seeds." He opened one of the cans and found . . . pumpkin seeds.

Fischer watched Kojak playing with his beloved white towel and wondered. Kojak is trained to alert to heroin and cocaine, not pumpkins. Knowing Kojak,

> REWARD AND PRAISE MADE KOJAK A MORE LIKABLE DOG.

Steve kept looking and so he sliced opened one of the pumpkin seeds. He found china white heroin. In all, two hundred grams, all in pumpkin seeds.

In four years, Kojak has made drug finds that resulted in over a thousand seizures of heroin and cocaine. He's found opium soaked into handmade paper and more opium hidden in vegetables; he's found cocaine when it's masked with other smelly items like coffee; he's found narcotics inside truck tires and behind the walls of airplanes.

Kojak is an aggressive alert narcotics dog—he doesn't just sit down when he finds his target, he attacks it. At the command—"Find it!"—he races through an area searching for the odor of narcotics. He is trained to take two sweeps. In the first, called a low search pass, Kojak runs through the whole area smelling quickly to get his bearings. In the second pass—the detail pass—he goes back to the spots that smelled promising for a more thorough search. When Kojak smells the goods—heroin or cocaine, for example—he digs and scratches and bites at the source of the scent, say a box or a piece of luggage. This is the alert to Fischer, who quickly throws the towel to Kojak so he'll stop attacking the box and start playing with his reward. It's important when a dog is trained to find narcotics and alert in this manner that he be diverted quickly before ingesting any of the drugs. Because of the aggressive nature of his alert, a trip through a cargo warehouse can leave a wake of torn boxes. (Kojak never searches people, only objects like boxes, luggage, vehicles, or buildings.)

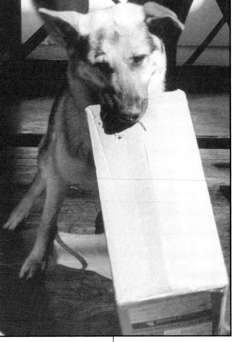

When Kojak was found on a street corner in Riverside, California, he was nearly feral. The man who ran the local shelter—who bore a strong resemblance to Telly Savalas—figured the dog had been living on the street for most of his life. Noting the dog's strong retrieval instinct—a surprise, given the rough life he'd lived—the shelter operator called the U.S. Customs Service to come and check the dog out. They found a dog whose retrieval instinct was so strong that it could be called frantic—which meant he was a good candidate for detector dog work. They named him Kojak in honor of the man who first noticed there was something special about this dog.

Kojak was trained by the U.S. Customs Service at Lackland Air Force Base four years ago. The training consisted of taking his frantic desire to retrieve a rolled up towel and changing that into a frantic desire to find narcotics, with the towel as a reward. This was done by putting the scent of narcotics on the towel and then transferring his desire from the towel to the scent of narcotics. It was the same sort of behavioral transference done by Pavlov, but instead of transferring the behavior from food to the sound of a bell, as Pavlov did, it was transferred from towel to narcotics. Because Kojak gets the towel as his reward, the finding of the narcotics is rewarded, and the desired behavior—finding narcotics—continues.

While he was trained to find and retrieve the scented towel, Kojak slowly lost his feral traits and focused his energy on his work. His scratching and digging were put to good use, and having his behavior rewarded and praised made him a more likable dog. Fischer says Kojak is the best dog he's worked with in fifteen years of canine work.

More than anything, Kojak wants to play with his towel. He knows this only happens when he smells a particular odor—narcotics—and so he will frantically try to find the odor. When he does, he plays.

KOJAK LIVES IN A PRIVATE KENNEL WITH THE TWENTY-FIVE other Customs dogs. His pen is fifteen feet by five feet and he stays there while he's not working. He is a Customs Service asset and, as such, needs to have his life sustained for as long as possible. Therefore, he eats only veterinarian-sanctioned food—no potato chips or ham sandwich snacks for this dog—and his weight is carefully monitored.

> KOJAK'S RETRIEVAL INSTINCT WAS SO STRONG THAT IT COULD BE CALLED FRANTIC.

The Customs Service has dogs working across the country. Part of their methodology is that the dogs do not live in the homes of their handlers. The thinking is that they want the dogs to be rewarded only when they work and find narcotics. Customs dogs do not get to play at the park or spend a relaxing evening on the couch, because this would be rewarding them when no work had been performed.

Kojak rotates through different areas of Customs, searching for drugs. He might sweep letter-class mail and parcels or work with the contraband enforcement team searching through warehouses, vehicles, luggage, or buildings. In addition, Kojak is part of a network of drug dogs loaned out to other agencies. He might sweep a prison for a call-out by the Bureau of Prisons, or a ship when requested by the Coast Guard.

When Kojak works he looks like he's playing his favorite game. He is a beautiful dog; his coat gleams with good health. After he makes his find and gets his towel, he spends a good half hour on his back rolling around on the floor and playing with Fischer, who refers to himself as Kojak's Dad. It's a complicated relationship they have, and indicative of the complicated nature of the life of a dog who is an asset.

It's a working dog's life. It's Kojak's life.

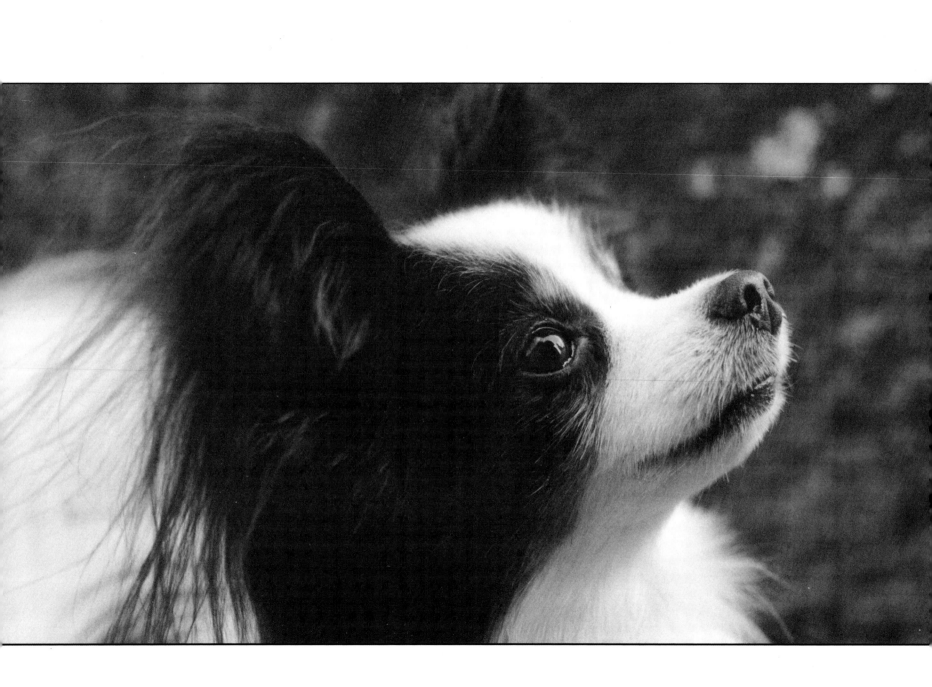

KIRBY

Show Dog

WHAT DOES ONE CALL THE DOG WHO WINS Westminster Best of Show besides *fabulous?* If we're talking about Loteki's Supernatural Being, a.k.a. Kirby, the Papillon who won the grand title this year, you'll have a hard time stopping yourself once you start describing this dog. *Astonishing. Delightful. Adorable. A perfect gentleman and a good friend.*

Kirby is perhaps the most popular dog in the world right now. In one short year, he

> KIRBY IS PERHAPS THE MOST POPULAR DOG IN THE WORLD RIGHT NOW

won the World Show in Finland, the Royal Invitational in Canada, and the Westminster Show in the United States, and this triple sweep has catapulted Kirby into a celebrity whirlwind. A week doesn't go by without an interview or guest appearance. His face has graced countless magazine covers. He's even been on *Oprah.*

And what does this celebrity do at home? He plays with his stuffed toys, loves taking walks, and eats canned dog food. He relaxes with his owner and handler, John Oulton, watching their favorite TV shows—*Dharma and Greg*, for instance.

At eight and a half years old, Kirby has recently retired from the rigors of show life. After winning at Westminster, there were no more grand mountains for the little pooch to climb. He now is Oulton's companion, his good friend, and will be doing his part to contribute to Oulton's Papillon breeding program.

Already, one of Kirby's sons, Cadaga's Civil Action, a.k.a. Nemo, is currently touring the AKC show circuit. Kirby feels sad when left behind, so Oulton usually takes him with Nemo to the shows. Although the superstar

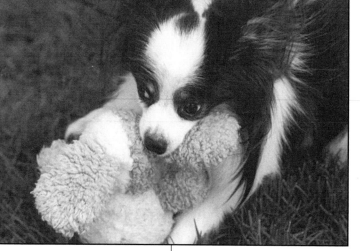

just hangs out off-ring, he is still the center of attention for his many adoring fans. People come from all over the world to see Kirby and vie for his youngsters, who are occasionally available to the fancy—that is, other breeders and Papillon-lovers.

A PROFESSIONAL DOG HANDLER AND BREEDER, OULTON works hard to groom his Papillons to win in the show ring. Special oils and shampoos keep Kirby's coat gleaming and fluffy, and Oulton pays special attention to the ear fringe and tail plume. Kirby exercises regularly to stay in tip-top condition. Oulton understands that the key to winning a big dog show is presentation, and he works harder than most to make sure everything is perfect.

Of course, one must start out with a dog who is capable of winning. The judges at AKC shows measure dogs against breed standards rather than against one another, and winning the coveted Best in Show award meant that Kirby, more than the other 2,500 dogs at Westminster that day, most closely matched the standards approved by the AKC.

For instance, the Papillon standards cover everything from nose (must be black) to tail (plume hangs to the side of the body). The AKC sets and maintains the standards so that breeds will stay consistent over the years. Thankfully, Kirby is perfect. The Westminster judge's critique said it all: "The Papillon was incredible." The judge also cited the relationship between Oulton and Kirby, saying it was overpowering and amazing to watch.

IN THE SIXTEENTH CENTURY, Papillons were called dwarf spaniels, and were coveted by European nobility: Marie Antoinette loved them; Madame de Pompadour named hers Mimi and Inez. At that time, the Papillon's ears drooped like a spaniel's, thus the name. Over time, as the ears became erect

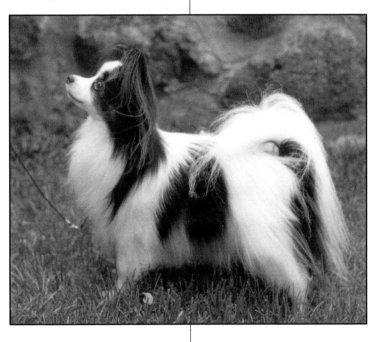

and spread like a butterfly's wings, the name changed to Papillon, which is French for butterfly.

Due to their small and dainty size, Papillons are considered toy dogs—along with the Pekinese, Chihuahua, and pug. Despite their daintiness, however, Papillons are hearty dogs, love an active life, and are

known to chase rodents. Kirby is no exception. Although he hasn't caught anything, and is described as not having an aggressive bone in his body, the little dog likes to try, especially if he happens to see a Connecticut squirrel.

Kirby gets along with everyone. He is affectionate to strangers and cats alike. In Oulton's house, there are nine Papillons, but Kirby is the only one with the freedom to wander where he pleases. Even so, when it comes time for sleep, Kirby jumps off Oulton's bed and heads for his crate.

After winning at Westminster, Kirby attended a luncheon at Sardi's in Manhattan. The guest of honor, Kirby sat on the counter and was presented with a hamburger on a silver tray. After he had eaten as much as he was allowed, Kirby posed for pictures and then took a little nap. For the most popular dog in the world, and Oulton's best friend, life remains good.

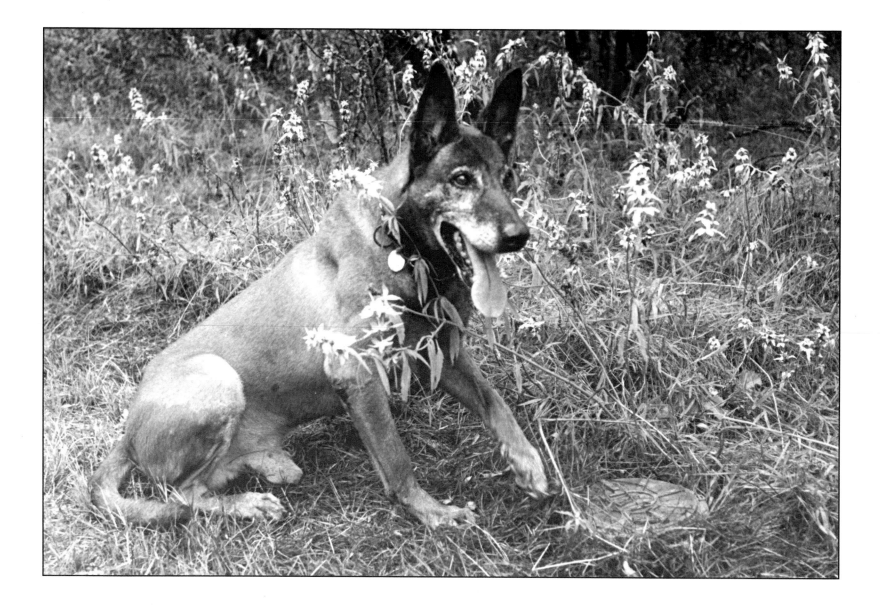

ROY

Mine Detector

IN BOSNIA AND CROATIA, ROY FOUND MINES BURIED underground by Serbs; he found mines buried underground by Muslims; he found mines buried underground by Croatians. When he got tired of the whole affair, and when the ground grew too hot for his nose, Roy was sent home to Texas. That's where he is now.

Land mines are among the most evil of human creations. Buried in the earth, they lie waiting, fifty years, a hundred years, to attack whoever happens to step on the ground above. The United

> THE BEST TOOL FOR DETECTING LAND MINES IS A DOG LIKE ROY.

Nations estimates 100 million mines are buried in sixty-five nations around the world. Anything weighing more than about five pounds can set one off. It could be a mother out for a stroll, it could be an animal looking for food, it could be a child chasing a ball.

While organizations around the world work to get land mines banned, these instruments of war keep getting made, and they keep getting buried. Once that happens, the only thing to do is get them out of the earth before they go off, and the best tool for detecting land mines is a dog like Roy.

Roy learned to find land mines at the Global Training Academy in Texas, where dogs are also trained for explosives and narcotics detection work. Global Training Academy has trained dogs for police departments across the country and for governments around the world. To locate land mines, Roy was trained to alert to the odor of TNT, C4, and smokeless powder. He can also recognize the odor of metal or plastic shell casings of mines. His reward for a find is a romp with a hard rubber ball.

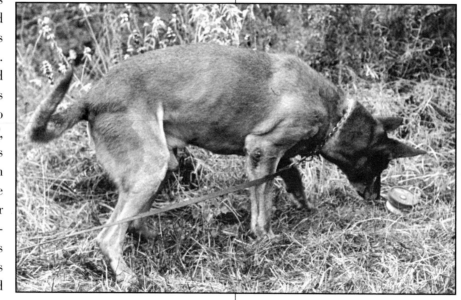

After training in Texas, Roy was leased to the U.S. State Department and flown with five other dogs and a trainer to the Tuzla region of Bosnia. While there, he trained with his local handler on mines lifted out of local ground. After eight more weeks of training, he went into the mine fields.

The methodology for working went like this: After a suspected mine field was identified, and boundaries were posted, the dog teams broke the land into sections and walked through those sections. Roy sniffed the ground ahead of him, sitting down fast when he detected a mine. Then his handler called him back and gave him his ball and a chance to play—in mine-free ground, of course. Roy's job was over. Another man moved forward with a metal detector and a probe and spent up to four hours gently probing the earth to find the bomb. Once found, the mine was safely detonated. Then Roy would continue his search. After the dog teams cleared an area, the metal detectors were brought through again. The team performed a final visual check before declaring an area free of mines.

SINCE MINE DETECTION dogs are leased to governments, they don't belong to their handlers and they don't go home with them. These dogs live in kennels. The people they work with change from year to year, and the countries they work in change even more frequently. Roy has

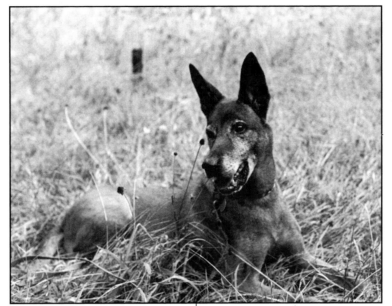

found mines and trip-wires, both above and below ground.

After two years, though, Roy retired. They had been transferred to Croatia in the middle of a hot and humid summer, and after a few hours of work each day, Roy's handler felt the dog wasn't using his nose as well as expected. He was nine years old. It was too hot for Roy. He was replaced and sent back to Texas.

traveled around the world for his job. Right now, aside from Croatia and Bosnia, other dogs from Global Training Academy are in Nicaragua, Costa Rica, Rwanda, and many other dangerous places. The only thing that stays consistent for mine detection dogs is the actual work.

It was hard work for Roy, day after day, nose to the ground, searching for mines. In the winter, the snow and ice blanketed the mines and prevented detection. In the summer, the heat made the work uncomfortable for both handler and dog. But that didn't stop Roy. He

Now, Roy takes it easy for a working dog and only works part time. Three times a week he gets to train and work, searching for bombs in schools and businesses near San Antonio. He always goes in as backup, with a younger dog doing the primary search. Compared to searching for land mines in Croatia, it's easy work.

Most dogs retire at nine or ten years old, but Roy is expected to keep at it for a few more years, at least. He takes walks and plays ball every day. He is an intense dog with an outgoing personality and a strong prey drive. What he likes best is working.

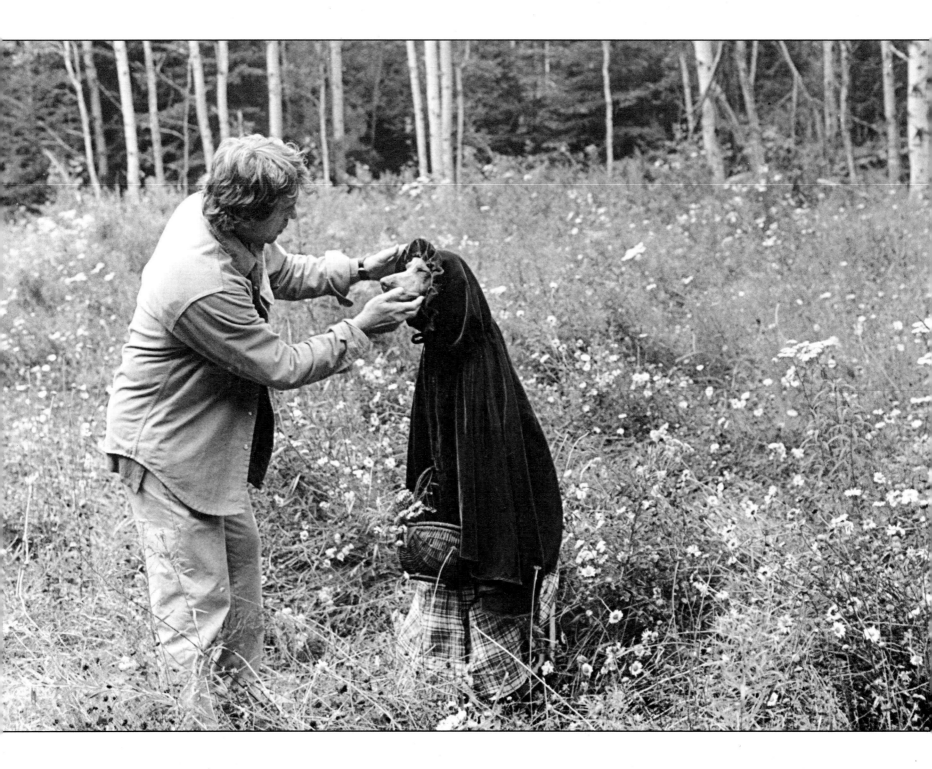

BATTY

Supermodel

IN THE WORLD OF WORKING DOGS, THERE IS NONE more glamorous than Battina del Ray. Star of the silver screen, television, literature, and fine art, this elegant Weimaraner is drenched with her own brand of feminine beauty and nonchalant charm.

Batty is part of artist William Wegman's famous Weimaraner clan. Daughter of Fay Ray, Batty was born into the life of the supermodel. She was the smallest in Fay's litter of eight, so tiny that Wegman had to hold her in place

> BATTY DAYDREAMS WHILE WORKING. SHE EVEN FALLS ASLEEP.

while she nursed. Right away, he got very attached to her and admired her feisty nature. She could send her six brothers off when annoyed; she was tough and vocal. Batty was catlike and elegant, standoffish and fond of playing games by herself. Batty was the runt, but she was beautiful and she was the puppy from this litter that Wegman kept to live and work with him.

From the beginning, although Wegman tried, Batty was actually trained by her mother. When Wegman

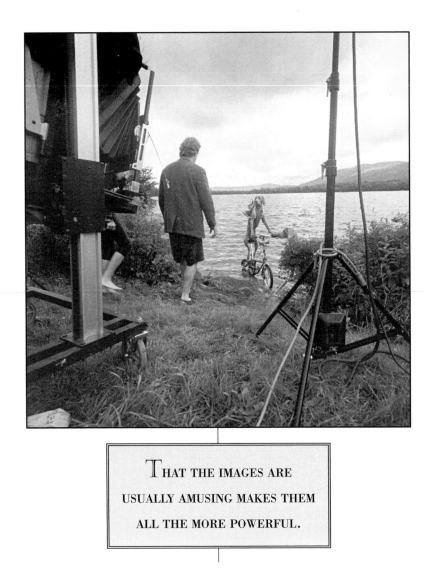

THAT THE IMAGES ARE
USUALLY AMUSING MAKES THEM
ALL THE MORE POWERFUL.

called Batty, she would look to Fay and then, only upon receiving approval, would go to Wegman. Fay didn't let Batty play with balls. She established the domestic arrangements. Fay slept on Wegman's wife Christine's side of the bed; Batty slept on Wegman's side.

When Batty was four, Fay became very ill and they found she had leukemia. The weekend before she died, it seemed that Fay and Batty somehow had a communication about arrangements and how things were going to change. Wegman was amazed by the change in Batty. She moved into the number one slot, staring at Wegman as if now she were responsible for him. When Fay died, Batty moved over to Christine's side of the bed.

Batty became very attached to her son, Chip, when she had her own litter of puppies. Eventually Chip moved into Batty's old spot—on Wegman's side of the bed—and Wegman had two Weimaraners living and working with him again.

WILLIAM WEGMAN'S ART IS IN THE WORLD'S MOST important museums and collections. His picture postcards are on refrigerators in kitchens around the world. Although not all of his photography includes images of

> BATTY IS USUALLY LAST, NOT BECAUSE SHE'S SLOW, BUT BECAUSE SHE KNOWS THERE ARE MORE IMPORTANT THINGS IN LIFE THAN BEING THE FIRST DOG OUT THE DOOR.

his dogs—he is also a prolific painter, filmmaker, and author—it is for the dogs that he is best known and loved. It is Wegman's dogs, after all, who decorate our T-shirts, and address books, and mouse pads. His dogs have given him access to a mainstream audience and all the benefits of popularity.

As he searches for transcendent beauty in his photographs, Wegman uses the dogs as shapes, pieces of meat with fur on them. The dogs get draped over rocky landscapes, and placed on boxes or jungle gyms. He also looks to capture the dogs' souls in the photographs, as they become portraits of his loved ones. These photographs are often melancholic and offer commentary on the nature of life. That the images are usually amusing, too, makes them all the more powerful.

When posing for Wegman, Batty is nonchalant and trusting. She is pliable and will go into whatever position he places her. She is indifferent even to her own well-being, as if sure that someone will catch her if she happens to fall. Batty daydreams while working. She even falls asleep and Wegman accuses her of being narcoleptic.

Batty and Chip and the Wegmans live in Manhattan, upstate New York, and Maine. They work year round. Some of the most famous photographs have been taken on the lake in Maine, others in the Manhattan studio. Wegman also photographs Batty's siblings, Crooky and Chundo, but they live with other people and just come in to work.

While in Manhattan, Batty and Chip accompany Wegman on twice daily bike rides to the park. They run with him for four miles and if someone recognizes them, it's usually, "Hey! Those look like those dogs!" Wegman might say, "They are those dogs!" or he might not. At the park, as in life, Batty retains her standoffish cool. She just isn't interested in socializing with strangers.

At the studio, Batty greets everyone who enters with a hearty bark. Then she retreats to her spot under the desk until the next arrival or her call to the set. When all four dogs are working, they rest on the couch and chair, and everyone else—that is, all the people—sits on the floor. Of the four dogs, Chundo is always the first one out the door. Batty is usually last, not because she's slow, but because she knows there are more important things in life than being the first dog out the door. Things like Wegman and what he's doing and the work they do together.

THIS ELEGANT WEIMARANER IS DRENCHED WITH HER OWN BRAND OR FEMININE BEAUTY AND NONCHALANT CHARM.

When Batty is dressed in clothes, she sits on a posing stool with a person behind her providing the arms and hands. The dogs often portray fairy tale characters. Batty has been Little Red Riding Hood and Cinderella. She always gets the ingenue parts, while her sister, Crooky, gets the character parts. This is typecasting, in a way, because Batty is the more feminine dog. Batty became a star posing for Wegman. Part of her charm, of course, is that she doesn't know she's a star. She knows she's loved and she has things to do. She's a working dog; Batty has her responsibilities.

Wegman admits to being deeply in love with Batty.

Batty enjoys posing, especially if she's outside and picking up the scent of animals or the trail of birds. She daydreams and closes her eyes. Wegman must call her name to get her attention, "Batty!" With the other dogs, Wegman can make promises or pretend he's leaving to get them to look at him and the camera. These tricks don't work on Batty. She is immune to teasers and knows the story. Batty has chosen Wegman, and him alone, and he does love her the best. She's his dog, and when he calls she will open her eyes and show him her soul.

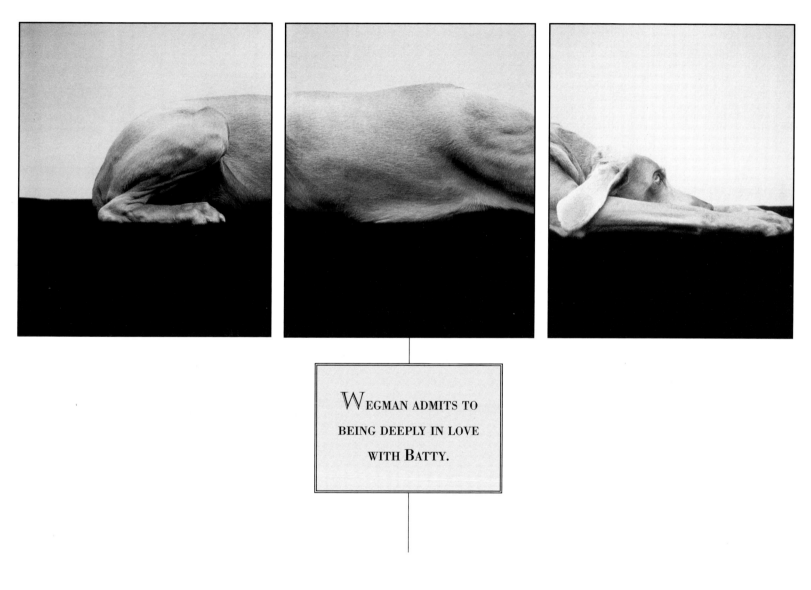

WEGMAN ADMITS TO
BEING DEEPLY IN LOVE
WITH BATTY.

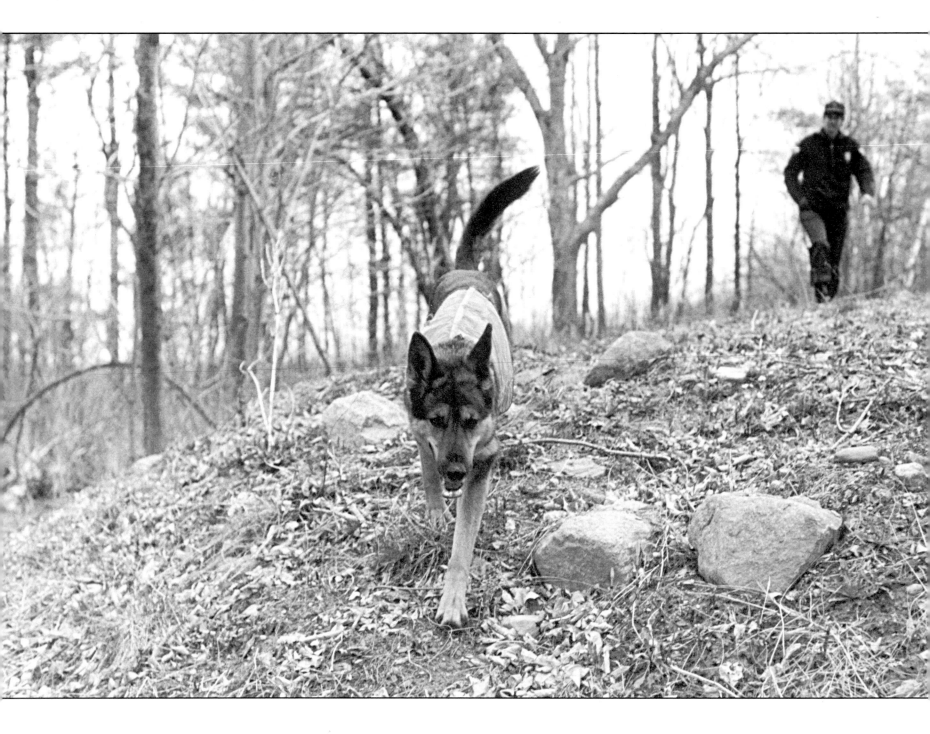

ANNA

Game Warden Dog

ALTHOUGH THE SKY WAS STILL LIGHT, THE SUN HAD already dipped below the pine trees when game warden Deborah Palman pulled her green patrol truck next to three fishermen who were packing up after a day of fishing. Palman had received a report of illegal fishing in these waters and needed to check it out. As she walked over to the men, she saw three ice coolers sitting beside their truck. The men looked at each other and quietly continued hooking their boat onto a trailer. The largest of the fishermen greeted Palman, "Evening, ma'am."

She told them of the report and asked if they'd seen anyone pulling more than their share of fish from the waters. "Nope. We didn't catch even one fish." The look he gave seemed to dare her to challenge them. Luckily, she didn't have to.

With a whistle, Palman called her German shepherd, Anna, from the truck. Anna is a delightful dog, full of personality and grit. Wearing a special orange vest, Anna jumped out of the truck and stood at Palman's feet, waiting for a command. Beautiful animal," the fisherman said.

TO ENFORCE THE FISH AND Wildlife laws in Maine, Deborah Palman sometimes needs a quick answer: Are there fish in that cooler, or not? To get the answer, she turns to Anna, trained in fish detection, who promptly sits down when the answer is yes. That gives Palman the probable cause she needs to request a peek in the cooler.

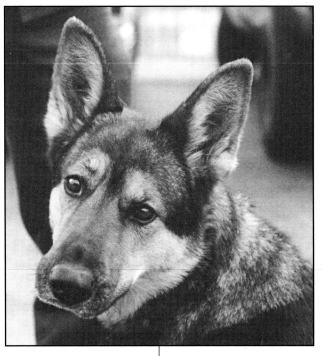

Anna's other responsibilities are as varied as Palman's: search and rescue, evidence retrieval, handler protection, tracking, and public demonstrations. In her little orange vest, Anna does it all.

To protect its wildlife, Maine, like other states, carefully regulates hunting and fishing, and it's the job of the game wardens to see that those regulations are followed. Game wardens also enforce recreational vehicle and litter laws, investigate hunting accidents, and perform search and rescue. If they're lucky, they've got dogs like Anna sitting next to them while they do it.

Anna was a rescue dog—given up for adoption by one of Palman's friends because she didn't get along with the other dogs in the household and had a little problem with chewing and knocking down trees. Although Anna doesn't get along with Palman's older dog, Rica—who is not a working dog—Palman manages to work around hostile situations by keeping the dogs separated. Palman realizes Anna and Rica are like siblings fighting for her attention and does her best to keep everyone happy.

When performing search and rescue, Palman relies on Anna's nose rather than her own eyes to find a missing person. People are constantly shedding skin rafts, tiny particles of dead skin cells—to Anna's powerful nose, we may as well be leaving trails of bread crumbs. After sectioning off the terrain and establishing a grid pattern with the other dog teams, Palman gives Anna a scent article to track, and says, "Go find!" When Anna finds the scent, she weaves in and out of the scent cone, with Palman following behind, tracking the scent to the source. Anna wears a bell on her collar to help Palman follow her.

While a lost hunter can usually be found through voice contact or fired shots, other people need someone to actually come and find them. Most of Palman and Anna's searches—usually four or five each year—are for children and people who are mentally or physically impaired. About 90 percent of the searches result in a found person the very first day. After that, the search becomes more difficult, but not without hope.

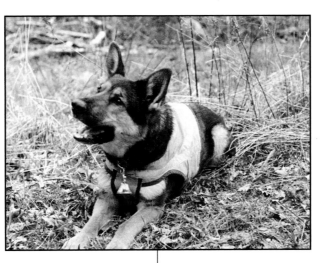

must pass stringent certification tests. Palman trained Anna over a period of two years, yet she is always keeping the training up through seminars and classes.

As they go through their work days, Anna is a help and a companion to Palman, sitting beside her in the patrol truck. Since she started working with Palman, Anna has stopped knocking over trees, though she does still enjoy a nice log to chew on now and again.

PALMAN NEVER KNOWS WHEN THEY MIGHT BE CALLED to work, and so she and Anna must always be ready. Last year, while vacationing in Vermont, Anna and Palman were asked to assist in finding a woman who had been missing for three days. Anna found her at the bottom of a cliff and, after seeing the woman safely to an emergency room for medical treatment, they returned to the hotel for the remainder of their vacation.

Game warden dogs are trained by their game warden owners. They aren't part of an official canine training program, like most official dogs. Nonetheless, they

Although some fishermen might not like it much when Anna gives the cue that they've been fishing illegally, most people respect the work of game wardens and know that they keep the forests and parks safe and beautiful for everyone. The laws they enforce keep the fish in the water—so the fishermen can come back year after year.

ON THIS PARTICULAR DAY, ANNA TOLD PALMAN THERE WERE no fish in the coolers in question, and the fishermen went on their way. Palman and Anna got back in their truck and continued their patrol of Maine's spectacular wilderness.

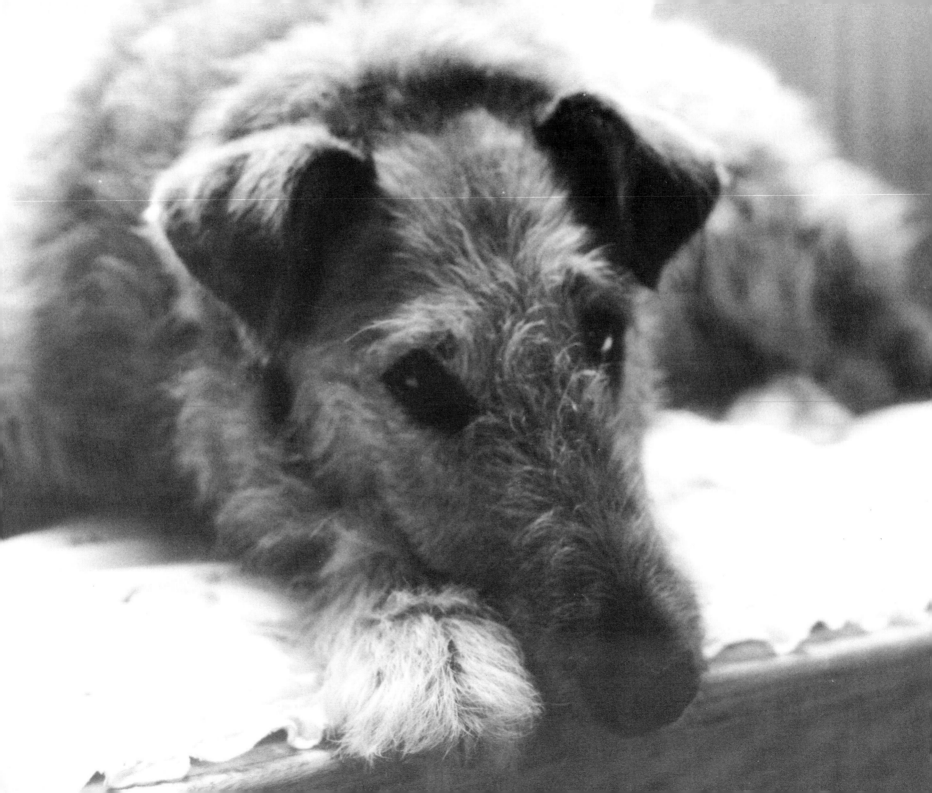

CINDY LOU

Actor

IN THE DOG-EAT-DOG WORLD OF ENTERTAINMENT, Cindy Lou has had her share of hard knocks and her share of success. After a brilliant run as Sandy in the national touring company of *Annie*, Cindy Lou was brought to New York City to audition for the same role in an upcoming movie. "Too ugly," said one movie producer. "Repulsive," said another, right to the poor dog's face.

LIKE MANY LEGIT ACTORS, CINDY LOU FOUND HAPPINESS by settling for a challenging role in a small, indepen-

dent film. She played the lead in *The Adventures of Thomas*. She was Thomas, a city dog sent to the country where he sees his first cat and promptly falls in love. She also recently played a villain—that is, a bad dog— in a television commercial.

Cindy Lou likes to work. When she's at home in Connecticut, waiting for her agent to get a call, she can get listless and moody. She strolls through the grounds of the country estate, watching the horses and the llamas and the other dogs playing. She naps on the couch. She follows her beauty routine. What she longs for is the excitement and attention of an audience, her co-stars, and her entourage.

While on tour as Sandy, Cindy Lou had a star's life, staying in elegant hotels and dining on fine dog food. Like many stars, she gave air kisses rather than actually licking anyone's face. She had her own understudy, Buster, who was allowed to stay in her hotel room but only if he slept on the floor. Cindy Lou took the bed and always turned down the bed-covers before retiring. She was a late sleeper and couldn't be roused before ten A.M., even for her fans.

CINDY LOU IS QUITE UNIQUE IN appearance. She is sleek and long-legged with strawberry blonde hair that is reminis-cent of Lana Turner. Cindy Lou follows an all-natural beauty regime: daily dips in the pond, exercise, sun-

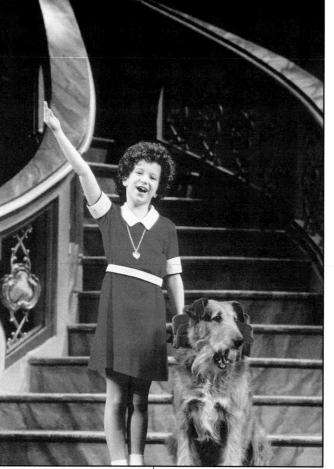

shine, fresh air, lots of beau-ty sleep.

In the troop of acting animals trained by Bill Berloni, Cindy Lou is top dog. She sleeps in the master bedroom, along with his wife's dog. The nine other dogs share a kennel and have the run of the farm during the day. Berloni has been train-ing animals for the theater and movies for twelve years. Although he doesn't come right out and say it, Cindy Lou is his favorite.

CINDY LOU WAS AN AGGRES-sive dog, a stray found living in the woods by the local dogcatcher. She came into Berloni's life via a phone call from his veterinarian. The vet had performed surgery on Cindy Lou to remove a puppy collar that had become embedded in her neck as she grew into an adult dog. She had recovered after the surgery, but now her time was up. The vet told Berloni that if he didn't take her right away she would be killed.

Berloni was a successful animal trainer and a soft touch. He went to see Cindy Lou but nothing made him think she would be a star, or even a performer. She was bedraggled and unfriendly. He felt sorry for her. Berloni took her home.

Right away Berloni had to go to Chicago for a job. He took Cindy Lou with him and they bonded. She slept in the hotel room with him and—after only two chairs—stopped chewing the furniture. Cindy Lou got the attention of the entire company of actors. Berloni enlisted their help in rehabilitating Cindy Lou and she slowly came to trust people. She blossomed. Berloni began to see potential for her to be an actor so he gave her a bit of training and got her a job. Cindy Lou's been a star ever since.

Berloni has a unique method of training actor dogs. Because Cindy Lou performs night after night with her audience only twenty feet from her, she can't fake her emotions. Cindy Lou bonds with the other actors in the play. Even if they're stars, part of their rehearsal job is to get on their hands and knees and make Cindy Lou love them. When she shows

> CINDY LOU FOUND HAPPINESS BY SETTLING FOR A CHALLENGING ROLE IN A SMALL, INDEPENDENT FILM.

emotions, they are real. She really is happy to be on stage because she loves the people she is with.

CINDY LOU HAS MADE AN AMAZING JOURNEY FROM HER early days as a stray dog. She is a famous actor. But, like many abandoned dogs, Cindy Lou has a past she can't shake. She still eats everything she finds as if fearful there one day won't be enough food to go around. Once, during an elegant day in Manhattan, she came upon a discarded pretzel and gobbled it up. Needless to say, she's always having to diet.

CINDY LOU HAS SO MUCH FUN WITH HER life that she does silly things that make people tease her for having gone Hollywood. She is surrounded by actors. She has her country estate in which to relax. Berloni loves her. And there's always the chance another Broadway show will come around that needs a very special, very beautiful dog.

Cindy Lou is grateful to be alive. Berloni is grateful to Cindy Lou, too. She is connected to him in a mysterious way and the time they spend together is filled with joy. Cindy Lou is a dog with a heart so big that by looking in her face one can see her soul. And that's not acting.

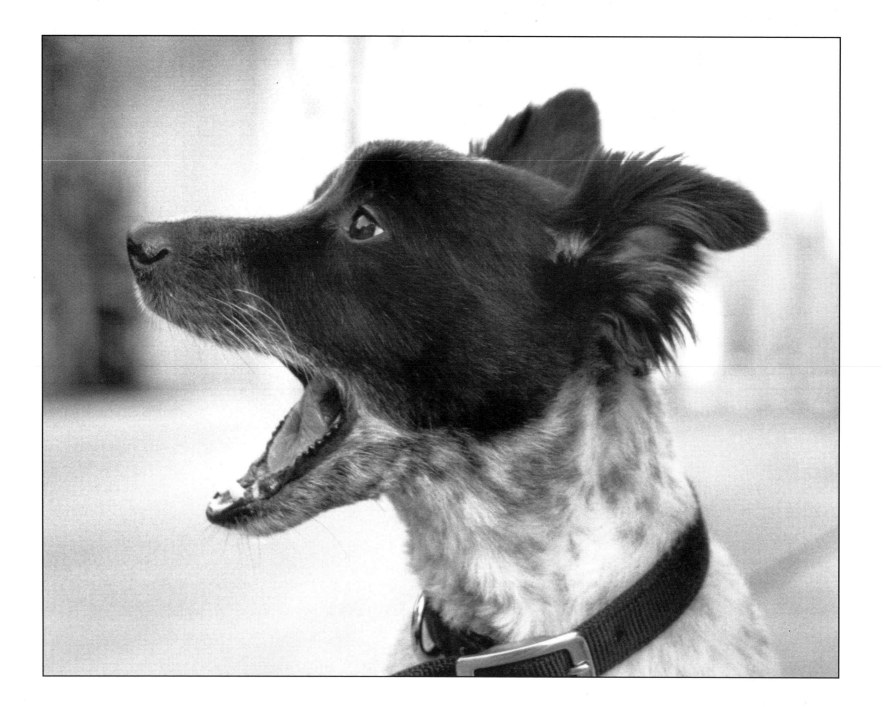

SPARKY

Guard Dog

IT'S BEEN SAID THAT WORK ISN'T WORK UNTIL YOU NO longer want to do it. If that were true, most working dogs would not be working dogs, because most of them love the work they do. Not so, Sparky.

Sparky approaches his job with, shall we say, reluctance. Or, perhaps, an intelligent hesitancy. He doesn't bark at the mail carrier; he lets cats pass through the backyard unchallenged; he tends to daydream and is often caught taking long naps in the sun on his family's porch.

> SPARKY APPROACHES HIS JOB WITH, SHALL WE SAY, RELUCTANCE. OR, PERHAPS, AN INTELLIGENT HESITANCY.

He'll never be retired, though. Mainly because of his performance one memorable night last year, when Sparky won the right to the title of Guard Dog, no matter what else he may do, for the rest of his life.

The father of Sparky's family works a night shift, as many people do, and bought Sparky from an uncle, who promised an excellent guard dog. The idea was that, since the father worked at night, his family needed the extra protection a dog would provide. Although Sparky's

45

sweet face and delicate manner—he is soft, with black and white fur—brings to mind a child's companion more than a guard dog, the father trusted in his uncle and brought Sparky home.

Right away, Sparky was willing to bark at anything and everything that passed in the night. So far, so good.

THE TROUBLE OCCURRED WHEN THE FATHER RETURNED from work, at 3:20 A.M., and Sparky ran to him, barking his head off and waking up the whole family of six children. This irritated the mother, who had never quite bought into the idea that she needed a dog to protect her.

To get Sparky to stop barking, the father started carrying biscuits in his right pant pocket, and soon Sparky was quietly running to him at 3:20 A.M. for his nightly biscuit. This went on for two years, during which time Sparky ingratiated himself with everyone in the family—except the mother, who still insisted she didn't need a guard dog, and loudly reminded the family—each morning—that she was the only person who remembered to give Sparky his water and food. As if she didn't already have enough work to do, taking care of six children and working full-time. She also doubted that any dog who received a bis-

> WHEN THE FATHER ARRIVED HOME HE FOUND HIS WIFE ASLEEP ON THE COUCH, WITH SPARKY CURLED UP ON HER LAP.

cuit each night would guard the house from an intruder, if one ever showed up, which would never happen.

Until the night it did happen.

The family was awakened by the sound of a girl screaming, and within a wink, the mother was downstairs with a baseball bat. Behind her, six children with saucer eyes and sleepy pajamas huddled together. They opened the door to the den—where the screaming sounded—and turned on the lights. And there a teenage boy stood, screaming his head off, while Sparky held on to what he had thought was the boy's pocketful of biscuits. "Get him off me!" the boy screamed in a surprisingly high-pitched voice. He clutched a roll of toilet paper in his right hand and, without much success, tried to bat Sparky on the head.

The oldest boy in the family recognized his best friend and started to laugh. He called Sparky, who let go of the boy's privates, and followed into the kitchen for a biscuit. The mother looked out the open window and saw that toilet paper covered three of the four pine trees in the front yard. The boy had run out of supplies, and come in the house to get what he needed to finish the job.

After everyone calmed down, and the young intruder's parents came to take him to the emergency room—

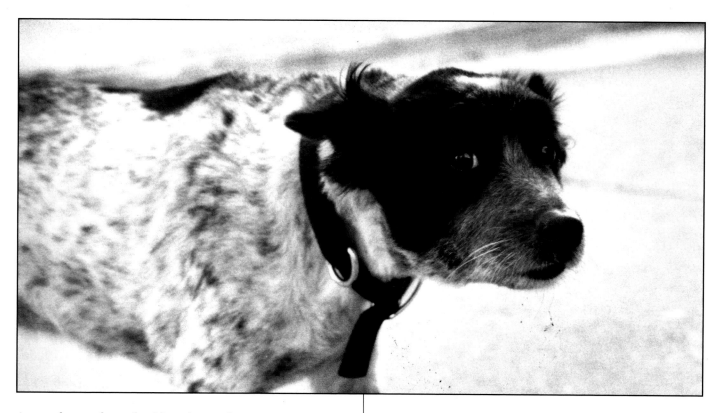

just to be on the safe side—the mother sent everyone back to bed. Then she sat down and had an excellent laugh. When the father arrived home he found his wife asleep on the couch, with Sparky curled up on her lap.

FROM THAT DAY ON, THE MOTHER NO LONGER COMPLAINS about being the only person who remembers to give Sparky his food and water. She's happy to do it. She also lets Sparky sleep on the bed at night and follow her around during the day.

As if they'd struck a deal, Sparky resists guarding and the mother provides him with more biscuits than he could possibly eat. She's got her sons to think of, after all, and her future grandchildren, too.

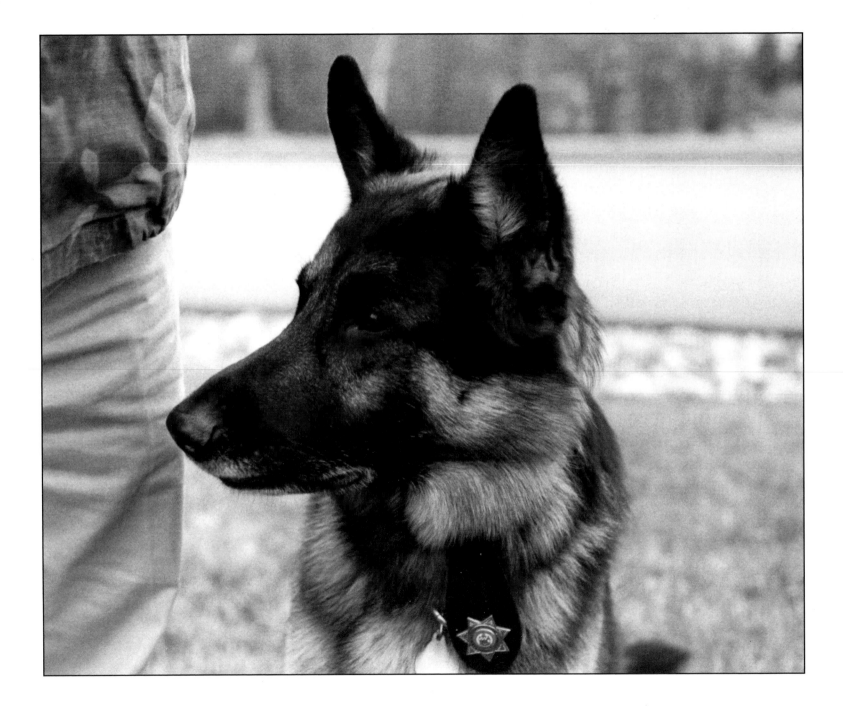

BUCK

Police K9

WHEN BUCK AND MELVIN GRAVES WERE CALLED to track down an escaped convict, the subject in question had already eluded the state police canine squad by crisscrossing a river five times. Buck got a good noseful of the escapee at his last known point of contact, sniffing eagerly at the trail, then hopped into Graves's car, ready for the pursuit.

Graves drove downriver, hopscotching ahead of where he figured the felon could be, and then the two headed back upriver on foot. At least, Graves was on foot; Buck jumped into the middle of the river and started swim-ming. He swam straight under an embankment to where the felon was hiding underwater. One peek at the aggres-sive German shepherd was all it took. "I give up," the escaped convict said. "Don't let the dog bite me."

DON'T TELL IT TO THE LOCAL CRIMINALS, BUT IN FOURTEEN years of canine police work, Officer Graves has never let one his dogs bite anyone. The threat has always been enough. Perhaps Graves has run into more than his share of intelligent criminals, because Buck cer-tainly knows how to follow through on his threat. He is trained to bite deep and hard. He also tracks, finds evidence, alerts to narcotics, protects his partner, and sits in the back of the patrol car, sharing each moment of each day with Graves.

Graves and Buck are the only canine team in Piscataquis county, a stone's throw from the Canadian border in Maine. This is the most rural county in the state, part of a vast wilderness, but the team still gets called twenty-four hours a day, seven days a week, to do what only they can do: track missing or wanted people and search for drugs.

Graves found Buck at a breeder of German shepherds on the Vermont–New York border when the pup was eight weeks old. When he got the dog home, Graves ran him through a series of puppy tests. For instance, Graves took an empty cigarette pack and threw it into the grass. When the young Buck pounced on it, a butterfly flew up and over the puppy's head. He glanced at the butterfly, but then went back to the pack, a sure sign that he would grow into an excellent working dog. Because he'd already had two other police dogs,

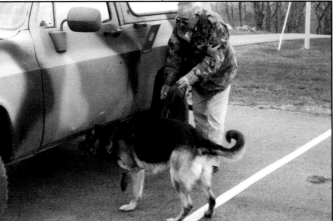

Graves new what he was looking for, and this dog had it all: He wanted to be trained, wasn't easily spooked, and didn't want to be dominated. All he needed was a new name—the kennel had called him Bruce, but as far as Graves was concerned no K9 in Piscataquis county was going to be named that. By the time they'd driven home, Bruce had become Buck.

NOW BUCK IS FIVE YEARS OLD, AND HE'S FULFILLED EVERY promise shown in those early puppy tests. In fact, he's so quick to learn that Graves has to be careful with the dog, for if Graves does something wrong more than twice, Buck will have learned it. Not only has Buck been certified by the United States Police Canine Association, but has also won top Schutzhund awards for tracking, protecting, and obedience. Moreover, he proves every day that he is excellent at his job.

For instance, recently Buck and Graves were called in to search a jail. The wardens had evidence of narcotics use, but they'd been unable to find drugs by searching the cell block. The minute Buck walked into the common area, he scratched on a television set. Graves pulled him into the cell block for the search but found nothing. Buck went back to the television set and scratched again. This time, Graves told the wardens to look into the set, and when they opened the back of it, they found the drugs. A new search of the cell block found the tool a prisoner had made to open the back of the television set, and that ended the drug problem in that jail.

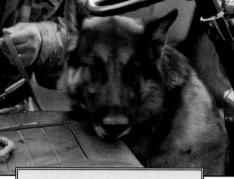

Graves uses positive reinforcement to train Buck. Although they still train all the time, Graves believes the first sixteen weeks are the most important time in a dog's life. He trained Buck from the beginning, but he always treated it as a game. For instance, when Buck learned tracking, it was always a fun track for food. When Buck and Graves played with his tug toy, Buck always got to win. And now, when Buck does a good job, he gets to play with that same tug toy and also receives praise in the form of food treats. He understands hand signals and voice commands in both German and English, and has learned everything that has been presented to him in his five years.

> OFFICER GRAVES HAS NEVER LET HIS DOGS BITE ANYONE. THE THREAT HAS ALWAYS BEEN ENOUGH.

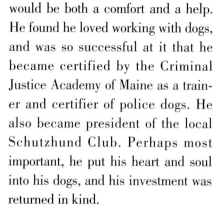

FOURTEEN YEARS AGO, AFTER TWENTY YEARS OF POLICE work, Graves was the head of the organized crime unit for the Maine State Police. He was under a lot of pressure from drug and smuggling units and saw that a dog would be both a comfort and a help. He found he loved working with dogs, and was so successful at it that he became certified by the Criminal Justice Academy of Maine as a trainer and certifier of police dogs. He also became president of the local Schutzhund Club. Perhaps most important, he put his heart and soul into his dogs, and his investment was returned in kind.

Buck follows Graves like a puppy, whether they're at work or at home. In fact, Buck sleeps right next to him on the bed each night. Buck is a beautiful dog. He is full of strength and life, yet he is sweet and gentle. Perhaps the most amazing thing about Buck is how fast he can switch from a friendly dog into an aggressive canine when Graves calls on him. And just as quickly, and also on Graves's command, he will turn back into that sweet dog. Buck is a police K9, and that's his job.

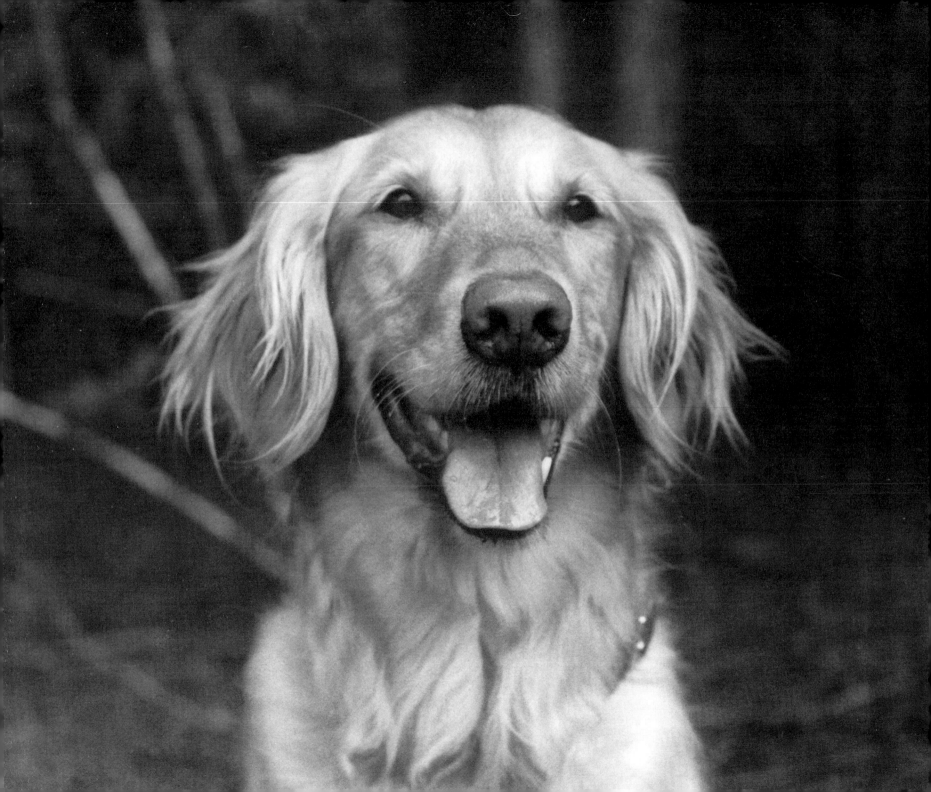

ROOKIE

Dancer

ROOKIE IS A GOLDEN RETRIEVER WITH RHYTHM. HIS favorite move is backward stepping, and he prefers a techno-beat.

Rookie regularly wins Freestyle competitions and is the only dog in the United States who has won a Musical Freestyle Excellent Individual title. Freestyle is AKC-sanctioned exhibition dancing for dogs and their human partners. It is obedience work to music with added tricks that would be right at home on a vaude-ville stage: lifting paws, moon walking, jumping, skating backwards, spinning, and twirling. After each successful routine, Rookie jumps into handler Carolyn Scott's arms and they head off-ring for his reward—a jackpot of snacks.

Rookie has overcome a fear of everything from elevators to shadows by traveling around the country competing in Freestyle events and making television appearances. The fear, which once kept him home, rarely surfaces now, although,

> **IF THE DOG HAS RHYTHM, THE TEAM SUCCEEDS.**

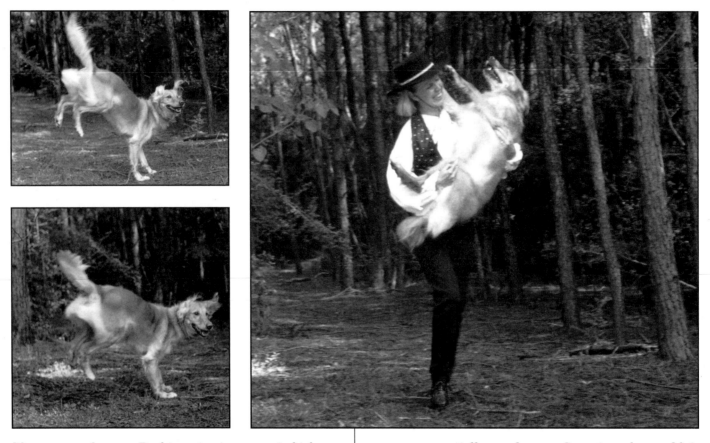

like many performers, Rookie maintains a certain high-strung personality.

Rookie's fear began when he was about nine months old. He was so fearful of his own shadow he would lie down and cower. He couldn't bear to be in a confined space, especially an elevator. Sometimes he wouldn't even take a treat—the sign of greatest distress in a dog who loves to eat more than anything.

In addition to his nervousness, Rookie had difficulty in the obedience ring, where Scott was training him to compete. Dogs compete for obedience titles by executing exact moves for a judge in a competition ring. Rookie was continually marked down in his score for his exuberance and enthusiasm: the wagging tail, the bouncing gait. Rookie was having too much fun. Where obedience requires smoothness, Rookie was loosey-goosey. Where obedience requires elegance and reserve, Rookie was bounce and swing. As his scores plummeted, he registered Scott's disappointment and became even more nervous. His obedience career ended sadly.

ONE LUCKY DAY, SCOTT SAW A FREESTYLE EXHIBITION, AND immediately thought of Rookie. They threw together a routine—her husband, Randy, videotaped them—and Scott was surprised to see how much Rookie's movement looked like dancing.

In Freestyle, a dog trainer like Scott choreographs a heeling routine to music with specific moves executed in a bravura dancing manner. If a dog bounces, it looks like dancing; if a dog is stiff, it looks like walking to music.

In other words, if the dog has rhythm, like Rookie, the team succeeds. What was once a deficit was now Rookie's greatest strength. Since that day, Scott and

> ROOKIE HAS THE LAST WORD IN CHOREOGRAPHY.

Rookie have been one of the premier Freestyle teams in the United States.

Rookie has the last word in choreography. Scott is never quite sure what he'll do in each routine. She trains him, and he performs, and somehow it always works for the music. Is he dancing? It sure looks like it.

ROOKIE TOOK SCOTT BY SURPRISE THE FIRST time he jumped into her arms at the end of a performance. The judges and the audience loved this flourish, so she encourages the dog to keep it up. Just as well too—as the audience applauds, Rookie feels her excitement and hup! he jumps whether she's expecting it or not. He also likes to add twirls to the routines. He never seems to get enough of those. These little tricks make Scott believe Freestyle is a creative expression for Rookie.

ROOKIE LOVES DANCING. AND HE LOVES SCOTT. PERHAPS most important, through his success, Rookie has overcome his fears. His nervousness rarely gets the best of him these days. Now when he walks into a scary situation—an elevator, a small room, the *Howie Mandel Show*—Rookie immediately turns to Scott for his jackpot. And he gets it.

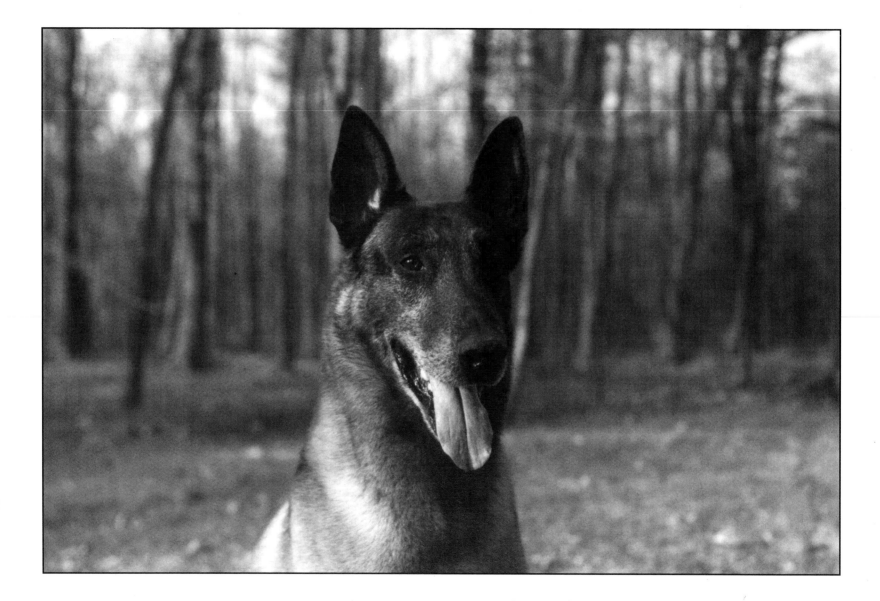

FREDDY

FREDDY

Ring Sport Champion

WHEN A DOG'S SPORT INVOLVES BITING AND ATTACKing, you would think that the dog would be a vicious, aggressive canine.

Not so! Freddy de Mallesagne knows when to bite and when to be cool, and most of the time he is cool. When he competed for the North American Ring Sport Championship, Freddy won the award through his incredible strength and canine intelligence. Freddy does well in Ring Sport by being a thinker. He anticipates. He calculates. Also, he has been meticulously trained by his owner, Debbie Seymour.

Freddy came to New Hampshire from France when he was three years old. A Belgian Malanois, he'd been rejected by his French owner for a number of reasons, mainly trouble with one of the Ring Sport exercises and being, in general, too quiet. At his new home, he was quickly loved and given years to perfect his skills.

RING SPORT DEVOTEES CONSIDER THIS TO BE THE toughest dog sport in the world. A dog is trained for months or even a year just to bite properly—that is, a hard, deep, unrelenting bite. The other exercises—

jumping over a nearly eight-foot-high wall and over a fourteen-foot-wide pit—seem incredible, and one must ask, why? For those who love Ring Sport, though, the question worth asking is, why not?

Ring Sport is a series of nineteen exercises that a dog is taught to perform one after another in a competition ring. They range from biting a man—wearing a padded decoy suit—in the face to ignoring food to performing incredible feats. It takes years of training and practice to teach a dog all nineteen exercises.

Ring Sport was introduced in the United States in 1986 by French devotees of the sport. Immediately, perhaps because the exercises seemed so incredible, people became interested in training their own dogs to do them. Now, there are Ring Sport clubs all across the country.

A dog begins the sport with 400 points and as he performs the nineteen exercises, any mistake—by the dog or his handler—

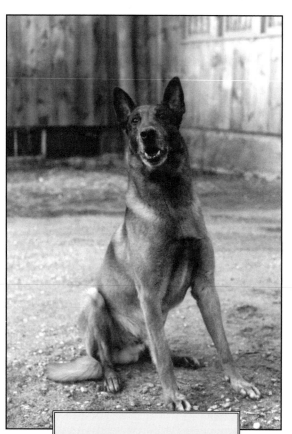

RING SPORT MAKES A GOOD HANDLER AS WELL AS A GOOD DOG.

results in points being taken away. When Freddy was awarded the North American championship, his score was 337.

The most difficult of all the exercises is called the Guard of the Object. The handler leaves the dog alone with an object, usually a basket, and the decoy tries to steal the object or draw the dog away from it. To keep his points, the dog must stay with the object while keeping it away from the decoy. It takes years of training to perfect this exercise—if it is ever perfected.

It took Seymour two years of training before Freddy understood what needed to happen in the object exercise. Freddy had an unfortunate tendency to bite the decoy and forget about the object. But it wasn't until the decoy assisted in training Freddy by grabbing his leash and pulling him away from the basket while Seymour ran out screaming and reprimanding, that Freddy really understood that he was not supposed to leave the basket.

Points are also taken away from the dog if the handler makes a mistake. The most common handler mistake is inadvertent signaling. Any body language—shifting weight, moving a hand—will result in a score of zero for the particular exercise. It is said that Ring Sport makes a good handler as well as a good dog, as everyone is under the same strict rules of discipline.

On the practical side of things, someone with a Ring Sport champion has a dog who can retrieve and guard objects, stay no matter the temptation, and protect his handler in a variety of situations. Aside from the competitions, Ring Sport trains dogs to an incredible level of obedience. Also, the time spent training usually bonds the handler and the dog into a loving team.

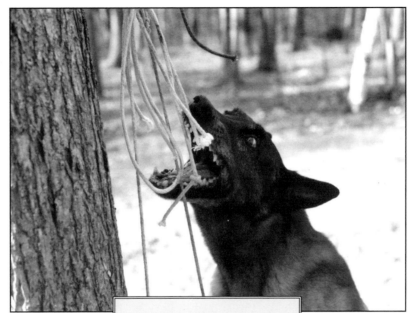

COOL OR NOT, FREDDY IS NOT A DOG TO BE TRIFLED WITH.

LIKE THE AMERICAN stereotype of a French-man, Freddy loves women. Especially Seymour. He is usually quite sociable and friendly, but when a man made a pass at Seymour, Freddy was right there, ready to attack. The man saw Freddy, poised and alert, and all Seymour had to say was, "Freddy's working." The unwanted lover knew what that meant and hit the road. Cool or not, Freddy is not a dog to be trifled with.

Seymour is continually amazed that his French owner rejected the dog. She says she can't imagine anyone not caring for Freddy. He is her best buddy, accompanying her every-where, even to work. If she's upset, he kisses her and cheers her up. He sleeps on the floor beside her bed each night. He's clean. He's protective. Freddy is a perfect gentleman.

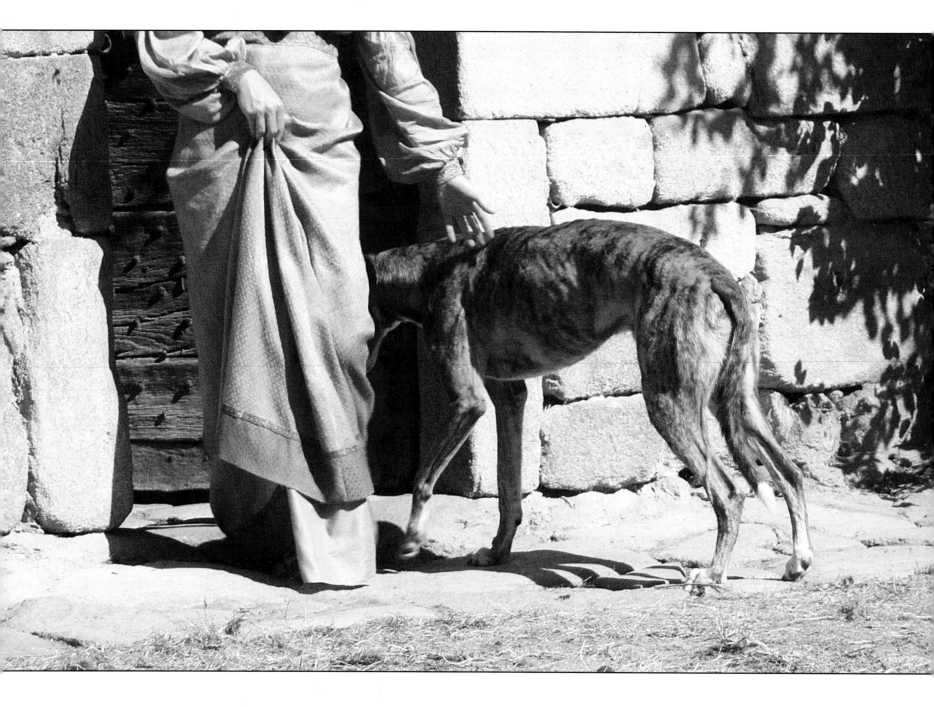

GUINEFORT

Saint

I N THE MIDDLE AGES, THE MOST BEAUTIFUL AND NOBLE beast, the greyhound, belonged exclusively to the aristocracy. A certain Lord Villars, living in a castle in France, owned such a creature and called him Guinefort. When Guinefort was not hunting with his master, it was his duty to watch over the master's infant son.

One day, while alone standing watch, an enormous serpent crawled into the nursery to make a meal of the son. Guinefort attacked the serpent and saved the baby, but the battle was bloody, and the dog was hurt. When Villars returned to the nursery, he did not see the ser-pent or the baby, only the overturned cradle and the bloody mouth of Guinefort. He immediately pulled his sword and killed his dog.

When the baby cried, Villars realized his horrific error, but it was too late. Guinefort was dead.

Deeply saddened, Villars carried the body of Guinefort outside and threw it down a well. He then planted a grove of trees around the well to honor his beloved dog. Soon after, the castle was destroyed and abandoned—no one knows what happened to Villars and his family.

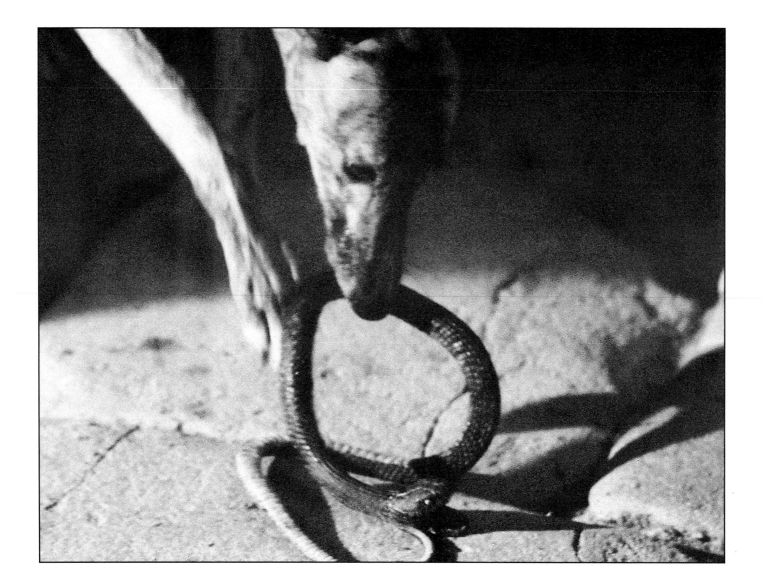

The local peasants heard this story and began to make pilgrimages to the woods to honor the martyred greyhound. They called him Saint Guinefort, and prayed to the dog when they were sick or needed something. Mostly, however, they brought their sick children to the well and prayed for Saint Guinefort to heal them. And so it went, in the French countryside, for hundreds of years.

Until, that is, a thirteenth-century Dominican friar, Stephen of Bourbon, traveled through the area in search of heresy and heard about the peasants' beloved Saint Guinefort. Calling the dog a saint was not only superstitious an idolatrous, but awarding sainthood was the exclusive domain of the pope and challenged the foundations of the Church. As one of the first inquisitors, Stephen of Bourbon knew what must be done.

He gathered the peasants together and preached to them the evils of superstition. He helped them cut down the woods, dig up the bones of Saint Guinefort, and burn everything in a huge fire. He told the peasants that anyone going back to the well for any reason would have his possessions seized and sold. With that, the friar left to continue his work, and the woods grew back and the peasants continued in their ways.

PEOPLE CAN'T HELP BUT OBSERVE THE CONNECTION BETWEEN THE LOVE OF GOD AND THE UNCONDITIONAL DEVOTION OF A DOG.

ALTHOUGH HE THOUGHT HIS JOB WAS COMPLETE, STEPHEN of Bourbon's efforts did not wipe out the cult of Saint Guinefort. In fact, pilgrimages to the well continued for hundreds of years. Even twentieth-century women prayed to Saint Guinefort. The last documented instance of a pilgrimage to the wood occurred in 1940, when a grandmother prayed to Saint Guinefort to heal her sick grandchild. In 1987, a French movie was made about Saint Guinefort and the cult that surrounded him. Released in America as *The Sorceress*, it features the dog pictured here as Saint Guinefort.

WHAT WAS TRUE IN THE MIDDLE AGES IS true today, and common people can't help but observe the connection between the love of God and the unconditional devotion of a dog. Whether the archetypal sacrifice of Saint Guinefort or the everyday loyalty of a child's pet, dogs have always known something important about love.

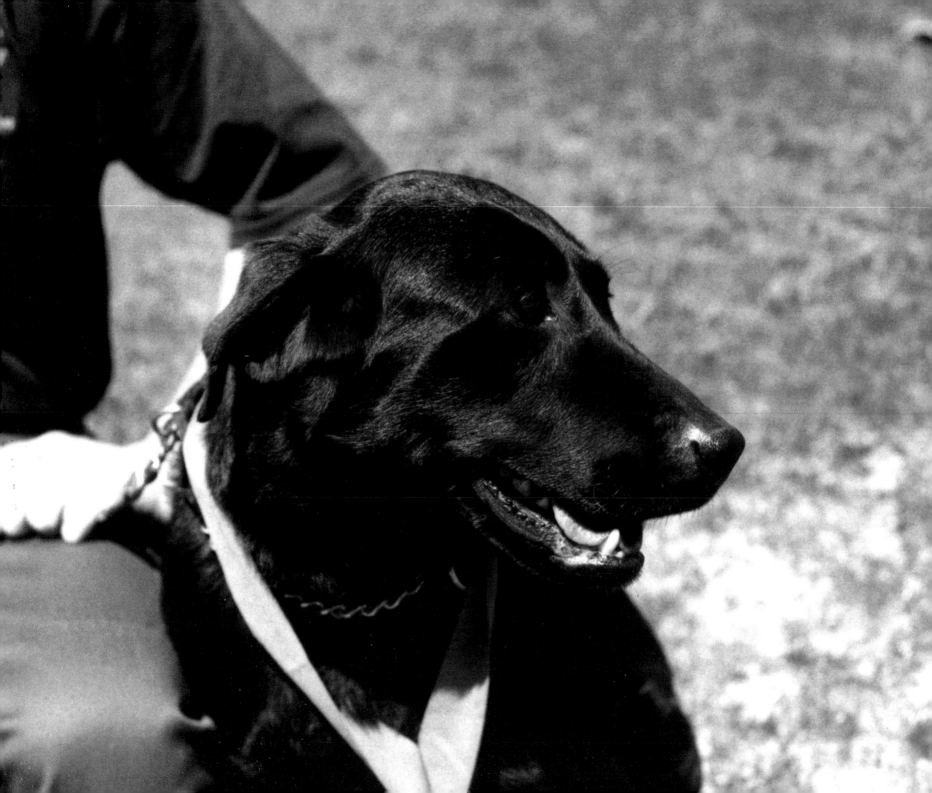

JAZZ

Iron Dog

AN UPSET OCCURRED AT THE NEW HAMPSHIRE Iron Dog Competition this year, when the only Labrador Retriever participating—and a quite lighthearted one at that—won by a landslide. All the German shepherd and Rottweiler owners could do nothing but swear to work a bit harder to prepare for next year's competition.

Jazz works with Donald McGee of Revenue Canada's Customs Border Service. Back home, they were Southern

> THEY WERE UP AGAINST SOME VERY TOUGH AND VERY SERIOUS COMPETITORS.

New Brunswick and Prince Edward Island's only detector dog team, trained to find narcotics and explosives.

Jazz was used to finding huge caches of narcotics as they were smuggled into Canada. Once, she found $2.5 million worth of cocaine hidden in the false gas tank of a vehicle that was being driven over the border. Jazz was used to winning drug dog competitions, and had won a competition in New Hampshire the night before.

Jazz was not, however, used to doggie drag races, obstacle courses, and three kilometer runs. Neither was McGee. That was what they were up against in the Iron Dog Competition. They were up against some very tough and very serious competitors—including the New Hampshire defending champ, Gunther, as well as the reigning New York and Pennsylvania Iron Dog Champions.

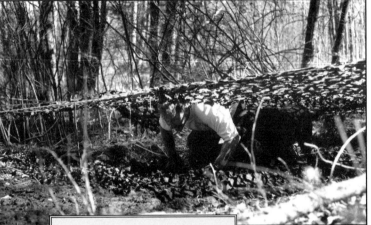

ON A CRISP APRIL MORNING, MCGEE AND Jazz began the day just hoping they wouldn't embarrass themselves. To avoid that, they went to check out the agility obstacle course before the race began. There was a swinging plank suspended by chains that wobbled ferociously when a dog walked across it. McGee saw that as a potential problem, so he had Jazz walk across it a few times, until she got her bearings. Although he knew they'd do better if Jazz also walked through the wooded obstacle course, McGee decided to pass because he knew that Jazz enjoyed new experiences, and since

> JAZZ'S REWARD FOR ALL OF HER WORK IS A BALL THAT NEVER BOUNCES THE SAME WAY TWICE.

they weren't there to win, he decided they might as well have some fun. As long as they weren't completely humiliated, that is.

As it turned out, Jazz and McGee had only one humiliating moment. Their trouble came during the doggie drag race. While the other dogs all chased after a decoy who screamed at them and ran through the finish line, Jazz ran the race in her own style. Jazz's reward for all of her work is a ball that never bounces the same way twice. She loves it. McGee knew the way to get her to run fast was to throw that ball for her to fetch—so that's what he did. Unfortunately, however, the ball hit the only thing on the field, a cone marking the finish line, and bounced 90 degrees off into the woods. Jazz, being Jazz, ran past the cone and then due right to get her beloved ball. No one could believe it. McGee had to join in the laughter—it was too funny. She ran the fourth fastest time, though, so at least there was no true embarrassment.

MCGEE GOT JAZZ WHEN SHE WAS three and a half years old from the Revenue Canada Customs Border Service College in Quebec. She was originally from Montana, where she had been bred to be a field dog, which she was prior to being sold to the college. McGee had two previous Labrador detector dogs, and when his last dog, Sammy, got sick and was retired into his home, McGee picked out Jazz.

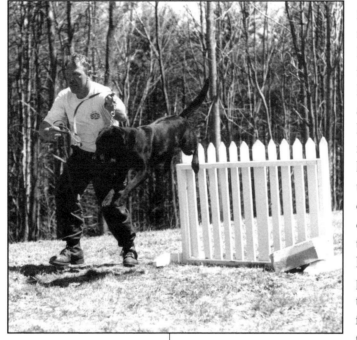

FOR MCGEE AND JAZZ, THE most difficult part of the Iron Dog competition was the endurance run. Three kilometers through woods, across streams and rock beds, through mud, under a net, over hurdles. McGee had to load and fire and unload a gun. Jazz had to collect evidence: a playing card, a rawhide bone, a tennis ball, a piece of leather that had been placed along the trail. If they didn't bring back all four pieces of evidence they would have been dis-

At first, Jazz didn't trust McGee. He could see it in her eyes: She worked for him, and did her job, but withheld her trust until he earned it. One day, after about six months together, McGee saw Jazz staring at him with puppy-dog eyes, and he knew he'd done it. Since then, they've been an amazingly well-bonded team, together twenty-four hours a day, seven days a week. Now she's six, but when Jazz retires, she'll live with McGee until she dies.

qualified—this happened to a lot of the competitors. It was a grueling course.

In the end, McGee and Jazz earned the top score. They won 198.33 out of a possible 200 points. Perhaps more important—with the exception of the bouncing ball incident—they didn't embarrass themselves.

The Iron Dog pits K9 against K9 in an intense ordeal of dog athleticism. When the day was over and the men were exhausted, one dog was victorious: Jazz.

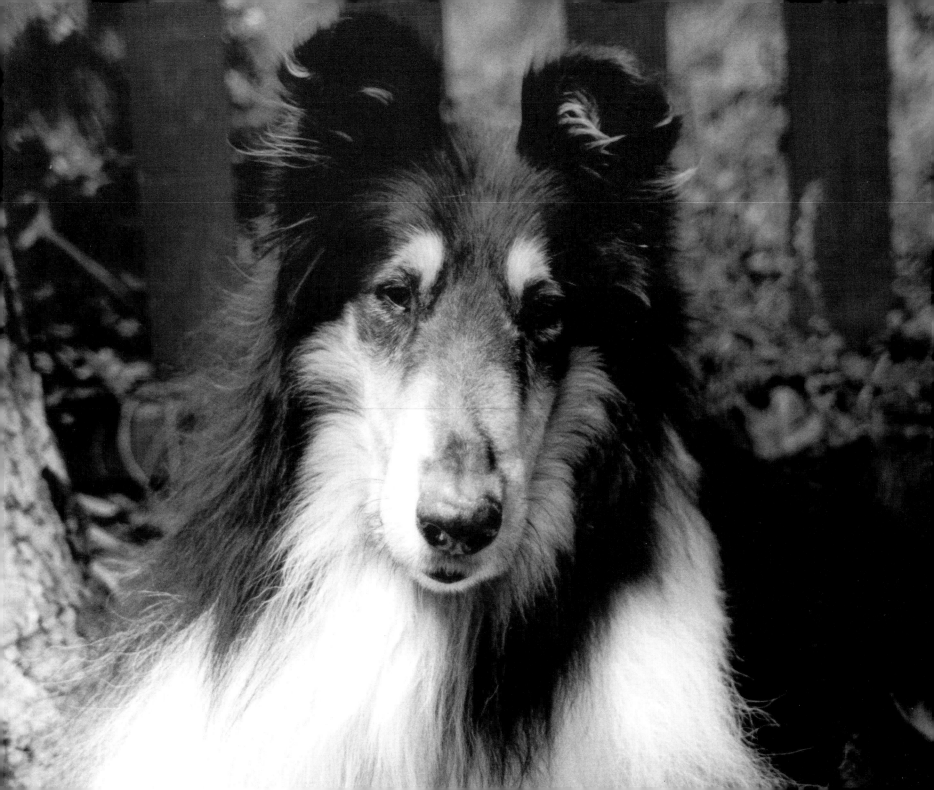

TUXEDO

Babysitter

CHILDREN LOVE DOGS. AND MANY DOGS LOVE children, too—usually one or two children at a time. But sometimes you'll meet a dog who loves all children, everywhere; a dog who runs to the sound of children's voices. A dog who can't resist a child. A dog like Tuxedo.

Nine years ago, this beautiful collie came to the Bracewell family on the Canadian plains. He was in a traumatized state with a tremendous fear of staircases and newspapers. He was also afraid of grown men, cowering in the corner whenever one came around. The Bracewells never found out exactly what happened to Tuxedo, but they gently coaxed and praised until he got over most of his fears.

From the beginning, Tuxedo drew children to him like a magnet. They loved his soft fur and long nose, and he loved them, too. Soon, he ran to the sounds of children's voices and laughter wherever he heard them, usually up the street to a park. And there the children flocked to him.

> TUXEDO DREW CHILDREN TO HIM LIKE A MAGNET.

TUXEDO'S WORK AS A BABYSITTER BEGAN WHEN THE Bracewell grandbaby, Miranda, arrived. Tux stood guard over Miranda while she slept. And, as the infant grew, Tux continued to watch, pushing with a gentle nose whenever the baby went somewhere she shouldn't, putting his body between the child and the staircase or the pond or the fire.

Miranda called him "Nana Tux."

Soon, Tuxedo kept Miranda safe on an eight-foot-square blanket in the backyard. Every time the

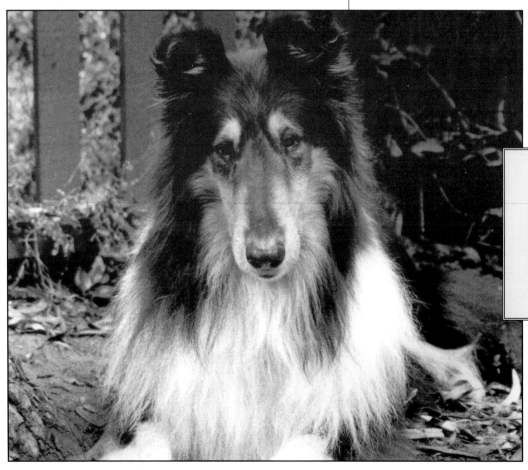

> TUX HELPED THE CHILDREN LEARN HOW TO BE GENTLE, HOW TO BE LOYAL, AND HOW TO SHARE.

baby crawled too close to the edge of the blanket, Tux would push her back toward the center. When Miranda's baby brother, John, arrived, Tux kept two babies safe on the blanket. And when cousins visited, four and then five young ones were playing safely under Nana Tux's watchful eye.

WHAT IS IT ABOUT COLLIES THAT INSPIRES CHILDREN? Is it their fluffy fur coat? Their aristocratic soft nose? Their gentle demeanor? Is it, maybe, that collies watch over children with the same dedication they once gave to sheep. And provide the children the love of a soft animal.

These are the lessons Tux taught while keeping his wards safe. As they learned to stand up, Tux was there to be tugged upon. When taking first steps, Tux made an excellent walker. Mostly, Tuxedo's gentle presence helped the children learn how to be gentle, how to be loyal, and how to share.

A FEW YEARS AGO, TUX MOVED TO California for a graceful and well-deserved retirement. He spends most of his time sleeping in the grass and barking at squirrels, but sometimes he slips away from the house. When Constance Bracewell needs to find him, she puts her head out the front door and listens for the sound of children's voices. She follows those voices, and there she'll find Tux. With the children.

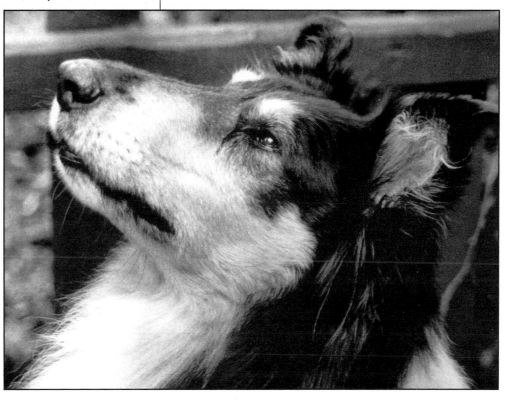

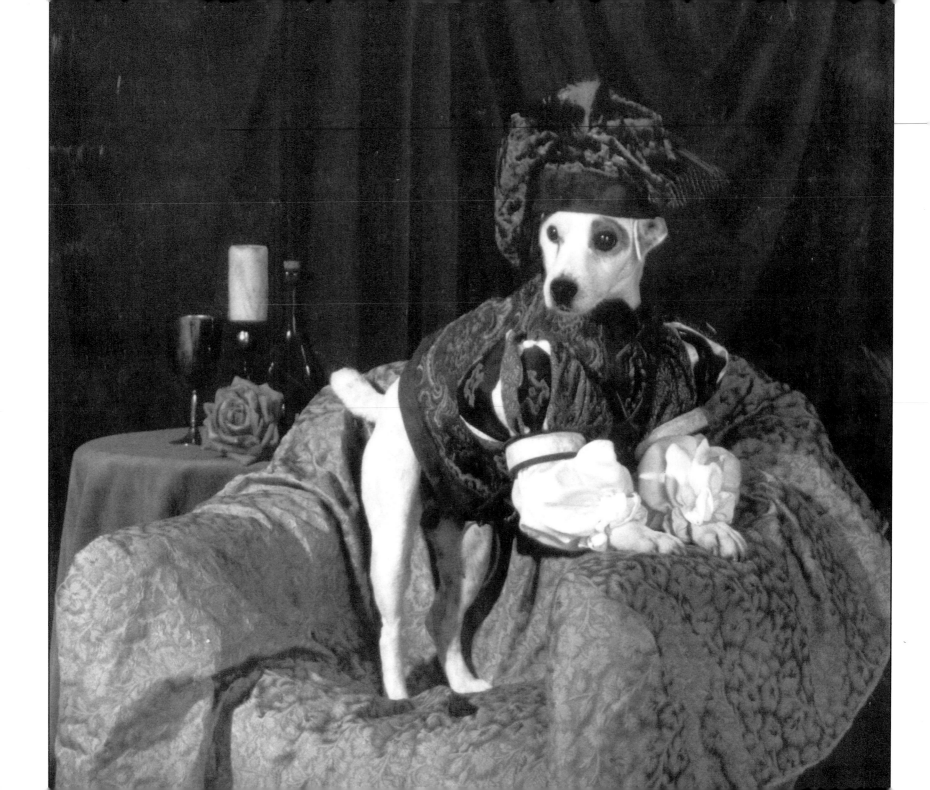

SOCCER

Television Star

EVERY DOG HAS HIS DAY. AFTER YEARS OF TOILING on television commercials for dog food he didn't even eat, Soccer hit the big time as the star of Wishbone, the award-winning PBS show about a dog who leaps into literature.

SOCCER IS AN EXCEPTIONAL NINE-YEAR-OLD Jack Russell terrier. He belongs to Jackie Kaptan, who trains animals for lots of movies and television shows. In fact, when Soccer's big break came,

> EVEN FOR A DOG, SUCCESS IS NOT WITHOUT ITS PRICE.

and the call to audition for the role of Wishbone arrived, Kaptan was on location with her yellow labs for the movie *River Wild*. She had to send an assistant with Soccer to show off his stuff.

No problem-o, as Wishbone might say. Soccer performed his back flips and scratch-a-fleas like a pro and aced the audition over 150 other hopeful dogs. The producers later said he was the most expressive dog—something anyone who has watched the show can confirm. He is fabulous.

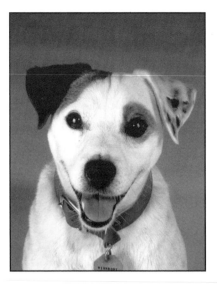

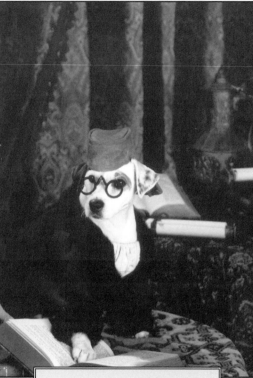

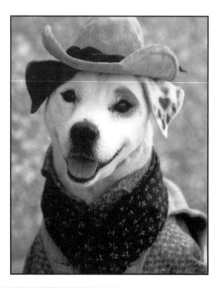

SOCCER WANTS TO WORK, HE WANTS to please, and he's very focused. In his role of Wishbone, he has worn hundreds of costumes, including armor, beards, and fantastic hats. Soccer can even do his most difficult trick, the back flip, while dressed in an elaborate costume and a hat.

The other actors on the set love Soccer. He is really fun to be around, always happy, always game to try a new trick. The stress of long hours of television production can be alleviated by a quick game of

Soccer is always willing to have his belly scratched, and you can't say that about most TV stars.

catch—both for human and canine actors. His only trouble on the set comes when he needs to give a prop to another actor and instead starts a tug-of-war.

After getting a scene right—which he almost always does on the first take—Soccer gets a food treat. His favorite reward is skinless chicken with garlic salt, specially grilled by Kaptan. Kibble rounds out his diet. He also receives a lot of praise and play time with toys while working.

SOCCER IS ONE OF KAPTAN'S FAVORITE dogs. She says he's one of the great ones, the kind of dog that comes around only two or three times in a lifetime. Kaptan's been training animals for twenty-five years, so she should know. There are forty other dogs living with Soccer. They live in kennels on Kaptan's five-acre spread outside of Los Angeles. When they're on location in Dallas, where *Wishbone* is filmed, Soccer has his own room in Kaptan's house, but even there he prefers sleeping in his crate.

Soccer was named for his fondness of miniature soccer balls. Plus, when he was a puppy, his markings resembled a soccer ball, with black spots over his eye, ear, and back. He still loves to destroy—that is, play with— miniature soccer balls.

Soccer has more toys than anyone could ever imagine, yet he still thinks he needs a new one every day. Soccer gets a toy and chew bone allowance from the production to spend each season as he wishes. He has

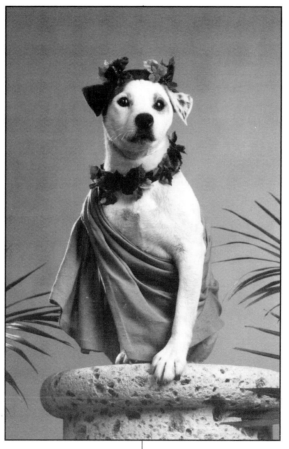

gone binge shopping at PetSmart, spending $200 on toys and chew bones in as little as three days.

Spoiled? Not compared to most TV stars. He does fly first class with a personal trainer. He does insist that the air conditioning be on when he rides in the car. He does stay in four-star hotels. And he does have bodyguards when making professional appearances. Still, Soccer is always willing to have his belly scratched, and you can't say that about most TV stars.

Even for a dog, success is not without its price. For many TV stars, that price is the loss of anonymity, the simple ability of common folk to be out among the people going about their business. For Soccer, that means being recognized everywhere he goes. Even if he's only ducking behind a tree or visiting a fire hydrant. There's a certain earthiness about Soccer. He may be a big star, but he never seems to forget that he is, after all, a dog.

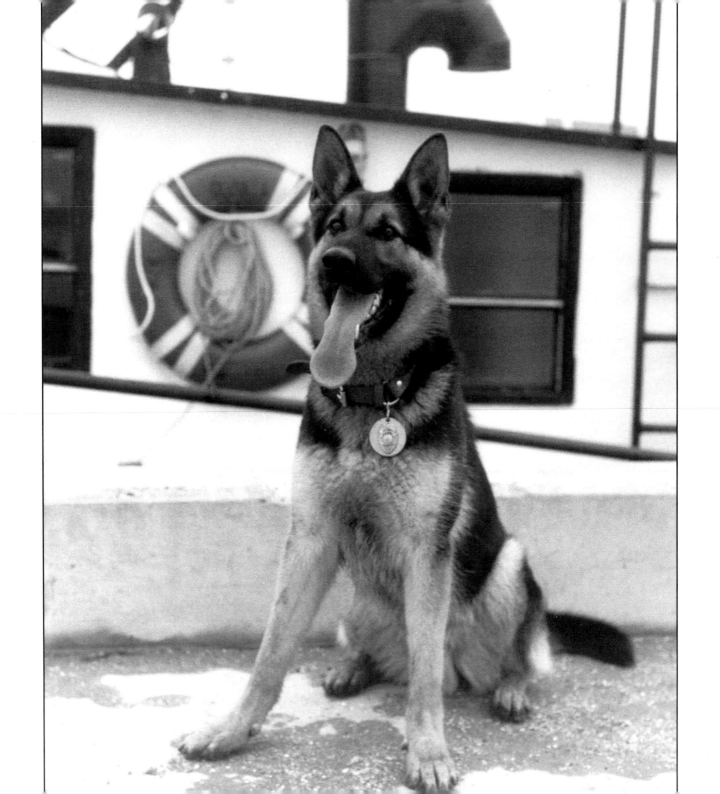

DUTCH

Coast Guard Dog

A DOG'S WORK IS NEVER DONE. AND DUTCH IS A DOG who never stops working. At the park, at home, even walking down the street where he might show a lot of interest in a particular automobile, Dutch searches for the presence of narcotics. That's when United States Coast Guardsman David Nilsen pulls Dutch back and gently reminds him they're just on their way to buy Milk Bones.

THE GERMAN SHEPHERD RESCUE FOUNDATION found Dutch in the New Jersey woods two years ago. He was starved, weighing less than thirty-five pounds, and was nearly dead. But he still would retrieve a thrown tennis ball. This strong prey drive alerted the rescue foundation to Dutch's potential as a working dog and they called the Coast Guard in Sandy Point, New Jersey, to send someone to check him out.

Nilsen had already tried two dogs from the German Shepherd Rescue Foundation. The first dog gave up too easily and lasted only one month; the second dog bit Nilsen and lasted one week. He was thrilled to find

"YOUR DOG'S GOT A GREAT NOSE."

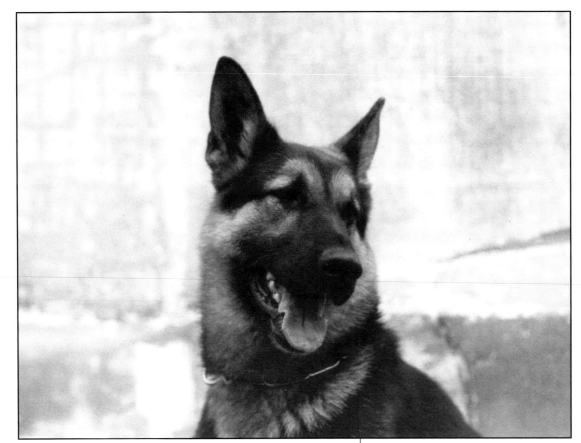

had already trained Dutch. He found German commands through an Internet search and tried them out, discovering that Dutch was already trained to search for drugs, explosives, and people. He was also a protection dog, trained to bite upon command. Dutch wasn't just trained—he was trained to do everything. How he ended up in the New Jersey woods no one ever found out.

BECAUSE DUTCH WAS so weak when found, he was carefully brought back to good health. Nilsen fed him very little at first, and took him on short walks, gradually increasing food and exercise. Now his weight is up to sixty-five pounds and he runs four miles a day

Dutch, especially when he looked closely and found a number tattooed in the dog's ear.

Nilsen traced the tattoo to Germany before losing the trail, but it made him wonder if someone with Nilsen, but they still must be careful with his diet. If Dutch eats anything other than his regular food, he vomits. Because of this, Nilsen is strict with regulating Dutch's diet.

AT THE SANDY HOOK COAST GUARD station, near the entrance to the New York Harbor, the Coast Guard relied upon the canine teams of local law enforcement before realizing they needed their own dogs to keep drugs from entering the country via ship and boat. Coast Guard canines are trained in the special marine environment in which they work, able to climb boat ladders and comfortable with being lifted into a ship, for instance. Dutch has been certified by the U.S. Police Canine Association, the U.S. Coast Guard, and the N.J. Attorney General.

Dutch proved himself with the local police when Nilsen was called out to assist in the search of a suspected crack house. Dutch ran into the suspect's bedroom and jumped onto a bed. He bit into a big pile of laundry on the bed, sig-

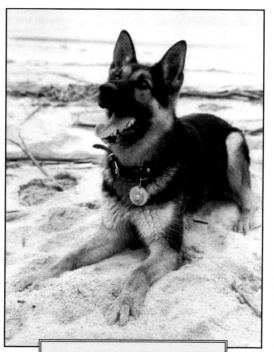

How Dutch ended up in the New Jersey woods no one ever found out.

naling Nilsen that he'd found the scent of narcotics. The police searched through the clothes. Nothing. They removed the blankets and sheets from the mattress. Nothing. Finally, the police removed the mattress and found, tucked into the bed's box springs, a notebook filled with complete records of a year's worth of drug sales. The suspect hadn't washed his hands after handling the drugs, so he left the scent of narcotics all over his notebook. Dutch's find gave the police listings of dozens of drug dealers and they gave Dutch the ultimate compliment. They told Nilsen, "Your dog's got a great nose."

DUTCH LIVES WITH NILSEN IN NEW JERSEY. They throw balls three or four times a day and take their runs together. His crate is on the porch, and when Dutch is tired he stands next to the crate to let Nilsen know he needs rest. Nilsen opens the door and the dog with the mysterious past climbs into his crate, finally stops working, and sleeps.

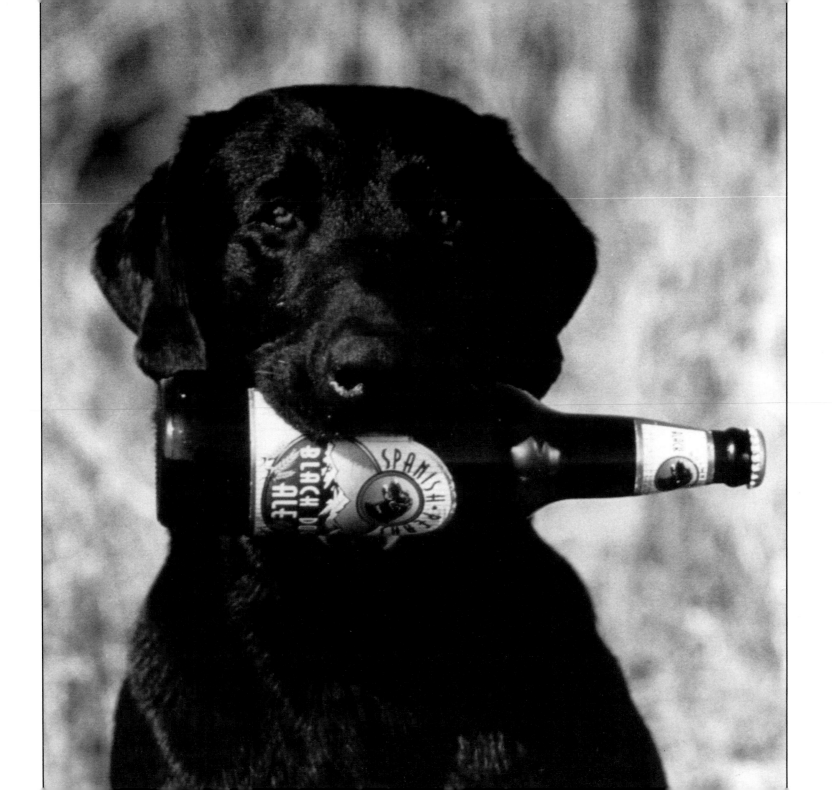

CHUG

Icon

IN CHUG'S LINE OF WORK, A DOG HAS TO WEAR A LOT of hats. In one day, he may pose for photographs, make sales presentations, attend fundraisers, and show off his gun dog abilities. At night, he could find himself sitting at a bar, signing photographs with his paw. He works all the time. And he's good at it, too. But what Chug loves most is sitting on someone's foot and getting his ears scratched.

Chugwater Charlie Hill is the black dog of Black Dog Beer. He's the Labrador with his mug on the label, holding a bottle of beer in his mouth. Chug belongs to Mark Taverniti, owner of the Spanish Peaks Brewing Company in Montana. Of course, Chug isn't the first dog to sell alcohol. Who can forget the Black and White Scotch terriers or Budweiser's own bullterrier, Spuds McKenzie? Chug wasn't thought up by slick advertisers, though; he is the living, breathing icon for Spanish Peaks. The beer was, in fact, named after the dog.

> THE BEER WAS NAMED AFTER THE DOG.

WHILE THE BREWERY WAS GETTING UP AND RUNNING, Chug accompanied Taverniti on his sales calls. They traveled around the country visiting liquor stores and distribution offices, and while they were at it, they participated in gun dog field trials. Chug is one of the few dogs in the country with master hunting titles from all three governing bodies of gun dog stakes: AKC, UKC, and NAHRA. Because Chug was so well trained, Taverniti knew he could walk into any situation and all the dog would do was make friends. While Taverniti

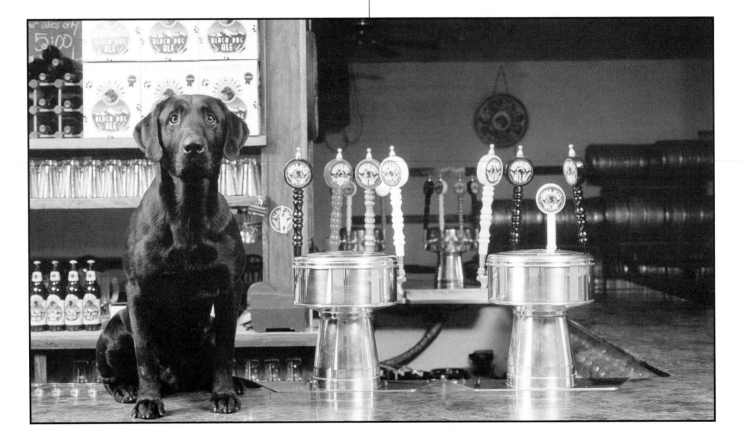

sold beer, Chug visited everyone he could, charming them and getting his ears scratched. The dog was irresistible, the beer was delicious, and sales skyrocketed.

Chug has a seductive quality; everyone wants to touch him. He's quite muscular, with the regal quality common in aging athletes. He also has a prodigious sideline as a stud. He has sired over a hundred puppies with a dozen bitches. He receives offers in the mail every week. He also gets fan letters. People send him their clothing for his paw signature. When a camera comes out, Chug knows just what to do. He vogues. He charms. He's Chug.

Of course, he isn't always accommodating. When he was a special guest on a radio show in Kansas City, a listener called in who didn't believe they had a dog in their studio. Apparently, despite all their appearances, some people don't think there really is a "Black Dog." Taverniti tried everything to get Chug to bark, but he wouldn't do it. Chug is a calm, sweet Labrador and

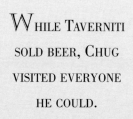

WHILE TAVERNITI SOLD BEER, CHUG VISITED EVERYONE HE COULD.

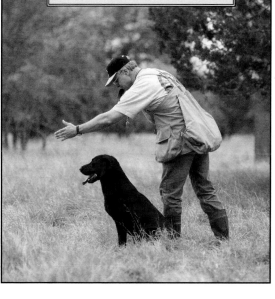

couldn't be better trained, but on that day, he would not bark for anyone.

ALTHOUGH CHUG HAS ALWAYS BEEN TAVERNITI'S FAMILY dog, lately he's been living with the Spanish Peaks publicity director, Vickie Andreassi. She takes him on sales calls and publicity events nearly every week, so it was decided Chug may as well live with her. Also, now that he is nine, Chug has earned a rest. Taverniti kept Chug in an outdoor kennel; Andreassi lets him sleep on the bed.

Since they travel so much, Chug ends up sleeping in a lot of hotels. He sits next to Andreassi while she makes sales presentations and he sits next to her at the bar when she organizes tavern promotions. He knows his job is to be friendly, so he walks around, greeting everyone, sitting on their feet. He allows Andreassi to use his paw to stamp autographs on hundreds of photographs. Chug seems happy to do it, as long as he gets his ears scratched.

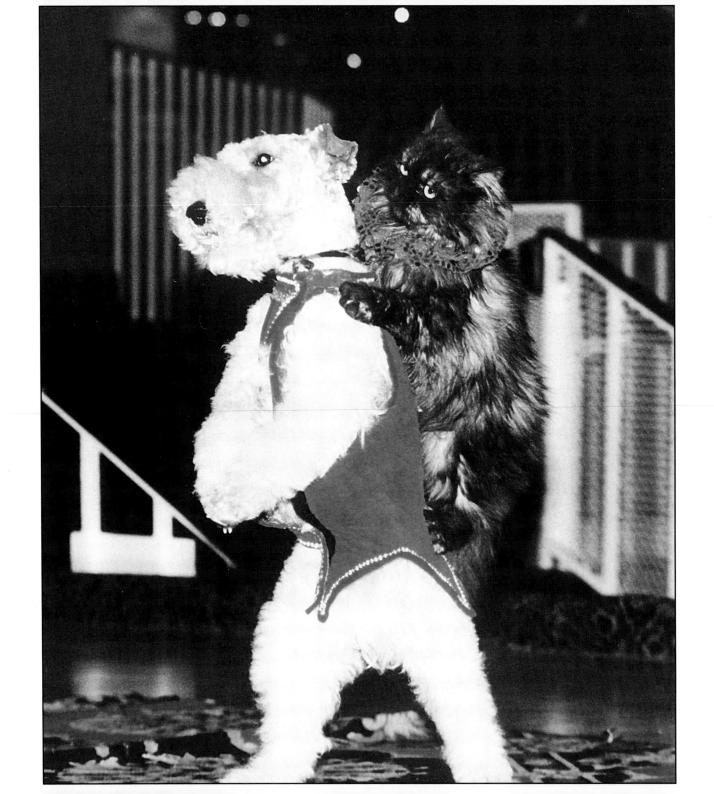

PHILLIP

Vegas Show Dog

As the only dog in a show called "House Cats," Phillip spends a lot of time with a cat on his back. He jumps over cats, lets cats jump over him, and lets a cat push him around in a baby carriage. Upstaged by house cats? Not this dog.

Phillip does a show-stopping routine of his own, balancing on his front paws on the hand of his trainer, Gregory Popovich, whose family has been in the Moscow Circus for four generations. Popovich is an amazing

> PHILLIP RECEIVES TWO REWARDS FOR HIS WORK: HOT DOGS AND RESPECT.

juggler and physical comedian, but it is for his animal act that he is best known.

Six years ago, Popovich trained two domestic cats to do a few tricks. Thinking of building an act, he went to a Las Vegas animal shelter to see if he could find more animals to train. Because there are no animal shelters in Russia, he was surprised to see so many beautiful animals sitting in cages. He wanted to take them all, but left with Phillip, who is cat sized and very cute. Even as a puppy, Phillip

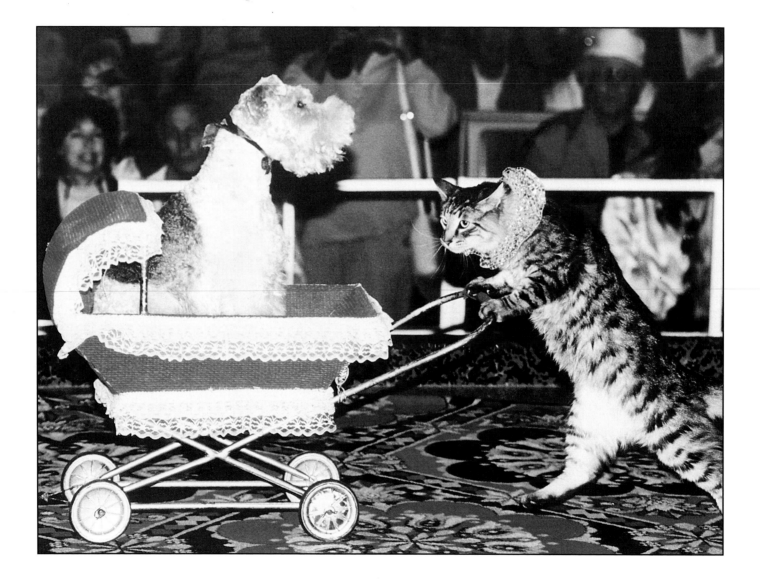

had an aristocratic air, with his neat curly hair and expressive eyes.

POPOVICH EVENTUALLY RESCUED THIRTEEN CATS FROM the shelter and built the act he calls "House Cats," which became very popular at Circus Circus. When Popovich and his animals perform, it's standing room only as the arena fills with laughter and children and many oohs and aahs.

As the cat show became more popular and the animals in the shelter kept tugging at his heart, Popovich expanded his repertoire to include a dog show, "Dog Classroom," and then turned both shows into "Pet Comedy Theater," a forty-minute act. Phillip is the only animal in all three shows; he works hard. Phillip has been performing twice a day, six days a week, for six years.

PHILLIP RECEIVES TWO REWARDS FOR HIS WORK: HOT DOGS and respect. He was trained by being encouraged to extend behavior he displayed naturally in play. For instance, he loved to stand on his hind legs and play with a knotted rope hanging from a tree. This gave Popovich the idea to have Phillip walk on his hind legs and eventually allow a cat on for a ride. It was a gradual process. Popovich is always watching his animals

> HE SEEMS STRANGELY ALOOF FOR A DOG. PERHAPS HE SPENDS TOO MUCH TIME WITH CATS.

for new ideas, although Phillip doesn't like to play so much anymore. He seems strangely aloof for a dog. Perhaps he spends too much time with cats.

Phillip is definitely interested in eating the hot dogs he earns. He also eats dried dog food mixed with canned dog food. The canned dog food had too much oil for Phillip's liver, so he was recently cut down to three times a week. Luckily, he didn't need to have his hot dog intake reduced.

Phillip lives in a special room in Popovich's home, which he shares with the thirteen cats and four other dogs. The dogs—Buba, Snow, Fekla, and Anthony, who perform with Phillip in the dog classroom show—all get along with Phillip, recognizing that, as Popovich's first dog, he has Alpha dog status. Each dog has a crate to sleep in and a special blanket of his own. There is a large backyard and every once in a while, the whole group is given the run of the house. There is no fighting, even between the dogs and the cats. They seem to recognize that they are all members of the same troupe.

Like most dogs, Phillip plays and eats and sleeps and vies for the attention of the people he loves. His life backstage is well-rounded and Phillip seems satisfied. He has animal companions and a kind human to work with, and he gets to eat hot dogs. Phillip's job is making children laugh and he knows how to do it well.

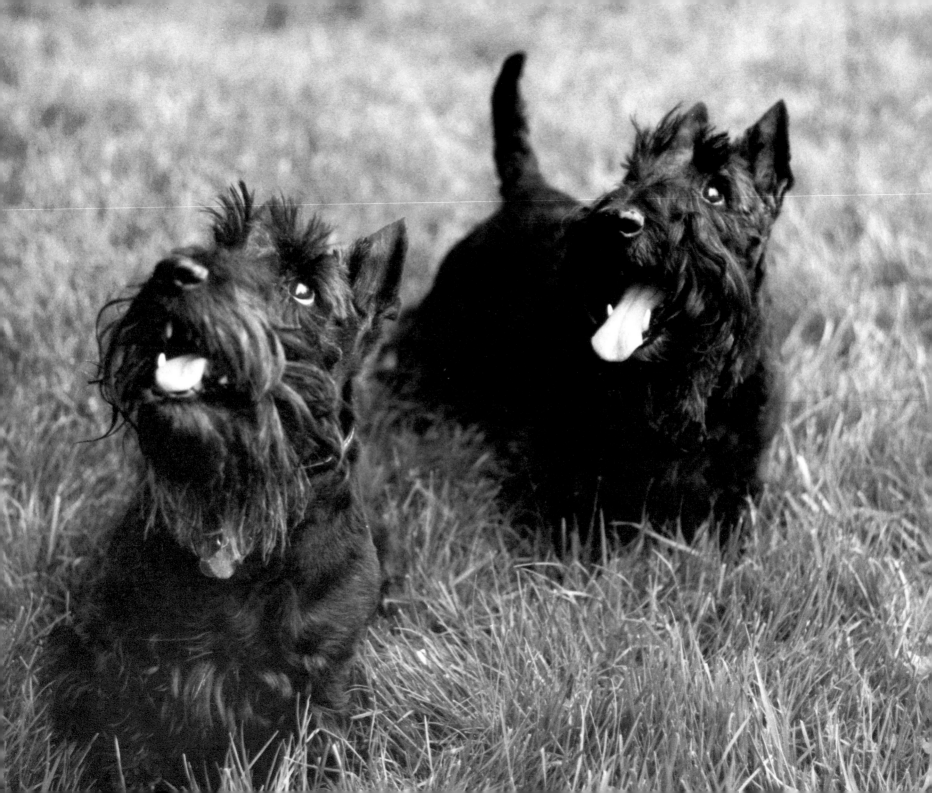

JOCK & CLYDE

Earthdogs

JOCK IS A DOG ON THE CONSTANT LOOKOUT FOR RATS, while Clyde remains behind, offering moral support. They are earthdogs. They work rats. But if one can't be found, these Scotties are more than happy to bark at a passing pedestrian instead.

UNDER THE AUSPICES OF THE AMERICAN Kennel Club, earthdogs are trained to run through tunnels and work rats, which are held in a cage at the end of the tunnel.

HAPPY AS HE WAS TO EAT THE MOUSE, CLYDE SAW NO POINT IN GOING THROUGH A TUNNEL TO BARK AT A RAT IN A CAGE.

"Working" involves barking and scratching in an attempt to get the rat—which is not allowed to happen. But don't tell Jock that.

Also, please don't tell him to not take his work home with him, because earth-dogging at home is even better for Jock. There are no cages at home and he kills the rats who make the mistake of moving into the woodpile in his backyard. Jock is a dog with a passion for rats and it's earned him the Master Earthdog title.

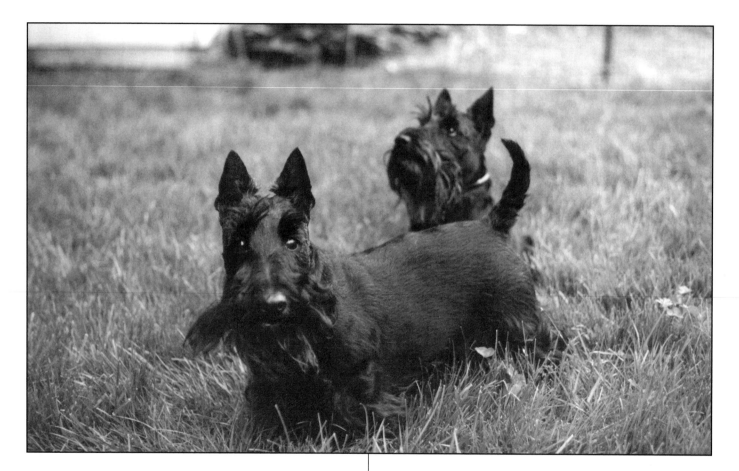

IN AKC EARTHDOG TRIALS, A NINE-INCH BY NINE-INCH tunnel is constructed, up to thirty feet in length, with false entrances and exits, twist, turns, constrictions, and obstructions. A caged rat is placed at the end of the tunnel to give the dog a simulated hunting environment. The dog is released a distance from the entrance to a tunnel. He must then follow a scent trail, also simulated, to the opening, find the rat, and work him. A

90

dog will have ninety seconds to find the rat, and ninety seconds to work him before being called off. When called, he must stop working, and come straightaway. Dogs who successfully complete the test are awarded titles, such as Junior Earthdog, Senior Earthdog, and the highest award, Master Earthdog.

To train Jock to go through the tunnels, his owner, Mary Rice, had to entice him with special treats. Like most Scottish terriers, Jock is especially interested in food. He received—and ate—cheese, chicken liver brownies, and finally a live mouse, before realizing he really did want to go through a small, dark tunnel to get a rat. When Rice trained Clyde, she offered him the same enticements—but, happy as he was to eat the mouse, he still saw no point in going through a tunnel to bark at a rat in a cage.

SCOTTIES ARE CONSIDERED BY MANY TO BE THE EARLIEST type of terrier, and the oldest indigenous dog of Britain. Terriers were bred for centuries to be ratters, dogs who can chase down and kill rats that would otherwise steal massive amounts of food. The very name terrier comes from the Latin root *terra*, for *earth*. Some Scotties, like Jock, have a strong instinct to get rats; others, like Clyde, just want to get along.

The Scotties have a lovely life in Virginia. Jock and Clyde enjoy playing with red balls in the backyard so much that they get blisters on their noses. They don't enjoy getting dressed up for the annual Scottish Christmas Walk in Alexandria, but that doesn't keep Rice from doing it anyway. She enjoys seeing Jock and Clyde in plaid. Who wouldn't?

A NINE-YEAR-OLD, JOCK STILL COMPETES IN AGILITY contests that require him to be thin enough to jump through obstacles. Clyde is in training for AKC Junior Earthdog and Obedience trials, but, like many Scotties, he's not really interested in obedience, and, for other reasons already mentioned, he doesn't do well in other sports.

Jock and Clyde's favorite food is whatever is available. Because Jock has a tendency to gain weight, especially since he was neutered last year, his weight is under constant surveillance and control. But that doesn't keep him from enjoying life. Rice gives the dogs a diet of steamed broccoli, solid-pack pumpkin, string cheese, green beans, tuna fish, yogurt, chicken liver brownies, and an occasional mouse. All in moderation, of course. And when it happens that Jock corners a rat in his backyard, his years of training will pay off in a quick kill. He's happy to leave the carcass on Rice's doorstep. It's the thrill of the chase that excites Jock. That, and the chicken liver brownies he's sure to receive afterwards.

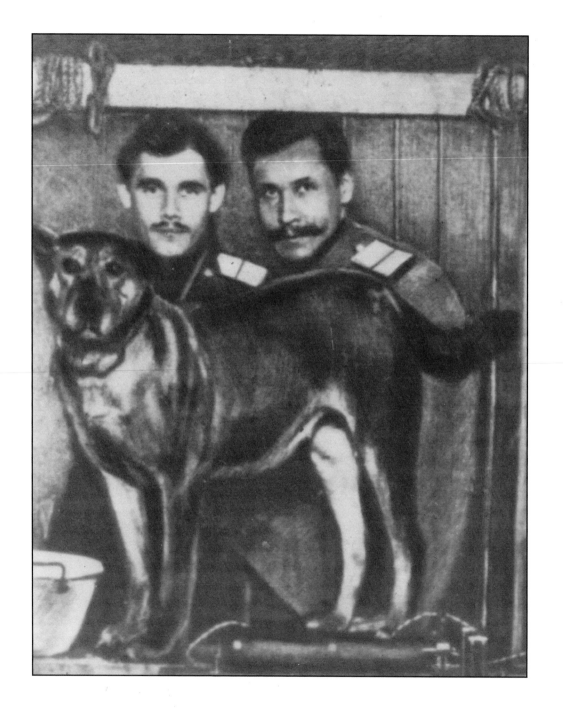

BORIS

Pavlov's Dog

ALTHOUGH THEY ARE STILL AMONG THE MOST FAMOUS canines, the names and histories of Pavlov's dogs were never recorded. Had they been, the story might have gone something like this. . . .

WHILE HIS CONTEMPORARIES, IN THE SPIRIT of true science, were experimenting on themselves (Hermann Ebbinghaus tested his short-term memory by memorizing nonsense syllables) and on their children (John Watson's experiments in child rearing included forbidding all affectionate touching of his infant sons), Ivan Pavlov brought his dog into his laboratory. Boris was whelped from Pavlov's bitch, Margarita, and he held a place of honor in the unique history of Pavlov's dogs.

Prior to 1897, Pavlov considered the wet mouths of his drooling beasts, the psychic secretions that were to make him a household name, to be a non-consequential by-product of his experiments. Although he noticed that the dogs started salivating in anticipation of feed-

> BORIS BECAME
> QUITE FAMOUS.

ing, what interested Pavlov were the properties of gastric juices produced by different types of foods. His question, essentially, was, do gastric juices have a variety of properties that are fine-tuned to digest whatever food is, at that moment, ingested? Answer: Yes.

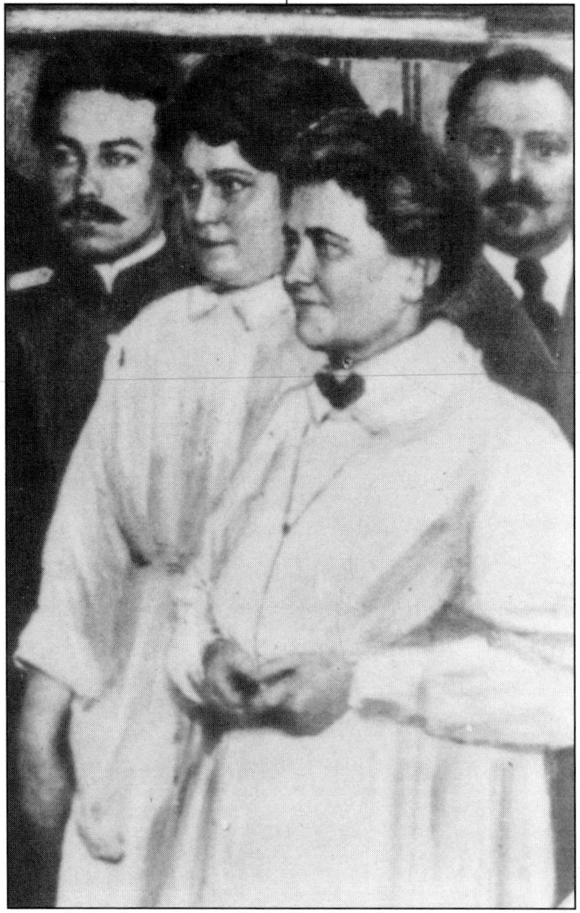

ASIDE FROM HIS LANDMARK STUDies in classical conditioning and gastric reflexes, Pavlov's place in the history of science was assured because he pioneered procedures in which surgery was performed on laboratory animals from which they recovered to live out somewhat normal lives. The surgery involved making a few minor adjustments in each dog to facilitate laboratory testing. First, a tube was inserted in the dog's throat to allow Pavlov to feed the dog without having the food actually reach the stomach, thus allowing one test animal to remain hungry in the lab. Next, he inserted a second tube into the dog's stomach so the gastric secretions could drip out for collection and subsequent analysis. Pavlov successfully analyzed gastric secretions for years. His fame rose. His fortune rose. He was in his fifties and many thought Pavlov had done all he could do with gastric secretions.

Then, one day, Pavlov brought Boris into his lab.

Boris was what Pavlov called a "vigorous secretor"—so vigorous, in fact, that Pavlov could no longer ignore the psychic secretions which flowed from Boris's stomach at the mere sight of Mikhail, the assistant in charge of feeding the dogs. The secretions flowed so prodigiously, in fact, that a crowd of observers would often gather to cheer Boris on. In St. Petersburg, in 1897, the gastric juices of animals were quite popular as a cure for stomach ailments, a tonic for an upset tummy or, more likely, a hangover. The Russian aristocracy would enjoy nothing more than popping down to Ivan's lab to watch gastric juices flow from Boris, which they would then purchase and drink on the spot. Boris became quite famous.

As Pavlov joined the crowd watching Boris drool, it struck him, quite suddenly, that there were more to these psychic secretions than met the eye. Excited, he brought a bell into the laboratory and changed his experiment. Pavlov rang the bell every time Boris salivated in anticipation of receiving food. And, as expected, Boris learned to salivate just at the sound of the bell.

BORIS WAS THE FIRST DOG TO BE classically conditioned. This dog, Pavlov's own Boris, was the one to secure Pavlov and his dog-testing apparatus a place in Introduction to Psychology textbooks for the rest of time.

After his spell in the lab, Boris was sewn up and brought home to be petted and pampered by Mrs. Pavlov, who loved nothing more feeding the dog each and every time he salivated, usually sweetmeats laced with vodka or her famous cheese doughnuts.

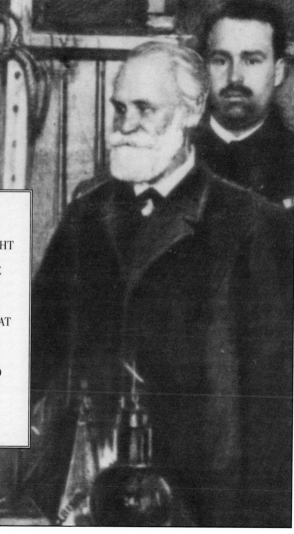

ONE DAY, PAVLOV BROUGHT BORIS INTO HIS LAB. THE SECRETIONS FLOWED SO PRODIGIOUSLY, IN FACT, THAT A CROWD OF OBSERVERS WOULD OFTEN GATHER TO CHEER BORIS ON.

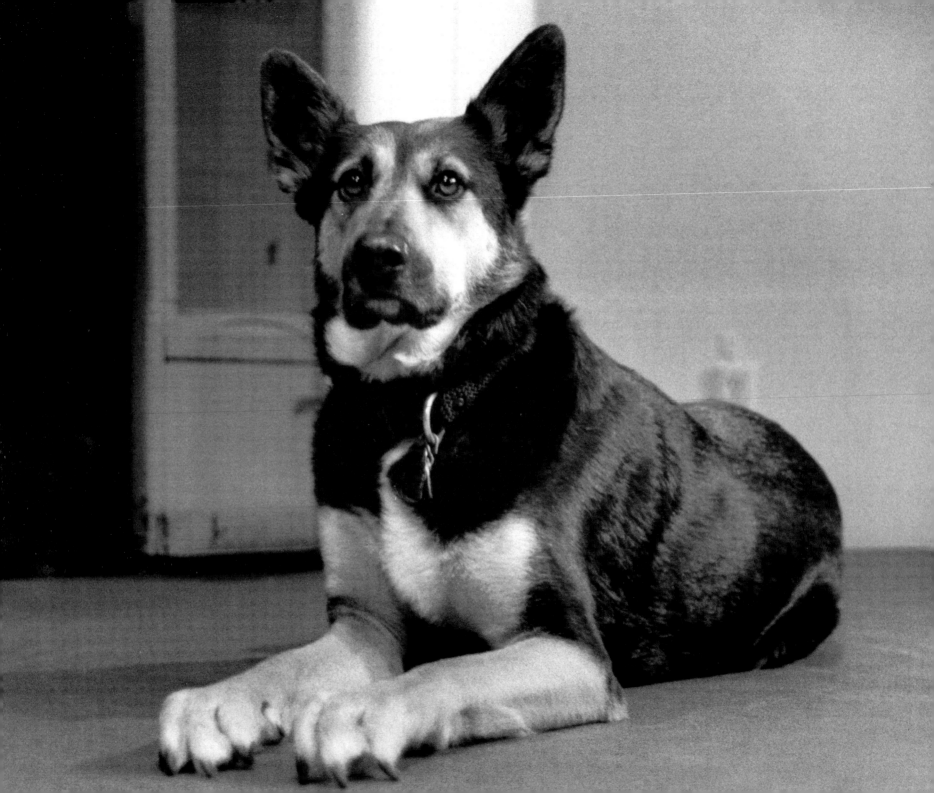

SHADE

Performance Artist

IT MUST HAVE BEEN FATE WHEN THIS PLUCKY MIXED-breed dog happened to be adopted by a member of an experimental theater company, because if dogs could be divas, Shade would have her name up in lights.

She's a lover of parties and staying up late. She's a show-off who climbs trees at the park, and who enjoys dressing up—but only in her favorite clothes. Shade flirts with everyone. But where she really shines is on the stage, in an improvisational theater piece. As a member of the Rachel Rosenthal

> IF DOGS COULD BE DIVAS, SHADE WOULD HAVE HER NAME UP IN LIGHTS.

Company in Los Angeles, she definitely landed in the right place.

HERE'S HOW IT WORKS. THERE'S NO SCRIPT. THE HUMAN actors performing with Shade (who consider her an equal collaborator) will give the dog cues—looks or gestures, or a line telling her what to do next. And they will work off the cues she gives them. And back and forth and back and forth, they make it up as they go along. Anything could happen.

It's experimental theater because it's mostly improvised and uses music and dance and video and movement and voice and light all at once. It can be spectacular.

What generally happens is Shade enters stage on her cue and finds a light. She sits in it and looks at the audience, and she reacts to the other actors and what is happening on stage. If they jump up, she jumps up. If they lie down, she lies down. She doesn't break character or wander off. She understands the etiquette of the theater and knows to come forward at the end of the show to accept her share of the applause.

NO ONE IS REALLY SURE WHERE CHARM COMES FROM. Of course, it helps to be on stage, but even there, cer-

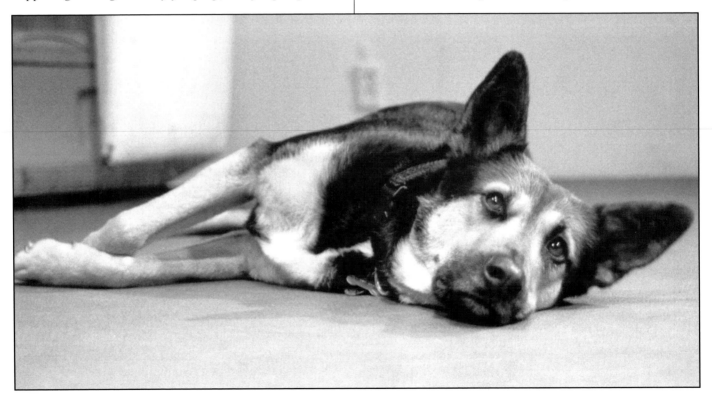

tain individuals will stand out, will be, somehow, watchable. All great stars have this quality, we like to watch them, even if they are just sitting there, watching us. It's star quality, an ephemeral, mysterious ability to be fascinating. Shade has that, somehow, and in her world, she's a star.

When not performing, Shade lives with her family in a Venice Beach bungalow and dines on sushi and cheese and smoked salmon—in addition to dog food. Her favorite treat is potato chips. She is often found grooming herself or attacking her squeaking hedgehog toy on one of her two beds. She doesn't bathe, she showers. If you were to meet Shade, and she didn't lick your hand, she might wink at you, or try to sing with you. Most likely she'd do something to make a charming impression.

WHILE CLIMBING TREES AND CHASING SQUIRRELS IN THE park earlier this year, Shade happened to blow out the knee on her back leg. The other members of her theater company banded around Shade and put on a benefit performance to pay for her surgery. Because they consider her an equal collaborator in the theater pieces she is in, the other members treat Shade more like a person than a dog. She only

> ALL GREAT STARS HAVE THIS QUALITY, WE LIKE TO WATCH THEM, EVEN IF THEY ARE JUST SITTING THERE, WATCHING US.

is asked to do those things she clearly enjoys, and is allowed to do most of those things at will—though there is a sign in the company bathroom reminding people to put down the toilet seat lid so a certain dog can't drink.

Rachel Rosenthal—the leader of Shade's theater company—takes special interest in animals and regards them as another species of people. Because animals are mostly invisible in our culture and lack the ability to protest abhorrent treatment, Rosenthal protests in their name. Often this means just presenting animals as visible beings in theater pieces, other times it means using her voice and her power in the world to actively protest the unethical treatment of animals. As one of the premier artists in America, Rosenthal is able to stir up imaginations and emotions to remind us all that animals are sentient beings with the ability to love and be loved. Just like the rest of us.

THE LIFE OF A PERFORMANCE ARTIST DOG IS A HAPPY ONE, with lots of attention and the opportunity for travel. It's a life many people would envy. Shade takes it all in stride. Her luminous eyes tell us she deserves it.

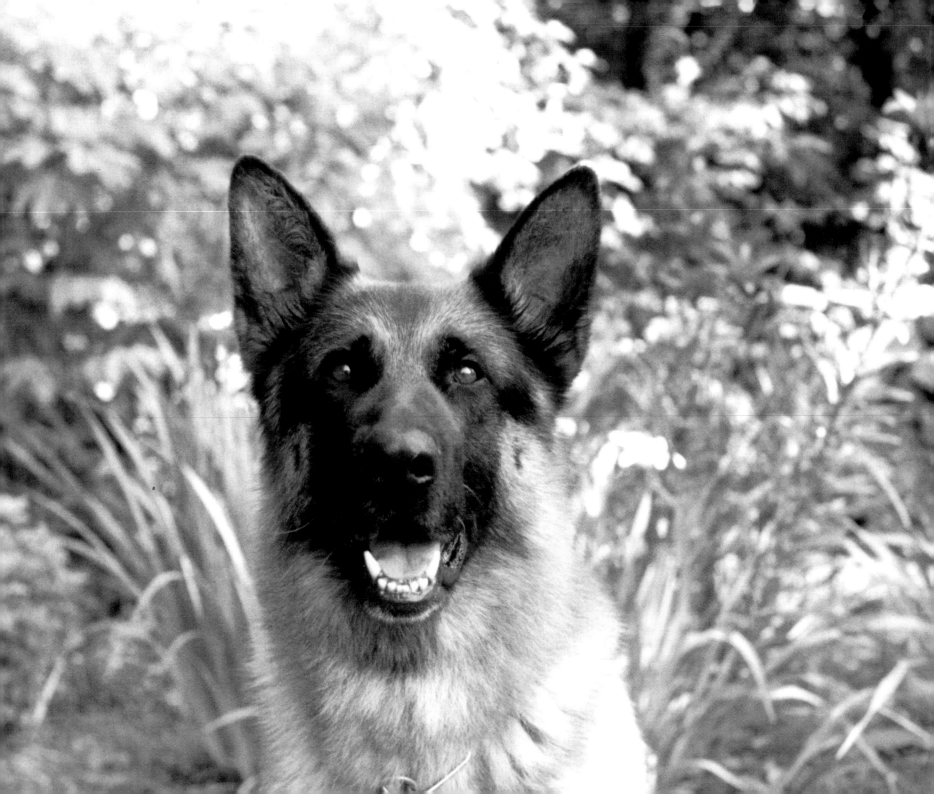

NAPOLEON

Schutzhund

STEVE GREGSON IS A GERMAN SHEPHERD GUY. WHEN he went to buy his first, he asked the breeders about all the titles listed after the dogs' names, found out about the sport of Schutzhund, and was instantly hooked. How were dogs trained so completely to excel in tracking, protection, and obedience? Because there was a Schutzhund club in Gregson's neighborhood, he was about to find out.

SCHUTZHUND—LITERALLY PROTECTION DOG— is a strenuous dog sport that began in

Germany. It was initially a testing program for breeders of working dogs to ensure that only those dogs who met certain standards were bred. Dogs were trained, tested, titled—and then bred. Soon, ordinary people wanted to test their dogs against those same standards, and clubs were formed around the world.

Although many Schutzhund dogs also work as police and protection dogs, for Gregson, Schutzhund is a sport. Unfortunately, Gregson's first German shepherd, Max, didn't quite work out. He is what is called

> NAPOLEON HAS FIRE.

a *angstbiter,* so insecure and afraid that he would bite out of fear rather than confidence. If a dog can't pass an initial temperament test, he can't train in Schutzhund. Max was retired into Gregson's home, where he now

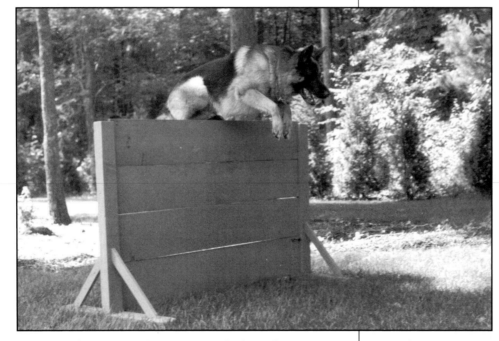

lives as a house pet. Gregson went looking for a new pet, and when he found Napoleon, he found a dog equal to the challenge of Schutzhund.

Gregson bought Napoleon from a dog broker in Boston, who had bought the dog from a breeder in Germany. Napoleon had no training, but he passed a temperament test and seemed quite trainable. Gregson brought Napoleon home and, after learning some German, got right to work training him.

Napoleon responded well to his training. He learned everything quickly. Eventually, though, Gregson came to see that Napoleon was a little rough around the edges. He was stubborn and only worked when he felt like it, not necessarily on trial days. It wasn't enough to train Napoleon with hot dogs and expect him to perform. Napoleon needed more.

IT ALL CAME DOWN TO STRATEGY. TO get Napoleon to win, Gregson made trial days peak days. The week prior to the trial, Napoleon stayed in his kennel without toys. He didn't get trained or played with. He was ignored. When he was finally brought out of his kennel, Napoleon was ready to focus and work. All Gregson had to worry about was his own nerves.

Gregson also developed a complex system of rewarding the dog. On the field, he wants Napoleon to just have a quick treat without being distracted, so he hands out sliced bits of hot dogs. When Gregson is introducing a new exercise, Napoleon doesn't get any toys. But once he's learned an exercise, and Gregson fears he may get bored, Napoleon is rewarded with his favorite toy—a pair of rubber hoses.

The German commands Gregson gives to Napoleon are the same commands given around the world, with a few exceptions: So *ist's brav*—that's good. *Pfui*—yuck! In Gregson's club they also say *ja wol*—yes sir—a lot, something perhaps picked up from old war movies. Schutzhund is demanding—for both dog and handler—but ultimately it is a way for people to have fun with their dogs.

SCHUTZHUND TRIALS TAKE PLACE IN ONE DAY, DURING which the dog and handler perform all three tests. The first, tracking, requires the dog to track footsteps and find dropped articles. The second test, obedience, involves a series of commands that the dog must execute. They range from the familiar stay, heel, and down stay to the unfamiliar—retrieve over a wall, or under the noise of a firing gun. The final test, protection, requires the dog to attack and stop attacking at the command of the handler.

IT WASN'T ENOUGH TO TRAIN NAPOLEON WITH HOT DOGS AND EXPECT HIM TO PERFORM. NAPOLEON NEEDED MORE.

The dogs perform the three test areas in increasing levels of difficulty as they proceed up the series of competitions—from Schutzhund one to three. On the day that Napoleon earned his Schutzhund one title, he got 266 out of a possible 300 points. He had the most trouble in the tracking exercise. Schutzhund dogs must track with their noses to the ground. He lost points because he picked up his nose, saw the tracking article lying in the grass ahead of him, and walked over to it. Pretty smart, really, but not what the judges were looking for. Nonetheless, he did well enough for the title. Trial judges noted Napoleon's intensity and snappy step—Napoleon has fire.

LIKE MOST SPORTS, SCHUTZHUND IS A PROCESS. DOGS and their owners work together and become better for it. Gregson says Napoleon is stubborn in the same way he himself is stubborn, and he is proud of his dog.

Although Max lives in the house and Napoleon lives in the kennel, there is no comparing the roles the two dogs play in Gregson's life. Napoleon is a working dog, fulfilled by the tasks presented to him, and he will be Gregson's partner if there are ever any confrontations that need to be dealt with. Napoleon is a dog Gregson can count on. For a German shepherd guy, that means a lot.

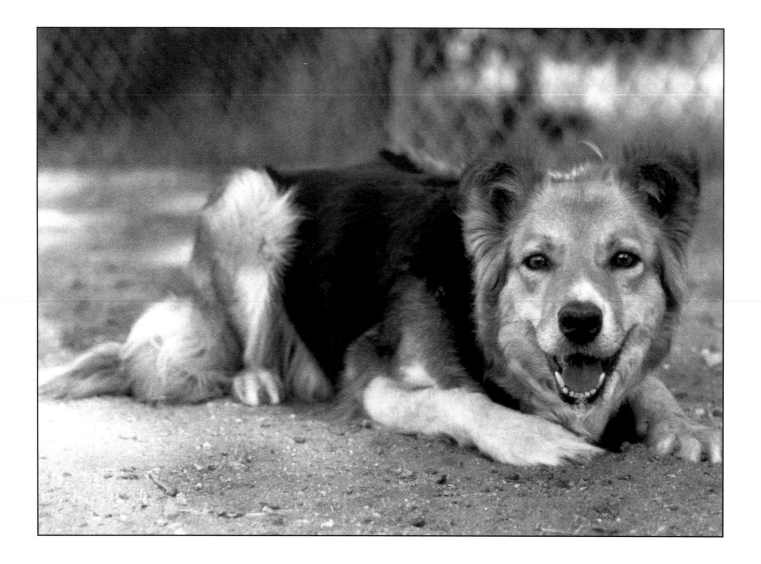

BRIDGET

Herder

SOME DOGS HERD: BRIDGET TEACHES OTHER DOGS HOW to herd. Rather, she demonstrates proper technique to people who want to train their dogs to herd. In practice, Bridget is fluid and focused. She moves sheep.

Bridget was given to Ted Ondrak six years ago. She was free, because her previous owner had decided she'd never learn how to herd sheep. Bridget had a lot of *eye*, that is, she stared at the sheep with a strong, intimidating glare. But she wouldn't creep close enough to scare the sheep and get them moving. She never followed through on the threat of her eye. Despite the

warning—"She's worthless!"—Ondrak decided to give her a chance.

When he was taking her home for the very first time, Ondrak got a feeling about Bridget. He knew she had been a kennel dog, only allowed out of her pen to work. He got a feeling that Bridget wasn't happy being a kennel dog. It seemed she needed affection, and Ondrak decided to give it to her.

The first thing he did was give her a big bowl of whipped cream. She ate it. He sat down on the couch, pulled her into his lap, and started petting her. They

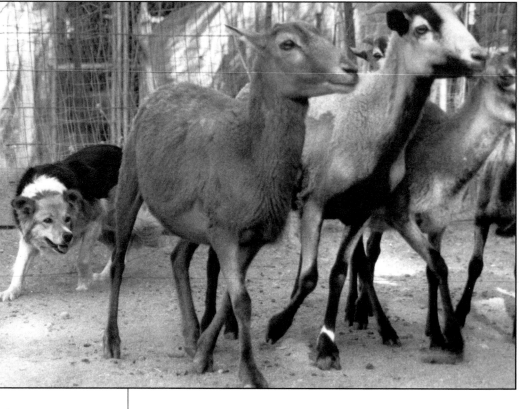

spent the evening watching television together, and that night she slept right there on the couch. The next day she followed him everywhere. The day after that she started moving sheep.

Ondrak trained her with language and emotion. "I love you, baby. Please, baby, do it for me." As she stared down the sheep, Ondrak gently tugged a line attached to her collar to get her to move in on the flock, crooning at her all the while. If she made a mistake, his voice was harsh, "What do you think you're doing?" This brought her to an instant halt. As she began to trust Ondrak, she moved in on the sheep more and more. She knew he'd never ask to go into a situation that wasn't safe. Now, Bridget is an expert.

At their ranch in Chatsworth, California, Ondrak and his wife, Jana, run the San Fernando Herding Association, where for $250 they teach people to teach their dogs to herd sheep. Lawyers with bouviers, teachers with border collies, actresses with Welsh corgis, even a judge with a schnauzer, all come here to have fun with their dogs. They watch Bridget and learn how to get their dogs to do what she does. Many of these dogs—and Bridget, too—also compete in sheep dog trials.

SHEEP HERDING IS INSTINC-
tual work for dogs. It's
based on the ancient talent
of wolves: the ability to
chase down, control, and
hunt a herd of prey ani-
mals. Of course, sheep
herding dogs don't eat the
sheep, but that doesn't
mean they wouldn't bite
them if they thought they
could get away with it.
Bridget drools if she even
looks at a sheep. That's why Ondrak needs
his harsh voice.

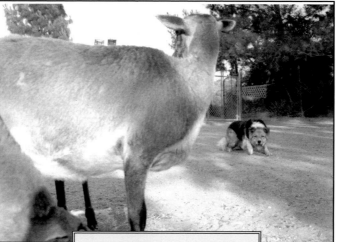

> BRIDGET WAS TRAINED
> WITH LANGUAGE, EMOTION,
> AND WHIPPED CREAM.

Herding dogs are known to have an
immense devotion to their duty. They
will herd their flock to safety in terrible
weather and protect it to the death, if
necessary. There is an old story of a border collie who was sent out to collect her herd of cattle from the fields at the far end of a large farm. On
this particular day, the dog was a very long time in
bringing the cattle in. The farmer started to go out to
see what was causing the delay when he saw the herd
and his dog, who trotted over to him with a new-born
puppy in her mouth. She placed the pup at the

farmer's feet and headed
back out to attend her duty.
Five times that night she
brought puppies to her
master, as she systemati-
cally herded the cattle into
their pen.

ALTHOUGH BRIDGET DOESN'T
have a flock of her own to
protect, she treats the sheep
at the herding school as if
they were her personal prop-
erty. The minute she arrives at the farm,
she hops out of the car and runs to where
the sheep are penned. She stares at them
like a dog obsessed, as if herding sheep
was her favorite activity. It probably is,
aside from eating whipped cream and
watching TV with Ondrak, which she still
does on a regular basis.

Bridget is a tri-colored border collie, with patches
of white and black and brown, and has stunning amber
eyes. As Ondrak says, she's one stylish bitch. And
when she gets near sheep, she will not look away. She
listens for Ondrak's voice. And, making it look easy,
Bridget herds sheep.

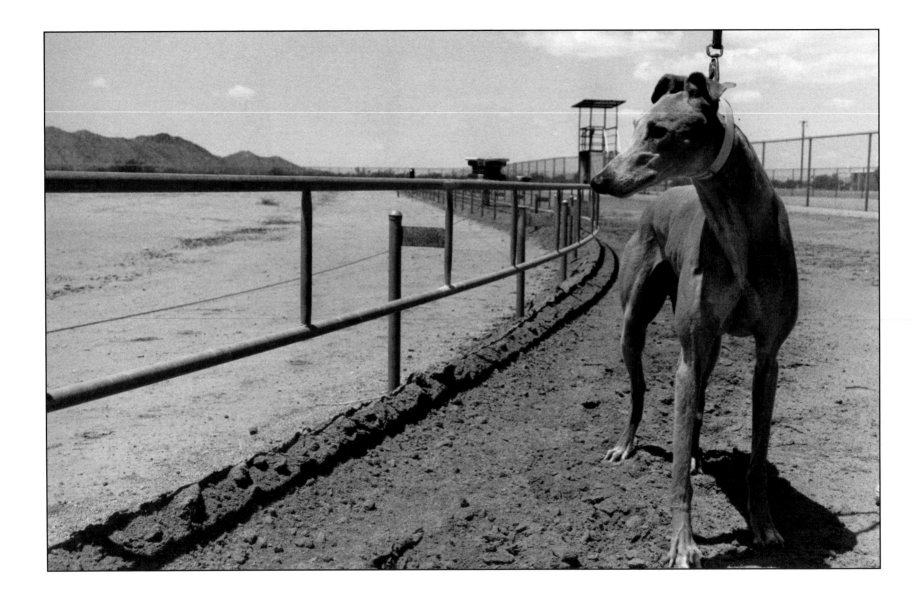

HUNTER

Racer

OLE HUNTER IS A GRACEFUL ANIMAL WITH POWER-ful legs. His demeanor is gentle, his eyes soulful, his color a rare blue fawn. Hunter is a money dog. He wins races at the Phoenix Greyhound Park and lives at the largest greyhound farm in Arizona.

Hunter was born at Gregory Wood's five-acre greyhound farm outside Phoenix two years ago. He still lives there—with nearly 200 other dogs. Hunter's mother, Ole K Sheila, was also a racer, though she was given up for adoption right after she gave birth to Hunter and his siblings. Although Wood regrets this

decision now—all her pups have grown into champions—at the time he thought Hunter and the others didn't look like winners. Hunter's father, Wigwam Wag, is one of the top stud dogs in the world; he makes $1500 a pop, fresh or frozen.

THE FIRST OPPORTUNITY FOR HUNTER TO SHOW HIS STUFF came when he was thirteen months old and began jack-a-lure training. A jack-a-lure is something like a fishing pole that Wood uses to drag a squawking lure on a thousand feet of monofilament line. This is where the adolescent dogs learn to chase the lure, which at this stage of the game is a fake raccoon hat with a jerk-activated squawker inside. The same brand of squawker is used by every racing organization so the greyhounds have a consistent sound to chase throughout their careers.

When he was fourteen months old, Hunter began training on the track. Wood has a regulation-size track with a motor-operated lure that moves faster than the greyhounds—who can run more than forty miles per hour. At the beginning Wood lets the lure drag in the sand—this kicks up dust the same way a rabbit would—to increase the dogs' natural desire to chase. Each day he lifts the lure a little higher off the ground until it's at regulation height.

From the beginning, Hunter loved to chase the lure. If a dog doesn't show this desire, Wood calls a Greyhound Rescue operation and puts the dog up for adoption. Usually one in each dozen dogs drops out at this point. Those who stay continue training until the age of eighteen months, at which time they are sent to the Phoenix Greyhound Park track for the races. Dogs are given six chances to finish in the top four spots. If they do not, they are sent to adoption organizations or, if Wood deems they are not suitable for adoption, they are euthanized by the veterinarian. If they consistently finish in one of the top four spots,

> HUNTER IS AS GENTLE AND SERENE AS HE APPEARS.

they move into the special air-conditioned building for money dogs.

HUNTER AND THE OTHER MONEY DOGS AT GREGORY Wood's greyhound farm spend most of each day resting in cages in a dark room, listening to rock and roll music from the radio. They wear muzzles except when they are eating. They go to outside kennels six times per day and to the exercise track in the mornings. Their lives are boring by design. Part of Wood's training strategy is to keep their off-track lives very quiet so they will give their all at the race. Hunter races every three or four days.

Like most professional athletes, Hunter eats a diet designed to provide the energy he needs to win. Olive oil with chicken, Weight Gain powder, sliced peaches, bananas, Gatorade, beef denatured with charcoal, Hi-Pro, electrolytes, T-F-15 Aveomycin powder for loose stools, honey meatballs, eggs, milk, lettuce. On racing days, Hunter doesn't eat until after he races, although he does get a treat of one marshmallow before he runs. The kitchen for the money dogs is almost as large as the air-conditioned room that holds their cages.

The weight of the dogs is strictly monitored. Before races, they are allowed a pound and a half

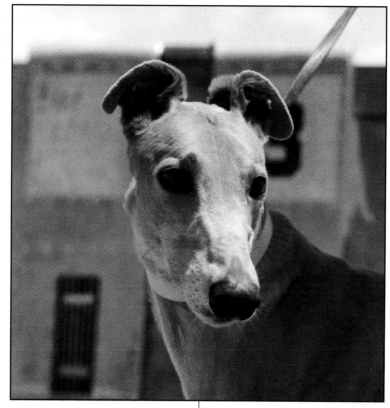

variance from their pre-set weight. The dogs are weighed twice before they race. Changes make gamblers nervous. Nervous gamblers don't place bets. Since Wood gets a cut of each dollar bet on Hunter, it behooves him to keep the dog's weight stable.

Although Wood and the gamblers who bet on his dogs all have strategies, none of it matters when Hunter is racing. Then he's alone, with whatever energy he has, chasing a lure. And when he's racing, he usually wins. Hunter is a crowd-pleaser because he paces himself and then comes from the back to win in the final stretch.

as the Greyhound Protection League are campaigning for their end. It's difficult for many people to see a gentle creature like Hunter and know that most of his time is spent alone and muzzled in a dark cage—even if that makes him a better racer. They believe he deserves better. When he's four, Hunter will most likely be retired and put up for adoption. With an estimated lifespan of between twelve and fourteen years, however, retired greyhounds have done very well in their adopted homes. They are as gentle and serene as they appear.

GREYHOUND RACING IS A MORE POPULAR SPECTATOR sport than professional basketball. No matter how many people enjoy the dog races, however, organizations such

FOR NOW, HUNTER WILL KEEP RACING. AND HE WILL keep winning. His grace and beauty will continue to be undeniable.

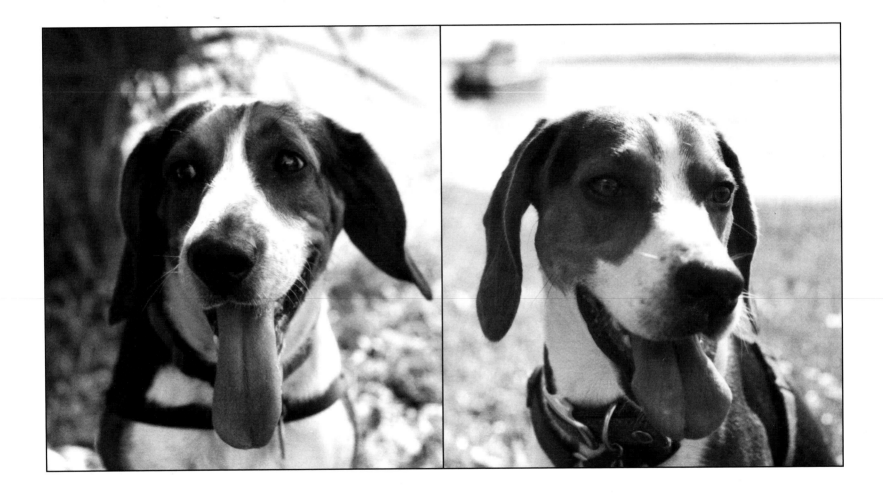

SHERLOCK & SCOUT

Insect Detectors

THEIR EDUCATION COSTS MORE THAN EXECUTIVE training at an Ivy League college. They are so valuable they are not allowed to roam off their leashes. Their skill? Finding bugs. Their names? Sherlock Homes and Scout.

THE PEST CONTROL INDUSTRY IS ONE OF innovation. Barrier treatment is being replaced by baiting and colony elimination, and the flashlight and screwdriver are being replaced by the dog. Not just any dog, but one who

> IT'S A LOT OF FUN TO WATCH A DOG INSPECT YOUR HOUSE.

has been trained and certified to find pests. At the Arrow Pest Service in Florida, one particular beagle was so successful that owner Terry Glover got another. Together, the two dogs have done wonders for his business.

Sherlock lives with Glover's son, William, while Scout lives with Glover himself. The two dogs can't live together because they just don't get along. They're ordinary house dogs, for the most part. They love playing tug of war with a rope bone. They like walks and

113

getting scratched and petted. They were trained to sleep in crates, but prefer, as it turns out, to sleep in the bedrooms of the Glovers.

On the other hand, they eat a specific daily diet of two cups each of chicken-based kibble. No table scraps. They are never off their leashes, except when indoors at home or the office. And they have a talent for finding bugs. As few as six carpenter ants or termites or powder post beetles will result in an alert. It doesn't matter if the bugs are in a wall or under a solid concrete slab. Scout and Sherlock know they're there, and know how to communicate that fact.

When they smell bugs, the dogs alert by scratching the wall or floor. "Are you sure?" Glover always asks. The dogs scratch again. They're sure. They're not wrong, either. Glover and his son have torn the walls off their own office and homes to prove it.

THE JOHN HENRY OF PEST CONTROL DOGS, A BEAGLE named Peaches, was tested at an entomology conference at Pennsylvania State University. He went up against the cutting-edge machines for detecting pests, the Termitech and the Boreoscope. They were all three used to locate termites that had been hidden beforehand by the researchers. When all was said and done,

> IT DOESN'T MATTER
> WHERE THE BUGS ARE,
> SCOUT AND SHERLOCK
> KNOW THEY'RE THERE.

Peaches found twelve infestations, the machines found one and two each. Afterwards, Peaches gobbled his handful of kibble and was ready for more.

Peaches and Sherlock and Scout were all trained by Dr. Andrew Solarz, of Beacon Dogs of Maryland. Solarz is a leading expert in training pest inspection dogs and has trained dogs now working across the country. Solarz charges $9,500 to educate a beagle. The initial training takes three months, and Beacon dogs are re-certified every ninety days via videotaped tests.

WHEN GLOVER AND WILLIAM BOUGHT SHERLOCK, WHO was their first pest detection dog, they set up a test termite farm in a garbage can in William's garage. Sure enough, Sherlock alerted in the garage, but he also alerted everywhere in William's house. After cutting the walls in the house without finding bugs, they called Dr. Solarz—who told them that the scent of the termites in the garage rose with warm air and traveled into the house via air ducts. To Sherlock, the entire house smelled like one big termite farm. They moved the termites out of the garage, and Sherlock only alerted to one spot in the house. They cut into that wall and found a termite infestation, which they decided to leave for use as a permanent testing ground. It's still there today.

WHEN THE GLOVERS FIRST STARTED working with Sherlock, they noticed he had a strange reaction in certain houses: he snorted.

They came to realize this snorting occurred only in houses that had cats, even if the cat had visited the house once and it was months before the inspection. It was clear they needed to get Sherlock his own cat. They got two. The cats, named Alley and Callie, live in the office and assist in training the beagles. They spend the days in cages, and run free at night, smelling the place up. Now used to cats, Sherlock has stopped snorting during inspections.

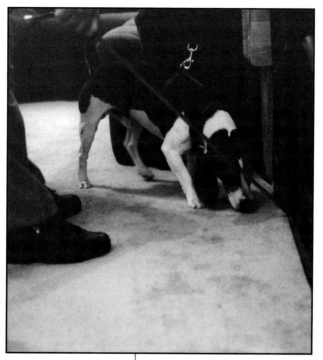

Sherlock and Scout always start inspections by standing on a box that has termites in it. Glover walks through the house tapping a stick on walls and floors, telling the dogs where to sniff. Every time they make an alert, the dogs get a few pieces of kibble. The working kibble is different from the kibble they eat at home. It has more chicken in it, so they like it better.

The dogs always get to eat when working. The Glovers hide small containers of termites to give the dogs something to alert to in case the house happens to be pest-free—and keep track of the food the dogs eat every day so they always get their two full cups of kibble.

WHEN NOT PERFORMING inspections, the dogs hang around the office with the Glovers. Scout sleeps under Terry Glover's desk and follows him everywhere. The Glovers are a family of animal lovers. In addition to the beagles and cats, two other dogs, three goldfish, and an iguana also spend the day at the office with the working animals.

In addition to being really good at finding pests, Sherlock and Scout have given Arrow Pest Service an added cachet. People like dogs. It's a lot of fun to watch a dog inspect your house. Especially a cute little beagle. At $200 per inspection, the dogs make more money in an hour than most executives. It seems their education was a wise investment.

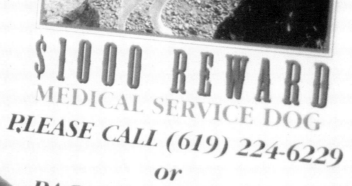

STILL MISSING

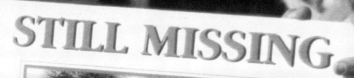

$1000 REWARD
MEDICAL SERVICE DOG
PLEASE CALL (619) 224-6229
or
PAGER (619) 333-2727
YOU HAVE SEEN THIS DOG   THANK YOU

NADIA

NADIA

Seizure Alert Dog

MANY PEOPLE KNOW THE STORY OF HACHI-KO, a dog in Japan who met her master's regular train every evening for five years when he was alive and for ten years after the day he died at the office. It's the kind of fidelity we expect in a dog. We would never expect a human being to return the favor, to wait patiently day after day for the return of a dog—but that's what Mike Cash is doing now.

FOR NINE YEARS, MIKE CASH RELIED UPON HIS DOG, NADIA, to alert him prior to epileptic attacks.

This beautiful dog is a malamute–border collie mix with three cow spots over her ribs. She has the long hair, curly tail, and affectionate temperament of an Alaskan malamute and the energy, intelligence, and markings of a border collie. Nadia had always been Cash's loyal, devoted companion, trained to come to his side, bark once, and sit near him when she sensed an oncoming seizure. This was the signal that told him to get to a safe spot and wait quietly. Within twenty minutes, the seizure would hit. Nadia always told him when an attack was imminent, and never missed one of them.

117

Nadia was excellent in other ways, too. She scored a perfect ten in the obedience exam given by her training facility (thus, the name, for Nadia Comaneci). She followed commands and could perform tricks. Cash could just talk to her and she would do whatever he needed. Nadia was Cash's partner, a companion with whom he went through life.

Nadia's only fault was that she was afraid of loud noises. Once, Cash took her on a shooting trip in Arizona, and at the sound of the first gunshot, she bolted. They tracked her down in the flat, empty desert. Next time, he left Nadia at home. He always remembered to tie her up prior to Fourth of July festivities. But sometimes one weakness is all it takes to foul up an extraordinary life. In September 1998, Nadia bolted at the sound of unexpected fireworks from Sea World in San Diego. Cash has been searching for her ever since.

NADIA ALWAYS TOLD CASH WHEN AN ATTACK WAS IMMINENT, AND NEVER MISSED ONE OF THEM.

SEIZURE ALERT DOGS AND THOSE THEY WORK FOR RELY ON a special bond. They pay uncommon attention to one another. The alert signal can be a special look or, as in the case of Nadia, a bark to warn of oncoming attack. When the attacks hit, the dogs are also trained to stay nearby to comfort and protect the person having the seizure—or to go for help, if necessary.

Epilepsy is a mysterious, incurable disease best described as a short-circuit in the brain's wiring. Although many people with the disease are barely affected or can take drugs that keep it under control, others must contend with unexpected seizures that knock them unconscious. Because these seizures occur without warning—even while driving a car or crossing a crowded street or walking down stairs—some epileptics must limit their activities to avoid harm. This is where the work of a seizure alert dog can profoundly benefit a person with epilepsy.

With an alert dog at their side, people who were housebound or forced to rely on other people to watch over them suddenly become free to do as they please. With a twenty-minute warning, they are safe to travel, work outside the home, or attend school.

NO ONE IS SURE HOW A SEIZURE ALERT DOG KNOWS AN attack is imminent. Perhaps there is a change in body-chemistry—prior to an epileptic attack—that causes a scent change detectable to dogs, whose noses are 1,000 times more sensitive than man's. Scientists cannot document this change, though, so no one can confirm the validity of seizure alert dogs. Cash has no such concerns; he knows what they can do.

His only question is, Where is my dog?

SINCE SEPTEMBER 1998, CASH HAS BEEN LOOKING FOR his dog in San Diego twenty-four hours a day and seven days a week. He has handed out thousands of flyers and spent hundreds of days on street corners holding up a sign. His life, once quite ordinary with the exception of Nadia, has become uncommon. Strangers give all kinds of advice and help—and sometimes even harassment. He has become the man looking for his dog, the man who doesn't give up.

While he stands on the side of a street, holding his sign, he remembers Nadia. How she loves to eat Barnum's Animal Crackers. How she waves at people with her paw. How, on their last day together, he took her to the airport to watch planes land and a tourist took Nadia's photograph and called her the most beautiful dog he'd ever seen.

WHEN CASH LOST HIS JOB AS A MAINTENANCE MAN IN Arizona, he came to start a new life in California. He had no friends there, but that didn't concern him as long as he had Nadia. Now that Nadia is lost, too, Cash

has found a reservoir of resolve he never knew he had. He'd always considered himself a man who never finished anything; now he is the man who is going to stay on the corner until he finds his dog. He is the man who knows that with loved ones, one must take special care.

This story will end, as all stories must, and Cash will put down his sign, for one reason or another. Maybe he will find Nadia, maybe he won't. In the meantime, Cash has received more from his dog than the signal of an epileptic seizure, he has seen into the depths of his own soul. This is the result of the bond between a service dog and the man who relies upon her.

A dog like Nadia can save a man's life. She can be a blaze of excellence in an otherwise ordinary life. The loss of such a dog can stop a man's life cold. Cash has been offered dogs and money and jobs and housing and religion and even love since he began his vigil, and yet he still waits for the return of Nadia.

> THE LOSS OF SUCH A DOG CAN STOP A MAN'S LIFE COLD.

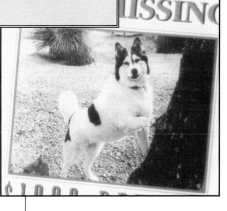

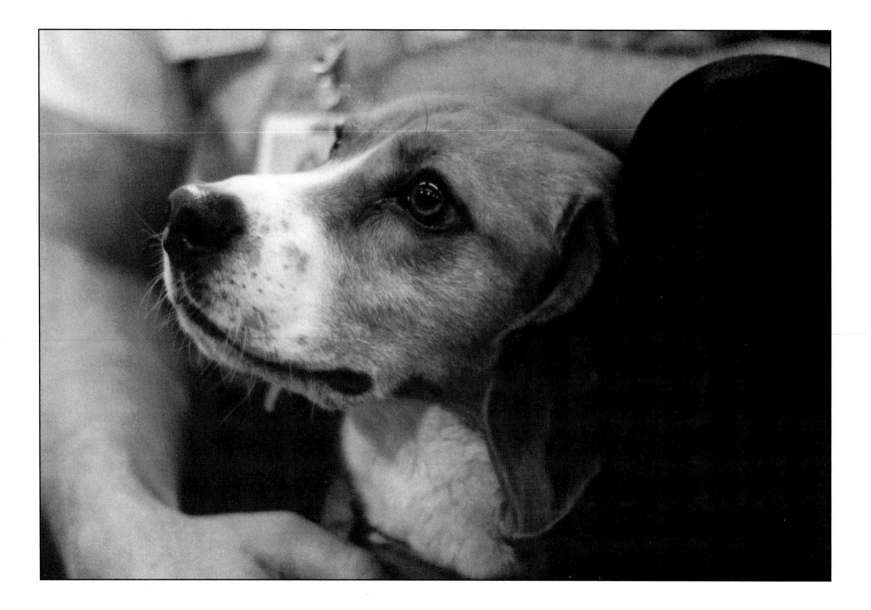

MANGO

Agriculture Detector

WHEN THEY SAY A DOG HAS A STRONG FOOD DRIVE, what they mean is that he'll do anything for food. Mango's food drive—which was tested prior to his beginning Beagle Brigade training—is right off the charts; he bit into luggage to get at chocolates. Needless to say, he was accepted into the program. Good thing for him, too, because Mango was one of the many beagles rescued by the Beagle Rescue Society and placed in the Beagle Brigade when a new home for him could not be found.

TO KEEP UNWANTED PESTS AND DISEASES FROM ENTERING the country, the U.S. Department of Agriculture initiated the Beagle Brigade in 1984. The dogs in green vests alert to the scent of fruits, meat, and plants at airport baggage claim areas across the country. Although he was named years ago at his job at Logan International Airport in Boston, Mango has become an expert at finding, yes, mangoes.

Mango has been working with Agriculture Officer Kevin Dailey for two years and they've established quite a partnership. Dailey reports his part of the job as paying Mango once the beagle makes his find. The payment? Special liver and garlic treats, which Dailey bakes in his own oven. Although Mango can't live with Dailey now because the normal food scents of the kitchen would be too confusing, when Mango retires in four years, he'll have a place in Dailey's home. Until then, Dailey drops Mango off on the way home each night at the nearby kennel where he lives in a relaxing, food-scent-free environment.

IN ADDITION TO FINDING A LOT OF SMUGGLED food, Mango has a track record of finding birds hidden in luggage. Although he doesn't alert to birds, his intense interest in them suggests a search to Dailey. Last year he kept sticking his face into a blanket-wrapped parcel until his nose came out bleeding. A canary, nearly dead inside the blanket, still managed to peck Mango on the nose. The canary was seized and put into quarantine. Mango probably saved the bird's life.

Accidents are an unfortunate part of the job for Mango and the other members of the Beagle Brigade. As they run through baggage claim areas at airports, searching for the scent of food, they are stepped on, rolled over, and even, sometimes, kicked. The USDA uses beagles exclusively in its detector dog program

> BEAGLES MAY BE CUTE, BUT THEY HAVE A WHOLE LOT OF ENERGY THAT NEEDS A CONSISTENT OUTLET. THEY'RE WORKING DOGS.

because they're small, cute, and nonthreatening. They also are readily available through Beagle Rescue societies, as many people who buy beagles don't realize the cute little dogs have a whole lot of energy that needs a consistent outlet. They're working dogs.

Like many workers, Mango goes through periods of lowered motivation during which he seems less enthusiastic than usual. In these times Dailey takes Mango on extra trips to the beach where Mango loves to play.

Last year, Mango's loss of interest didn't go away after a romp on the beach. He tired quickly and Dailey got worried. A trip to the veterinarian revealed the dog had a heart murmur and needed a special low-sodium diet to prevent further damage to his heart. Because the beagle was rewarded with food treats, Dailey went on a search for a low-sodium replacement. He found none. That was when Dailey began making special liver treats for Mango. By boiling and then baking beef liver with garlic, he made something Mango loved that wouldn't hurt his heart. Now Mango is crazy about his treats and is more motivated than ever.

MANGO WORKS WITH ANOTHER BEAGLE NAMED MR. CASEY, a lemon yellow beagle who has become skittish in his years in the Beagle Brigade. Mango and Mr. Casey romp while waiting for passengers and their luggage to arrive. When he sees baggage, Mango knows it's time to get to work. He stops socializing with Mr. Casey and

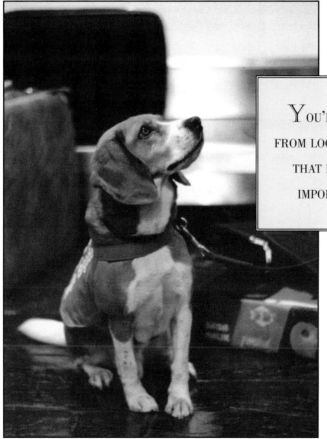

YOU'D NEVER KNOW FROM LOOKING AT MANGO THAT HE DOES SUCH IMPORTANT WORK.

focuses on the task at hand. It's a lot of work, too. When a 747 empties of passengers, Mango will run through the baggage claim sniffing hundreds of pieces of luggage. He gets a twenty-minute rest, then he needs to be ready for the next flight.

This is important work. The Department of Agriculture wants to prevent a catastrophe like the Mediterranean fruit fly from entering the United States again. Mediterranean fruit flies are considered the most threatening pests worldwide. They burrow into fruits and vegetables and destroy crops. The Medfly, which is believed to have come through the Tampa airport in 1997, cost more than $3 billion in damaged and destroyed produce. Two hundred square miles around Tampa were sprayed with the pesticide malathion for months before the flies were eradicated.

DESPITE HIS GREEN VEST, YOU'D NEVER KNOW FROM LOOKING at Mango that he does such important work. He's affectionate and playful and a bit of a goofball. He's quite at home in the airport baggage claim, not a bit startled by the loud sounds and masses of harried people. He approaches his work with gusto, filled with the hope of earning a liver treat or maybe even stumbling across a hidden canary.

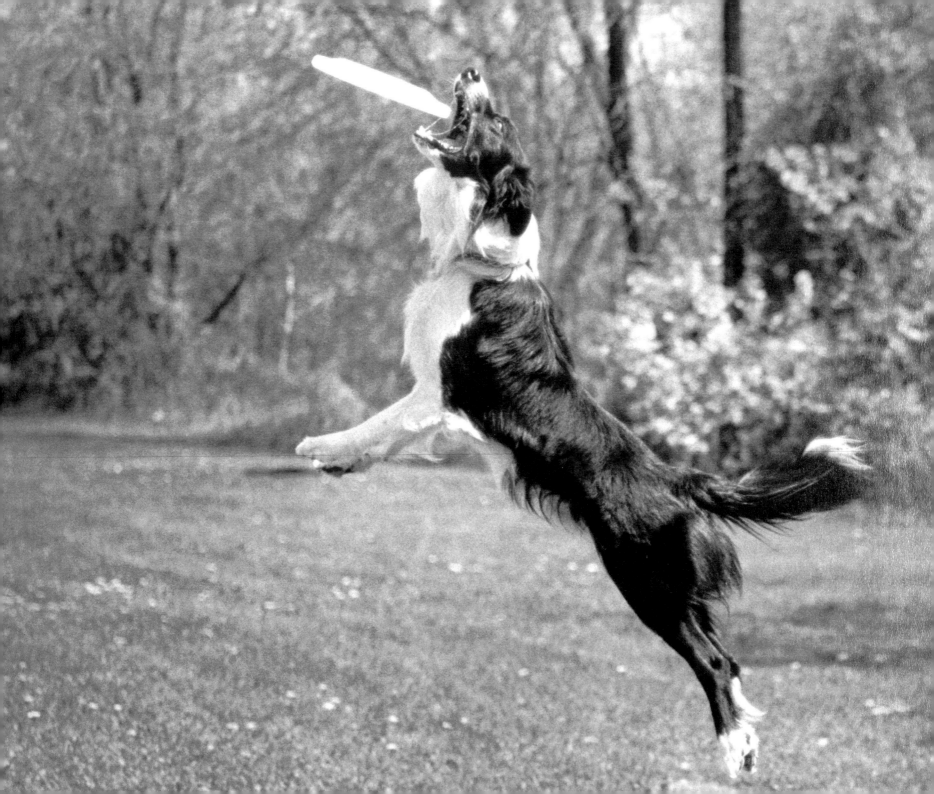

WIZARD

Disc Dog

AFTER WINNING THE HUMAN WORLD FRISBEE Championship at the age of nineteen, Peter Bloeme found a border collie pup who liked to play catch. Within two months, he had a Disc dog. Within two years, that dog was the Champion of the World.

WHIRLIN' WIZARD WAS A MAGICIAN ON THE Frisbee field. His innovations to the sport are still remembered and imitated. With Bloeme, Wizard was the first dog to have a choreographed rou-

> WIZARD WAS THE FIRST DOG TO HAVE A CHOREO-GRAPHED ROUTINE.

tine, the first to perform simultaneous moves, the first to have a pre-routine. The level of difficulty of his moves blew everyone away at the 1984 World Championships, the first and only time Wizard competed.

The routine started with Bloeme and Wizard on the field in front of thousands of spectators. While everyone was waiting for the first throw, Bloeme joined Wizard on all fours. Together they sat, then lay down, then rolled over twice. In ten seconds, they had the audience eating out of their hands and paws, and *then* they started throwing the discs. They were not only polished, they also scored a ten out of ten for the difficulty of their routine. From back flips to butterflies to multiples to tapping, Wizard astonished everyone with his abilities and grace.

Tapping was a particularly thrilling move. No one had seen anything like it. Bloeme tossed the disc to Wizard. Wizard bumped the disc back to Bloeme with his nose. Because Wizard spent his whole life catching Frisbees, it was the most difficult trick to get him to not catch the disc. Bloeme did it by holding Wizard's collar, and saying "Tap," while preventing him from catching the Frisbee, thrown softly upside down toward Wizard's nose. Eventually, Wizard understood what was being asked of him, and he would tap without having his collar held. Later, Wizard learned to tap the Frisbee into the air and catch it himself as it returned to earth.

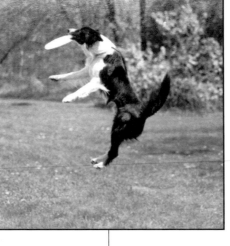

WHEN BLOEME PICKED WIZARD OUT OF A LITER OF PUPPIES, he didn't know what a life-changing moment was occurring. Bloeme had been traveling across the country giving demonstrations of his ability to play with a Frisbee. Everywhere he went, people asked him if he had a disc dog. Finally, he got tired of saying no.

He taught the little dog to eat his food from a disc and chase one as it rolled across the floor. They practiced together for fifteen minutes four times a day, every day, no matter the weather, and an incredible bond was formed. By the time Wizard was sixteen weeks old, Bloeme added Wizard to his demonstrations, letting the pup chase the Frisbee and be adorable.

When Wizard was eight months old, he performed with Bloeme at half-time at a New York Mets game. The first and only time he suffered from nerves, Wizard got sick in a Mets office before the show. After that day, Wizard was a professional and he spent the rest of his life performing.

Together with Bloeme and their Frisbees, Wizard traveled around the world. Wizard was the youngest dog to win the World Canine Frisbee Championship. Bloeme was the first person to win both the human and canine championships. They were on television everywhere, in front of audiences around the world. They even helped tear down the Berlin Wall together.

Wherever they went, they tossed and caught and tapped Frisbees.

AS HUMAN FRISBEE CHAMPION OF THE World, Bloeme was well known. With Wizard, he became a true celebrity. Everyone wanted to see them perform. Something unique was added when the little dog joined the act, something more than another performer. That something was Wizard.

He was a dog who loved to play catch. He didn't really care if he was tossed a disc or a ball or even a sock. He would catch it and bring it back for more. When he saw a Frisbee, Wizard crouched down and stared at it, just like a herder staring at a sheep. Wizard gave the disc a lot of eye. He transferred all of his intense sheep herding energy into play intensity.

BLOEME STILL TRAVELS AROUND THE WORLD FOR Frisbee sports, but Wizard died last

WHEN BLOEME SPEAKS OF WIZARD IT IS WITH A KIND OF AWE. WIZARD ENRICHED THE FRISBEE CHAMPION'S LIFE IN WAYS THAT ARE SOMETIMES MYSTERIOUS AND ALMOST SACRED.

year, at age sixteen. Now he accompanies his dear friend only in spirit. When Bloeme speaks of Wizard it is with a kind of awe. Wizard enriched the Frisbee champion's life in ways that are sometimes mysterious and almost sacred. Bloeme credits the dog with changing his life, his hometown, his career, even his marital status. Not a small order, unless you happened to be a little border collie who just loved to play catch.

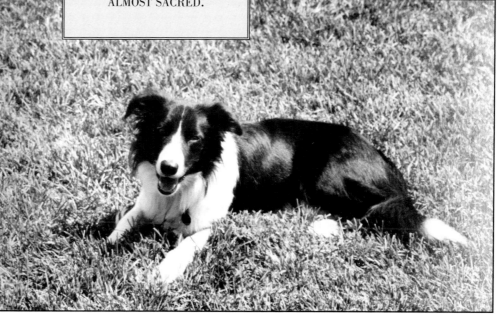

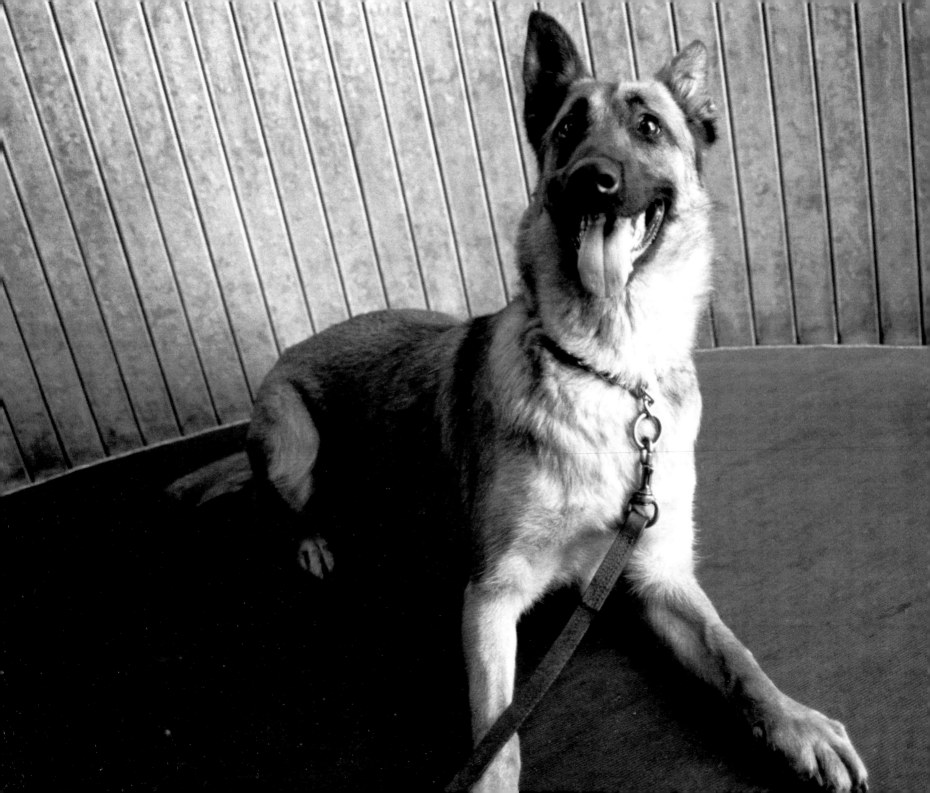

MITA

Currency Detector

IF A DOG SNIFFS THE AIR AROUND YOU WHILE YOU ARE boarding an international flight, check your conscience. She might be Mita and she might be searching for cash. Lots of cash.

Mita is a currency detector dog, trained to alert only to five hundred bills or more. She does this by knowing the scent of the ink on the bills—a special, top-secret formula used only by the U.S. Mint. Mita can recognize the distinctive oily scent of this ink so accurately that

> IF YOU'RE CARRYING FIVE HUNDRED BILLS OR MORE, MITA WILL SMELL IT ON YOU.

she knows when someone is carrying more than the legal limit.

WHEN LEAVING THE USA, ONE MUST DECLARE ANY CASH IN excess of $10,000. That's the law. Prior to the work of dogs like Mita, the Customs Service had to rely on random searches to find cash as it was being smuggled out of the country. Now Mita can point the finger—or the nose—and determine who will be searched. If you're carrying five hundred bills or more, Mita will smell it on you. There's no masking the odor.

That's when Customs Officer Roy Key will approach to ask if you're carrying $10,000 or more. This would be your last chance, as they say, and if you've got the cash, you'd better declare it because Mita has already told him where it is. She does this to get her reward: a chance to play with Key and a white towel.

TECHNICALLY, U.S. MINT INK IS MORE DIFFICULT TO FIND than narcotics, as it's strictly controlled by the Treasury. Mita and her handler have a small case filled with bottles of the ink to use for training aids. Every four or five months, the U.S. Mint sends replacement bottles. Mita also trains with cash swapped at a local bank, to keep her alerting to the cash itself and not the scent of Key's hands combined with the ink, for instance.

MITA'S PRIMARY PLACE OF WORK IS THE AIRPORT JETWAY. International flights are targeted based on the countries being flown to and, sometimes, on the passenger lists. As the passengers walk down the jetway, Mita and Key pass by them with Mita working the air around each passenger. If she gets to the last passenger without making an alert, Key will look for a volunteer to wear a special fanny pack filled with five hundred $1 bills. Mita needs to earn her reward, a long play session

with Key and a towel during which Mita nearly bounces off the jetway walls. It's important that Mita gets to make a find each time she searches in order to keep her drive up.

Not that Mita seems to need it. She is highly motivated and eager to work. She gets so excited to do her job, in fact, that as they drive to the airplane hangar in Key's van, she spins in circles in her crate. Other officers call her the spin-cycle dog. Key knows she's just thrilled to work.

TWO YEARS AGO, THE CUSTOMS SERVICE BOUGHT EIGHT Belgian Malinois dogs from Holland and brought them to San Antonio for currency training. Mita is a passive alert dog, sitting down rather than scratching at the source of the scent. This is what enables her to search people, rather than cargo. She has a partner dog, Macomb, who searches packages and luggage at LAX and alerts aggressively, scratching and biting at the source of the odor. Together, they have found hundreds of thousands of dollars of cash.

Mita was bred in Holland for work, and that is what she does. She lives in a kennel near the airport with the other Customs dogs, and works nearly every day.

WHEN THE NEW $20 AND $100 BILLS WERE issued last year, they caused a problem for Mita: Too much ink. The new bills have maybe five times as much ink on them than the old-style bills. Mita started alerting to fewer than five hundred bills. There was nothing to do but wait for the new bills to be absorbed into

TOGETHER, THEY HAVE FOUND HUNDREDS OF THOUSANDS OF DOLLARS OF CASH.

circulation. Mita gets better at her job over time. As the months pass, she finds more and more smuggled cash. And she gets to play more and more with her beloved towel.

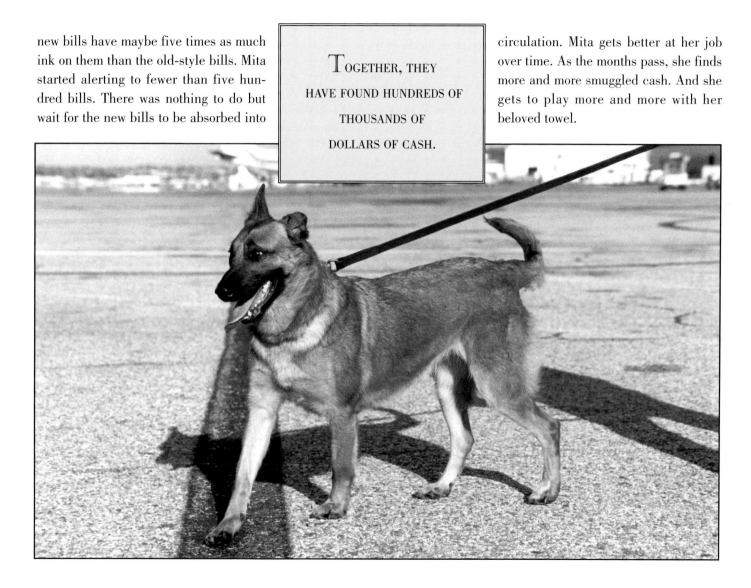

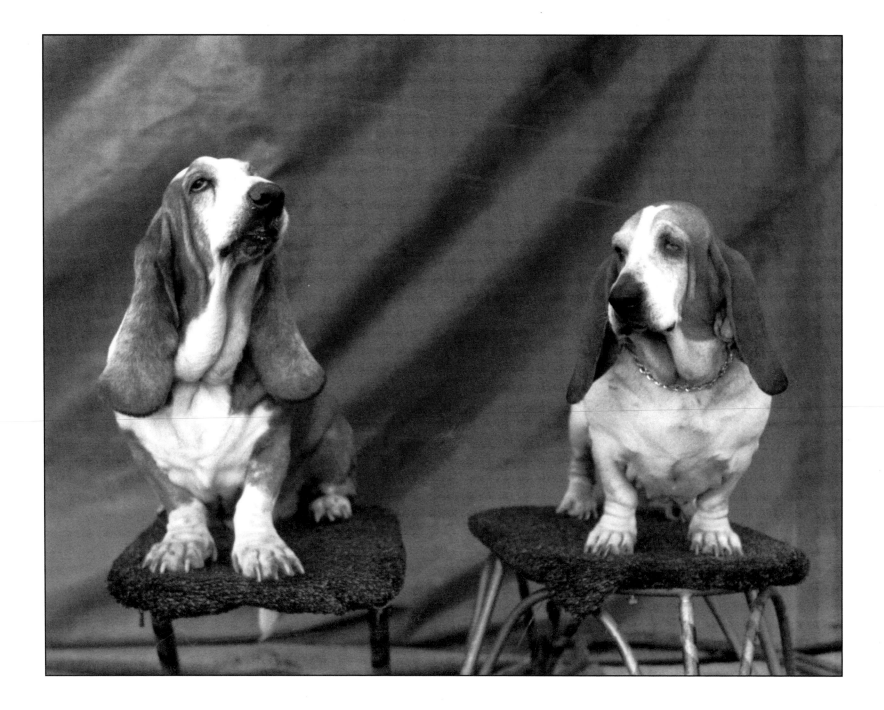

CARLUCIA & ICAR

Circus Dogs

WHEN PEOPLE THINK CIRCUS DOGS, THEY'RE LIKE-ly to think poodles. Maybe a terrier. But basset hounds?

It can work. Especially for these two charmers.

Carlucia and Icar came from Russia last year with Ella Levitskaya to join the Big Apple Circus. Since then, they've been living in a red trailer attached to a motor home, traveling all across the United States. They've spent the year under the big top, jumping onto stools and rolling over for the applause of children. It looks like performing, but to these two it's all a game served up with delicious food.

The show begins with a fanfare as the fifteen dogs take their places center ring on stools. Carlucia and Icar perform with a Great Dane and twelve dachshunds. The dachshunds jump over Icar, one of them rides on Carlucia's back, and the Great Dane jumps over the lot of them. With amazing orchestration the dogs perform

> TRAINING DOGS IS EASY; IT'S TRAINING THE HUMAN THAT IS DIFFICULT.

trick after trick, in groups and alone, for ten minutes. The finale, with all fifteen dogs moving at once—in carts, over hurdles, through hoops—is an amazing spectacle.

LIKE MANY BASSET HOUNDS, CARLUCIA AND ICAR ARE MORE agile and friendly than their low-slung and melancholy appearance suggests. Levitskaya plays against this discrepancy between appearance and fact in their act. The greatest laugh comes when Carlucia tries to jump onto

her stool and can't quite make it. She tries again. And again. And finally hauls her bulk onto the stool. With the applause of children comes a treat from Levitskaya, usually a bit of chicken.

LEVITSKAYA COMES FROM A FAMILY OF CIRCUS PERFORMERS and grew up under the big top in Moscow. When she was six years old, her father gave Levitskaya her first dog. This wasn't a pet, like the first dog of many chil-

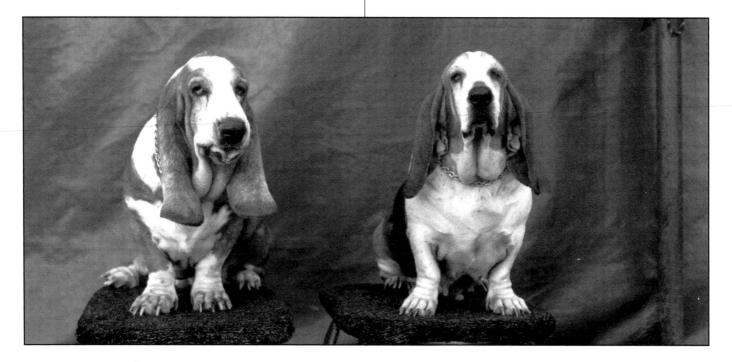

dren, but a working dog. She trained that dog to perform in the ring and has been training dogs ever since.

Forty-five years have taught her a few things about circus dogs. First, they aren't supposed to perform in the ring, they're supposed to play. Second, training dogs is easy; it's training the human that is difficult. Third, the only way to find a trick a dog will perform in the ring is to watch his behavior at play and develop that into an act.

For instance, Carlucia and Icar like to roll over and over on the ground of their play yard. Quite humorous. It's especially funny when they do it under the big top while dachshunds jump over them.

THE BIG APPLE IS UNIQUE AMONG CIRCUSES BECAUSE IT is nonprofit—its manifesto is to make children happy. It has clown units in residence at children's hospitals and gives special performances to children who especially need something to make them laugh. Certain dogs have the ability to delight. Certain children need something delightful.

PERHAPS THE MOST IMPORTANT RULE LEVITSKAYA HAS learned about training circus dogs is that if she serves them food from her own table, they're quick to learn a new trick. And so she will cook something in her trailer

and carry it back to the dogs' trailer when she wants to tell them she is happy with them. Which is quite often.

Carlucia and Icar eat delicious food. They make children laugh. They go for walks every day with Levitskaya. And they have each other.

CERTAIN DOGS HAVE THE ABILITY TO DELIGHT.

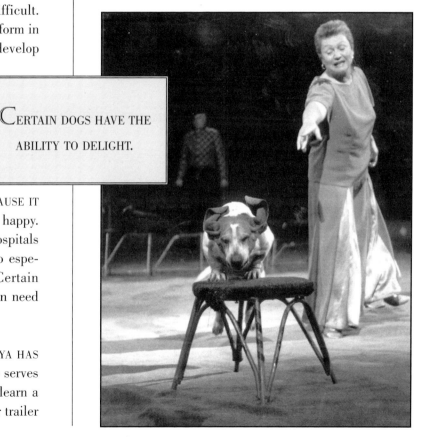

135

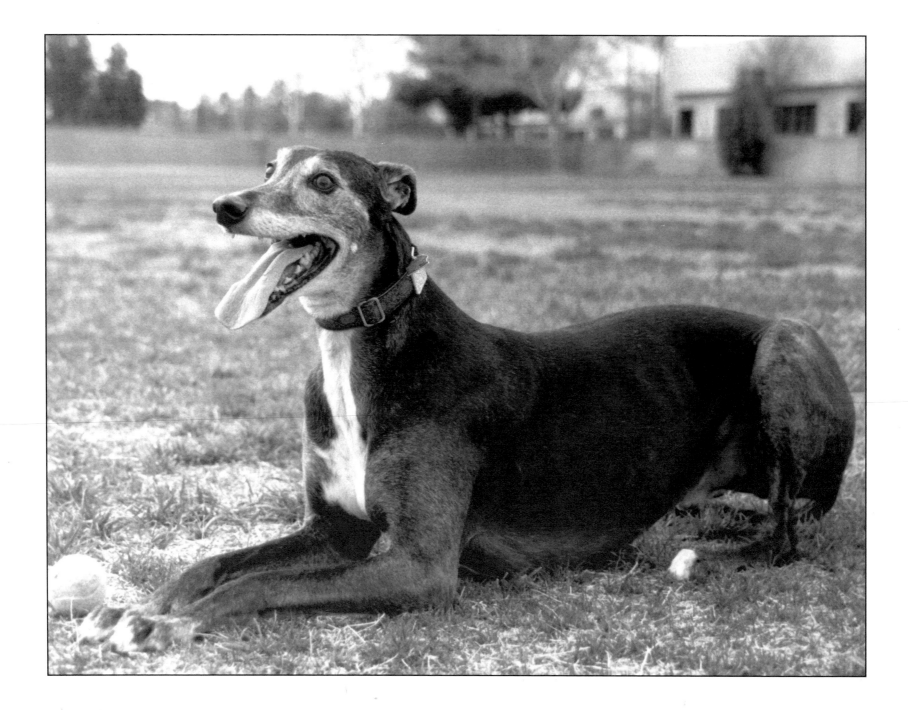

STEALTH

Flyball Player

THE FIRST THING MOST PEOPLE NOTICE ABOUT Flyball competitions is the incredible sound of cheering dogs. The only team sport for dogs, Flyball is as noisy as a professional basketball game, but with a definite canine flair. While dogs race, those waiting on the sidelines howl and bark nonstop. It's easy to see why. Flyball is fun with a capital F.

Two teams of four dogs race against each other and the clock. Each dog on the team takes a turn running over four hurdles, pounding a box with his paws to release a tennis ball, grabbing that ball in his mouth, and running back over the four hurdles to the finish line. A fast Flyball player runs the entire 102-foot course in four seconds.

That's right. Four seconds. The fastest team in the world has a time of just over sixteen seconds for all four dogs to complete the course.

THE FLYING COLORS FLYBALL TEAM WAS FORMED IN Nevada in 1995, and their fastest official time is 18.8 seconds. The fastest dog on the team, Mirk, runs the course in four seconds flat. Many of the other dogs run in the low fours. Flyball is for all dogs, although the fastest are often border collies and Australian shepherds. The dogs on Flying Colors come from all over, from animal shelters to purebred kennels. They are Labradors, shelties, border collies, German shepherds, mixed breeds, and one greyhound, Stealth.

A nine-year-old retired racer who started playing Flyball just last year, Stealth has a best official time of 5.6 seconds. That is nowhere near that of the fastest Flyball players, but it is fast enough to rank him in the top five greyhounds playing Flyball in North America.

THE GOVERNING BODY FOR FLYBALL, THE North American Flyball Association (NAFA), ranks dogs by breed and by points earned. Flyball players rack up individual points during competitions to earn eight titles, from Flyball Dog at 20 points to Flyball Grand Champion at 30,000 points. Each dog earns points based on his team's performance at a competition. Stealth earned his Flyball Dog title at his first competition early this year.

Since the fastest teams are usually filled with border collies, NAFA has a special category of races just for four-breed teams. Flying Colors has two teams, one with three border collies and a height dog, and one with

> FOR STEALTH, FLYBALL
>
> IS ALL ABOUT
>
> TENNIS BALLS AND
>
> ALL ABOUT FUN.

four breeds. The four-breed team; in addition to Stealth, usually consists of a Labrador named Shelby, a German shepherd named Frei, and a border collie named Captain. Stealth runs as the anchor dog, the last dog to go, and the team relies upon his phenomenal speed on the return leg.

The hurdles are set at a height four inches below the shoulders of each team's smallest dog, with a minimum of eight inches and a maximum of sixteen. Therefore, most teams have a height dog—a small, fast dog like a Jack Russell terrier—to keep the hurdles low. Flying Colors has a Boston terrier–Chihuahua mix named Watson who plays on their regular team and keeps the hurdles at nine inches. This is part of the strategy.

Strategizing behind the play also includes deciding at which point to release each dog. When one dog is finishing the course, his nose must pass over the finish line just before the nose of the next dog to run passes over the starting line. If the starting dog begins too early, he is red lighted and must run the entire course again after all the other dogs have finished. If he starts too late, precious seconds are added to the time. The dogs pass as close to nose to nose as possible. When Stealth was first trained to run Flyball, he was started far back from the starting line so he could build up speed, but he got distracted. Now he is released near the start line after a quick run and the word, "Go!"

Because of his background as a racer, Stealth needed some extra help to learn Flyball. People with adopted racing greyhounds are warned never to let their dogs run off leash—otherwise the dogs will start running and never stop. This was a great concern for the Flying Colors team. Stealth must be turned around at the box when he gets the tennis ball and stopped after crossing the finish line. He is obsessed with tennis balls and, as a sight hound, he focuses on visual stimuli. Stealth's owner, Dana Provost, holds a tennis ball behind her back and runs away from Stealth so he will race to cross the finish line. By stopping with the ball, she gets Stealth to stop running, too.

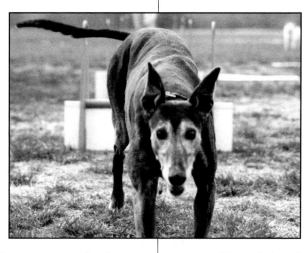

IN THEIR HOME, PROVOST HIDES TENNIS BALLS THROUGHOUT the house for Stealth to find. She hides them under the bed and in the closets. She hides them in the backyard. This is part of Stealth's training. He eats a special high-protein diet supplemented by steamed vegetables, cottage cheese, and yogurt. In an attempt to get him to run faster on the return leg, Provost made a mock-rabbit to lure Stealth down the course. He didn't like it, though. She tried special food rewards and toys, none of which made him run faster. Stealth runs best for tennis balls.

When Stealth earned his Flyball Dog title last fall, the team was as excited as they ever get. Like any athlete who has overcome special challenges, Stealth has a lot of heart behind him. To many on the Flying Colors team, although Mirk is the fastest dog, Stealth is the star.

At their biweekly practices, Stealth spends a lot of time running around and playing with the other dogs. The field often looks more like a dog park than a competition field. He grabs tennis balls when he can and runs to the other side of the field. When it's his turn to run the course, Stealth concentrates and does it, but after a few runs, he's ready to play again and runs away to find lost balls. For Stealth and the other members of the Flying Colors Flyball team, Flyball is all about tennis balls and it's all about fun.

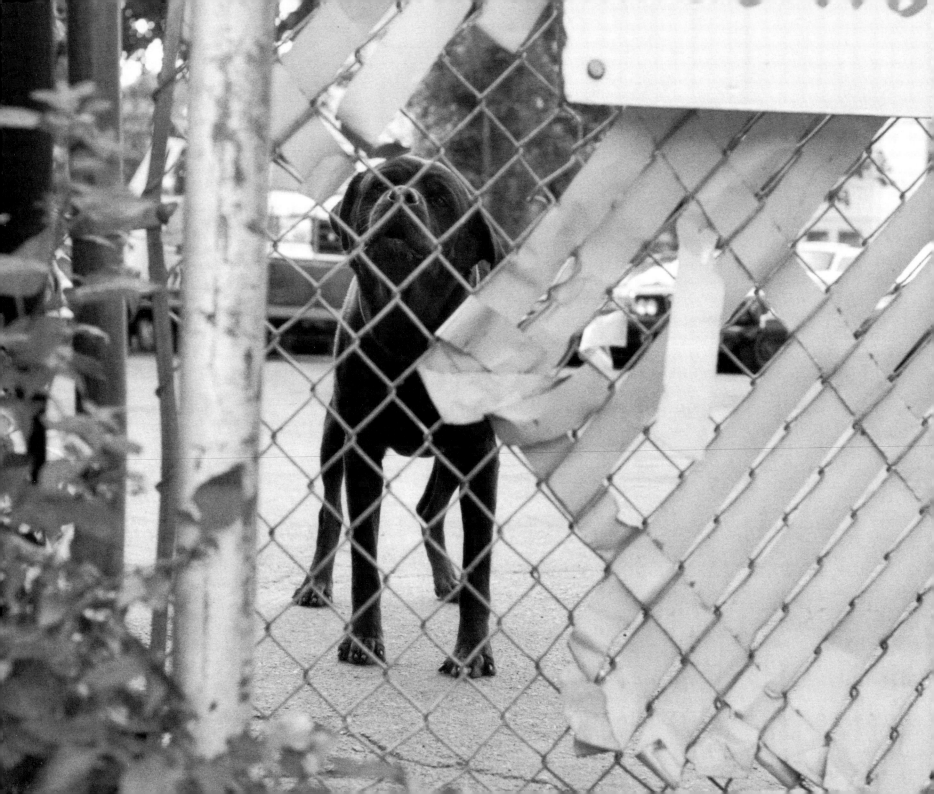

AXEL

Junkyard Dog

AXEL'S WORLD IS A FIVE-HUNDRED-SQUARE-FOOT automobile junkyard. He guards it as if there were no more precious plot of land on this earth. Maybe he's right.

When a junk man has security concerns, he doesn't go looking in the yellow pages under burglar alarms; he goes to the dog pound. That's where Axel came from, five years ago. He was just a fluffy black pup with enormous paws, but somehow he seemed to have the potential to be vicious.

Once Axel was on the job, the security concerns went away. All he needs to do is wander free in the yard at night, barking when appropriate, rushing the fence and showing his teeth when absolutely necessary. As far as the yard workers know, the guard dog has never had to actually bite anyone. It seems the threat of Axel has been enough.

Axel's shelter is a doghouse in the back of the yard. He spends his days there, tethered to a pole. That way, he can still do all the barking he wants, without anyone's needing to fear a bite. Most days, though, he spends curled up sleeping, tired from the long and lonely nights guarding the junkyard. Axel has a big responsibility, though he didn't always shoulder it alone.

Three years ago, a female German shepherd wandered into Axel's junkyard. She was a delicate dog, thin and tentative. There were no tags on her frayed collar.

Axel had always barked his head off at any dog he saw, but with this German shepherd, he was different. She came over to him, and they touched noses and sniffed bottoms. Then she had a long drink from Axel's water bowl. He lay down in his doghouse and peeked out at her while she ate from his kibble dish. When she finished, Axel didn't move. He seemed to be waiting to see what she would do. She looked around, seeming to evaluate the spot, then, as if judging it satisfactory, she curled up in a bit of shade and slept.

The guys in the shop cheered. Although he was held in a different regard than their pet dogs at home, Axel was still close to their hearts, and they wanted him to be happy. For some reason they could never recall, the guys named the German shepherd Cootie. They gave her a kibble bowl of her

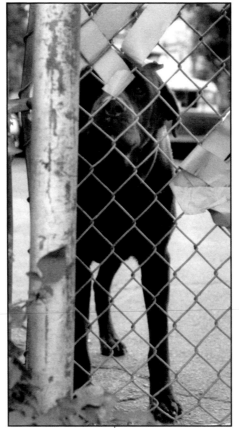

own, and she quickly set up residence in the junkyard. Next thing they knew, Cootie was pregnant.

Axel and Cootie seemed genuinely happy together. They both enjoyed barking at strangers. She accompanied him on the rounds of the yard at night, and spent the days curled up next to him near the dog house. Dogs are pack animals, and need fellow canines as mates and companions.

Cootie and Axel's puppies were adorable. There were only five of them—three boys, two girls—and they favored Axel's look, with short dark hair. Cootie was a patient and sweet mother and spent most of every day nursing and caring for her litter.

After the guys found homes for her pups, Cootie changed. She stopped eating, and spent her time hiding under the burned out shell of a '67 Mustang. The guys in the shop brought her pig's ears as special treats. They gave her a squeaky stuffed bear. Nothing snapped her out of it, though, and one day, she was gone.

Poor Axel was absolutely morose. He howled for hours and kept wandering through the yard searching for her. For days, he lay by the front gate waiting for Cootie to appear the way she first had: looking for food and shelter, but finding much more.

Although that was over a year ago, Axel still spends part of each day waiting quietly for Cootie. And, although he still does his job and barks at strangers, it's not with the same gusto he once had. He doesn't seem to be having fun anymore.

ONCE AXEL WAS ON THE JOB, SECURITY CONCERNS WENT AWAY.

The guys from the shop keep Cootie's kibble bowl filled and try to cheer Axel up. One guy took him home for the night, but Axel nearly tunneled out of his backyard. Another guy takes Axel on regular trips to the park to play ball. Whenever Axel returns to the junkyard, however, he runs straight to that old Mustang and looks underneath for Cootie. Nothing.

The guard dog hasn't given up hope, though. She wandered once into Axel's junkyard. It could happen again.

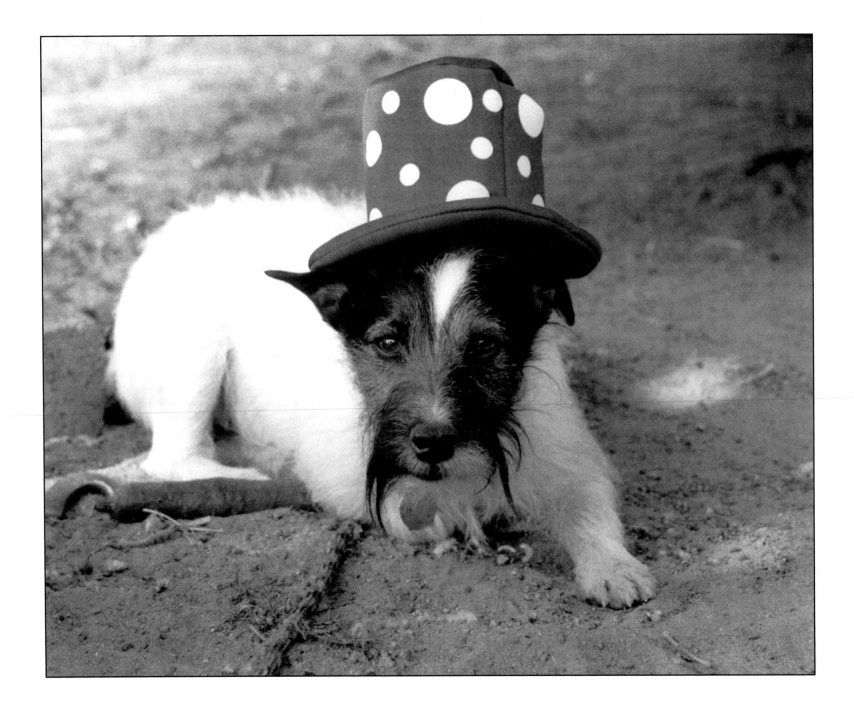

ZIGGY

Rodeo Clown

IN HIS LITTLE FOAM FISH COSTUME, ZIGGY WATCHES from the sidelines as Charlie "Too Tall" West tells the rodeo audience about his brilliant career as a fisherman. He's caught every fish in the world except for the one who eludes him: the Humboldt River Dog Fish. Behind the fence, Ziggy gets so excited to perform that he must be held back. He whimpers and yips and finally squeals with excitement. West works the crowd and pretends to fly-fish with his special pole until he hears Ziggy squeal, then he taps his head to give his partner, Michelle Melville, the signal to release the dog.

Ziggy shoots like a rocket straight to West and grabs the end of the fishing line. As the crowd cheers at the sight of the intense little fish, West and Ziggy battle back and forth. It goes on for as long as the crowd will laugh. Then West falls to the ground. The Dog Fish wins. They run together from the arena and the next rodeo contest, calf roping, quickly begins.

Ziggy's reward for a good performance is a few beef treats. He waits for his costume to be removed, then stands patiently by the trailer where the treats are kept. He has a long drink of water and takes a nap in the shade. Later, during the bull riding, when West performs from inside a barrel, Ziggy watches intently from the sidelines. West tells jokes like, "I think that bull is sick—he just threw up a cowboy!" Ziggy stares straight at West, but doesn't yip or squeal. He knows he has finished performing for the day.

THESE DAYS, RODEO IS BIG-TIME entertainment, but it started as annual cattle roundups in the eighteenth century when Spain occupied most of the land that became the American West. After the roundup work was completed, the vaqueros, or cowboys, would blow off steam by competing at bronco busting, cattle roping, and bull riding. When the fascination with the American West produced shows like Buffalo Bill Cody's Wild West in the 1880s, rodeo became an organized event, much like it is today.

A rodeo clown's job is to entertain the audience between the heart-stopping cowboy competitions. If the clown is also a barrelman, like West, he stays inside a barrel during the bull riding, making commentary and telling jokes to ease the tension of the arena. West has been

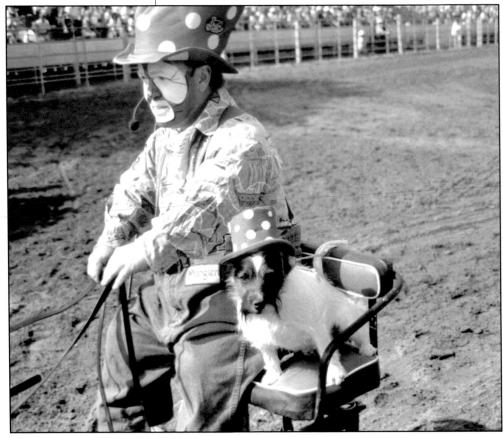

working in the rodeo for eighteen years and Ziggy is not his first dog.

Several years ago, West worked with a little dog named Bingo who dressed in a bull costume, complete with horns. Unfortunately, Bingo had a problem with hot dogs. No matter what West did, when he called Bingo into the rodeo arena, the little dog in the bull costume would head straight for the hot dog stand. West realized Bingo had lost his taste for rodeo, and it was time to look for a new dog. He found Ziggy.

ZIGGY IS A JACK RUSSELL TERRIER WHO HOLDS ONE EAR up and one ear down. He has the fuzzy face of a wizened old man and the temperament of a seasoned professional. Touring the rodeo circuit with West, Melville, and their miniature horse, Thunder, Ziggy is happy with what he has. He is always the first one to jump into the cab of the truck when it's time to hit the road. In the summer, they average three shows per month, which means constant travel, hotels, and all-night driving. Through it all, Ziggy never tires or stresses. He always squeals with excitement before his act.

At their home base in the foothills above Sacramento, California, they live on a ranch with the twenty miniature horses Melville and West breed and

> BEHIND THE FENCE, ZIGGY GETS SO EXCITED TO PERFORM THAT HE MUST BE HELD BACK.

train. They often visit Bingo, who now lives with West's mother and still enjoys eating hot dogs. In the off-season, they work on their act, looking for new ideas. They've been trying to teach Ziggy to stand on Thunder's back, but he doesn't like it much. Who would?

When building acts for Ziggy, West and Melville look at his natural behavior for ideas. Last year, Melville was training Thunder with a lunge whip when Ziggy ran up and grabbed the tip of the whip. He thought it was a great game of tug-of-war and would not release his end of the whip no matter what. Since the whip resembles a fishing pole and line, this game gave Melville the idea of a dog fish. She and West had a little fish costume made and an act was born.

ZIGGY DOESN'T HAVE A NATURAL INSTINCT FOR RIDING on the back of a horse and so it hasn't become part of the show. They watch him for new ideas, though, so they'll have a fresh act for next year. In the meantime, everyone is happy with the Dog Fish act. Because it's built around Ziggy's own idea of fun, he is always excited to perform. A true professional, he never misses a cue. Ziggy never heads for the hot dog stand.

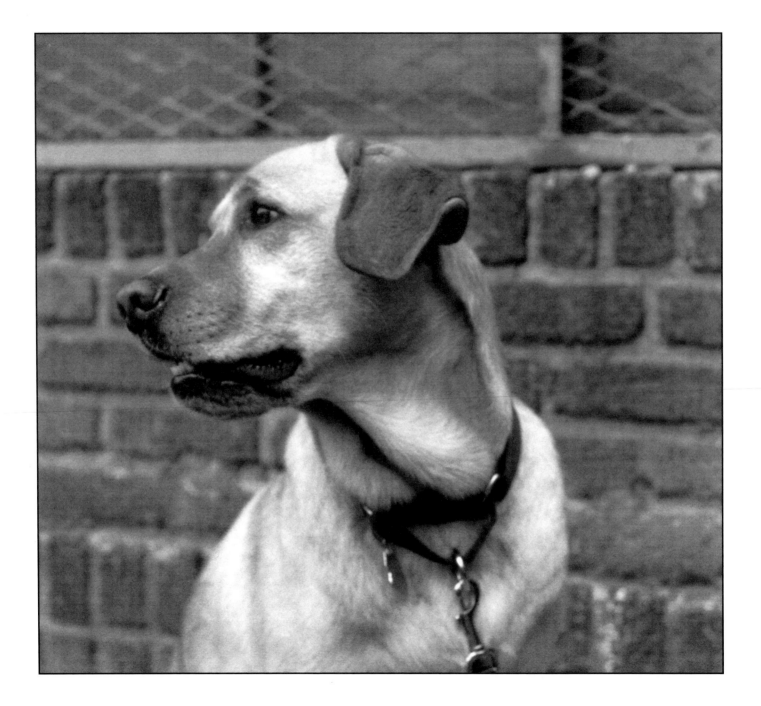

GARRETT

Explosives Detector

ALTHOUGH SPECIAL AGENT RAY NEELY GIVES HIS Labrador partner, Garrett, pink squeaky toys to play with at home, they maintain their professional demeanor while investigating crime scenes. All toys stay in the car.

A GRADUATE OF THE PRESTIGIOUS EXPLOSIVES DETECtion program run by the Bureau of Alcohol, Tobacco, and Firearms, Garrett is trained to alert to the odors of more than nineteen thousand explosives. That means he can find bombs, guns, and shells, both before and after they've detonated. ATF canine teams like Garrett and Neely fly around the country sweeping buildings and investigating crime scenes. They spent two weeks finding bombs in Littleton, Colorado, after the Colombine High School murders, and they regularly sweep the United nations building in New York. They work to prevent crimes and solve them. Garrett's alerts result in search warrants, convictions of criminals, and a generally safer world.

Garrett came to the ATF from the Guiding Eyes for the Blind in New York. The trainers there determined that he liked to sniff more than is desirable in a guide dog, who needs to focus on the ground in front of him. Since Garrett had already been socialized for work by a special puppy-raising family, he was given the chance for a new career at the ATF. The new career, as it turned out, was much better suited to his curiosity and to his nose.

Garrett's explosives training began with six weeks of imprintation, during which time he was presented with the scent of explosives just prior to eating kibble. This was repeated more than 125

THE ATF HAS BROKEN DOWN EXPLOSIVE MATERIALS INTO THEIR BASIC ELEMENTS AND COME UP WITH FIVE FAMILIES FROM WHICH COME ALL NINETEEN THOUSAND KNOWN EXPLOSIVES. GARRETT WAS TRAINED TO ALERT TO ALL OF THEM.

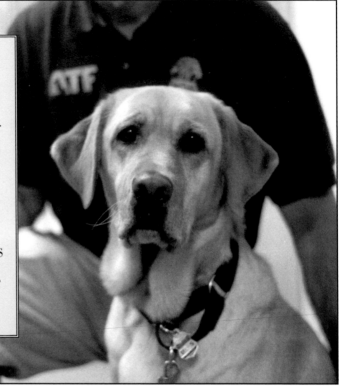

times per day until Garrett associated the desirable act of eating with the formerly neutral act of smelling explosives. Garrett learned that he eats only when he smells explosives, and, because he really likes eating, he has learned to really like smelling explosives. The ATF has broken down explosive materials into their basic elements and come up with five families from which come all nineteen thousand known explosives. Garrett was trained to alert to all of them.

During the next ten weeks, Garrett underwent operational training with Neely. Together they learned the methodology of following scent cones and communicating with each other. The ATF strictly controls the methodology used by its canine teams so that any handler can work with any dog. At the end, Garrett was run through testing by a forensic chemist and passed with a score of 100 percent. That is, they could not present Garrett with an explosive to which he would not alert.

OVER THE YEARS, GARRETT has proven himself to be especially good at finding residue, the microscopic amounts of explosives left on the scene after criminals have made bombs. Because residue is often evidence of bomb building at investigations, Garrett can help build a case against a criminal, and his alerts have resulted in the end of criminal careers.

At the beginning of each day, Neely measures out Garrett's kibble for the day and puts it into a special food pouch. When Neely attaches that pouch to his belt, Garrett knows it's time to work. He begins searching and when he smells explosives and sits, he gets a few pieces of kibble. Because he's fed throughout the day, he will work throughout the day. If Garrett doesn't find an explosive to alert to, or they

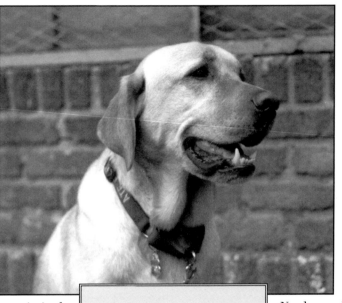

GARRETT REALLY LIKES EATING, SO HE HAS LEARNED TO REALLY LIKE SMELLING EXPLOSIVES.

happen to have a day off, Neely will hide a training aid—usually his gun—so Garrett always has something to find and always gets fed.

NEELY SAYS HE THINKS OF Garrett as he would a child, concerned if the dog makes a noise in the middle of the night, bringing a special cushion with them so Garrett is comfortable while traveling. Although Garrett won't sleep in the bed with Neely—a habit learned from his days training to be a guide dog—sometimes, to help the dog sleep, Neely will lie on the floor next to Garrett. And, just like a child next to his father, Garrett will curl up and fall into a deep slumber.

Garrett is also a comfort to Neely, who often investigates grisly crime scenes. After all, who wouldn't want a big Labrador next to him while searching for evidence of man's inhumanity to man. At the ATF, they always say, "Trust your dog." Neely does.

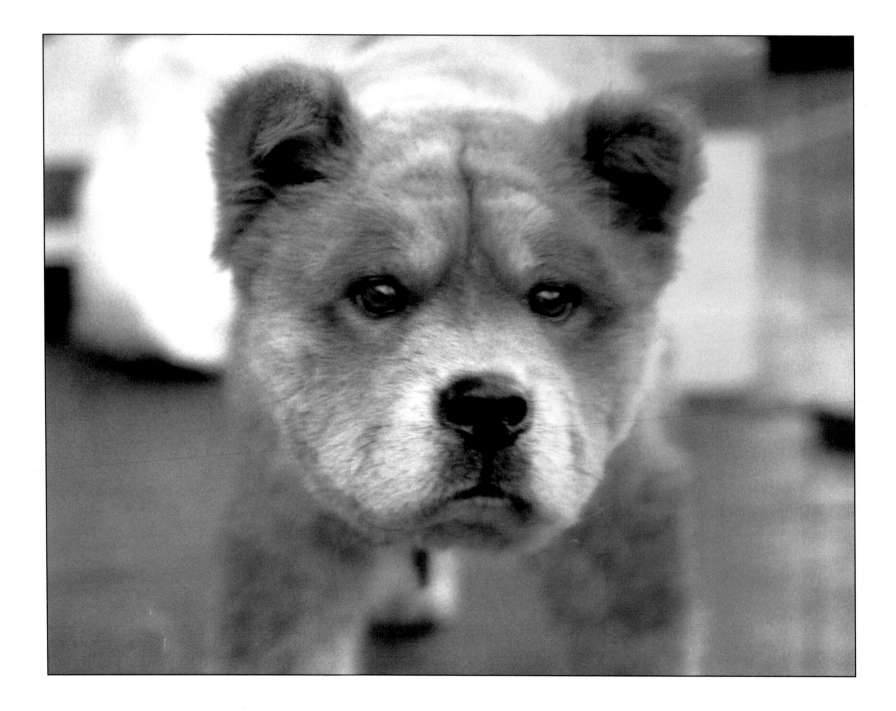

ANGEL

Panhandler

IN THE BEGINNING, DOGS AND HUMANS WERE RIVALS, preying upon the same animals for food: bison, mammoths, and reindeer. As early humans evolved, developing the brains that allowed them to invent weapons such as the spear and the bow and arrow, however, this relationship began to change.

Humans noted with interest the natural hunting and guarding skills of wolves. These animals tracked game by its scent; they heard noises from far in the night and barked warnings to their pack. The humans used their newly-developed skills to domesticate the talented wolves, and soon the two species were working and living together.

> ANGEL WEARS HIS STREET SMARTS LIKE A BULLETPROOF VEST.

THAT EARLY ASSOCIATION RESULTED IN relationships much like the one Angel has with Morris. Morris lives in an urban area; he is without a home and makes do, for now, with a shopping cart filled with various belongings: a clock radio, jugs of water, a tan cashmere sweater. Morris sleeps under a particular freeway overpass. It's not an especially safe place, and Morris, being a heavy sleeper, used to get robbed fairly regularly. That is, until the day he woke up to find a warm dog sleeping next to him. He named the dog Angel.

Angel is a sturdy little dog who wears his street smarts like a bulletproof vest. He knows how to avoid sticky situations; he knows how to get out of them, too. Angel sleeps next to Morris and guards him at night, and if anyone gets too close, the little dog barks. Once Angel began to sleep next to him, Morris stopped getting robbed.

Morris stands next to a freeway on-ramp each morning from 6:30 to 7:45. He holds a sign that reads, "Please help me feed my dog." Angel stands next to him. Each morning they get a few dollars, enough to make it through the day. By 9 A.M. they are at McDonald's, where Morris buys three hamburgers, extra pickles. Angel eats two. They have some water. Morris drinks a large coffee.

The rest of the day is their own. Sometimes they spend it together—they might go to the park, or just walk. Once they went as far as the beach and both swam in the ocean. Other times they each go their

> By RELYING ON EACH OTHER, BOTH BECOME A BIT MORE CIVILIZED.

separate ways. Morris figures Angel spends those days marking fire hydrants or looking for females. Morris usually heads for the library to work on his manifesto, or he might spend time socializing at a particular pub. They meet up again at night, under the freeway overpass.

Morris doesn't know why Angel started sleeping next to him, and he never tethers the dog. Angel was just there one morning, curled up at his feet, and Morris got the idea to modify his sign. Right away, his earnings doubled.

His costs went up, too, though. Angel likes to eat, and Morris makes sure the dog gets his two hamburgers and water each day. On particularly successful days, and as a special treat, Angel gets a carton of milk—Angel really likes milk.

LONG AGO, WHEN ANGEL'S ANCESTORS WERE MAKING friends with Morris's ancestors, an important relationship was formed that changed the lives of both species. The dogs became better fed and domesticated; the men became better hunters and were able to rest at night under the watch of their dogs. By relying on each other, both became a bit more civilized.

Since then, dogs and humans have had a unique connection, unlike that between man and any other animal. Dogs continue to work for humans, but they have become companions and friends in a way that horses and even cats have not. We love our dogs. And they love us. It's what's at the heart of the canine-human relationship.

Morris and Angel have been together for two months now, and

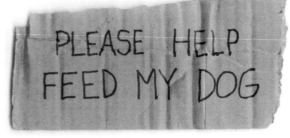

already Morris can't imagine life without the dog. He's trying to think of a way to get a place for the two of them. Somewhere safe, somewhere quiet. Maybe with a little yard. And a refrigerator where he would always keep a big carton of milk for Angel.

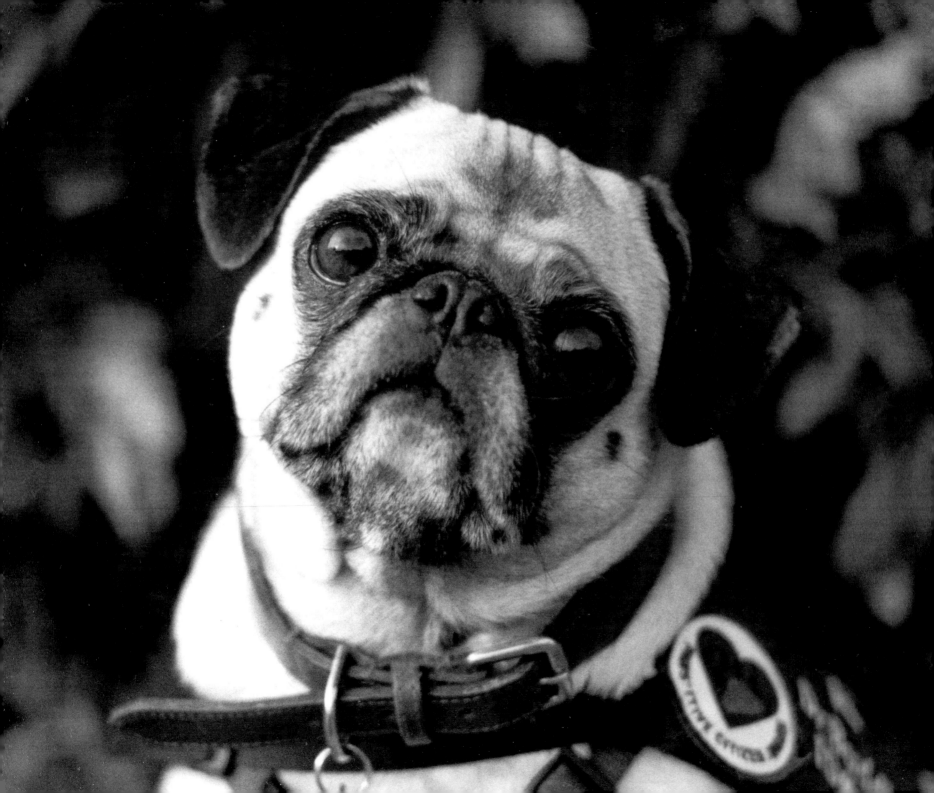

DR. BUDDHA

Therapy Dog

"WANT TO COME SAY HI TO THE DOGGIES?" THE SHY boy wearing a large baseball hat isn't sure about coming over to see the little pug named Dr. Buddha, but he can't stop watching her. Three other children are already lavishing the small dog with pets and kisses. They were here the last time she came to visit at the Ronald McDonald House—a residential facility for terminally ill children and their families—and know where to find the stethoscope in her bag. Dr. Buddha knows to stand still while the children take turns counting her heartbeats and their own.

WEARING A RED HARNESS THAT READS "Therapy Dog," Dr. Buddha takes her responsibilities, seriously. Her fur is as soft as fine velvet and she permits nonstop attention from children. She climbs into a wagon to be pulled around a playground and slides down a slide that's four times her height—all for the amusement of a child. With a spe-

> MIRACLES ARE JUST
> PART OF THE JOB.

cial leash that has two handles—one for Buddha's owner, Daniela Ortner, and one for the child Buddha is with— sick children and their siblings take her for a walk.

She moves from person to person, then sits on the lap of one child long enough to make a special bond. She sits near shy children, coyly leaning into them until they lose their resistance and scoop her up. Buddha seems to know what each child needs and how best to approach.

Later, at a nearby center for abused children, Dr. Buddha sits on little laps and listens to secrets that children won't tell the adults. When anyone gets upset, Buddha is right there for a hug and a lick. For an hour, children forget their circumstances and focus on the simple joy of loving a dog.

> DR. BUDDHA TAKES
> HER RESPONSIBILITIES
> VERY SERIOUSLY.

RESEARCH SHOWS THAT THERAPY WITH ANIMALS LIKE DR. Buddha benefits people of all ages. Animal-assisted therapy will lower blood pressure, decrease anxiety, and speed the healing process. A child may not realize he is receiving physical therapy each time he picks up a tiny treat and offers it to a dog, but doctors and researchers do. That's why more and more dogs like Dr. Buddha are allowed into health facilities. One child took his first steps out of a wheelchair when he wanted to take Dr. Buddha for a walk. These sorts of miracles are all part of the job for the little pug.

Buddha comes by her talent naturally. Her dad, Magic, is also a therapy dog. Buddha was the runt of a litter that was the result of a weekend Magic spent with a supposedly-spayed pug neighbor. At birth, Buddha was so tiny that her veterinarian said she would never make it, but after being nursed with a tiny bottle by Ortner, her belly became so fat she earned her name.

Now she's six and a half years old and has been a therapy dog for most of her life. Her calm but friendly temperament makes her a favorite with the children she visits. Before Buddha leaves—but after they wash their hands—each child receives an instant photograph to remember the little pug's visit.

At eight and a half inches tall, Dr. Buddha is so adorable no one can help petting her, yet she is sturdy enough to endure an hour of intense attention. Like most pugs, she maintains her poise while still seeming happy and friendly. This makes her a perfect therapy dog. During her weekly rounds she visits hospitals, nursing homes, shelters, and special education and day care centers. As the number one member of the Create-A-Smile animal-assisted therapy team,

Buddha has visited hundreds of children.

Buddha doesn't take her work home with her. When she is not wearing her harness, she is a different dog, a more playful dog, given to excitability and curiosity. She shares her comfortable home with three other dogs, a cat, and a hamster. Her favorite treat, dried liver, is handed out liberally.

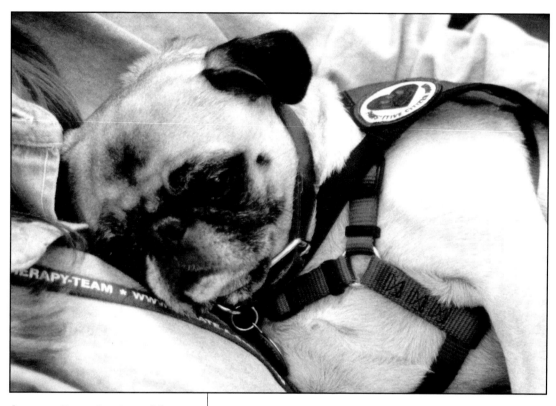

PEOPLE ALL OVER THE world know to bring their dogs with them when visiting sick loved ones. Organizations like Create-A-Smile, which trains and certifies animals and their handlers, make it possible for dogs to go places where they wouldn't ordinarily be allowed, places like hospitals and shelters. Places filled with people who most need visits from a dog like Dr. Buddha.

AT THE END OF HER VISIT TO THE RONALD MCDONALD House, Buddha gets sleepy and her eyelids droop over her big eyes. She crawls into the nearest lap, and, sitting upright, begins to snore. The sound is loud, more like a small rhinoceros than a small dog, and it makes even the shy children laugh. Dr. Buddha peeks out from beneath her eyelids. It's all part of the job.

Photo Credits